CW00701681

A Daring Game

'I will not conceal from you that I am playing a daring game, and it is very possible that when I least expect it I may be seized, tied to the tail of a mule, and dragged either to the prison of Toledo or Madrid. Yet such a prospect does not discourage me in the least, but rather urges me on to persevere; for I assure you (...) that I am eager to lay down my life in this cause, and whether a Carlist's bullet or the jail-fever bring my career to an end, I am perfectly indifferent.'

George Borrow:
letter to the Reverend Andrew Brandram
14 July 1838 from Vila Seca de la Sagra

A Daring Game

George Borrow's sales
of the Scio New Testament
(Madrid 1837)

Peter Missler

DURRANT PUBLISHING

Gabicóte Publication nº 1

Copyright © 2009 Peter Missler
All rights reserved.

Published in 2009 by Durrant Publishing, Norfolk

ISBN 978-1-905946-04-4

The right of Peter Missler to be identified as the author of this work has been asserted by him in accordance with the Copyright, Designs and Patents Act 1988.

This study was published with the generous backing and support of the George Borrow Trust.

The cover illustration, which may be understood to show George Borrow throwing the police spy Pedro Martin de Eugenio out of his apartment on 30 April 1838 (*The Bible in Spain*, chapter 39), comes from '*Maria Espanhola ou A Victima de um Frade*' by Wenceslau Ayguals de Izco, Lisbon 1849.

Illustration 4 is from the 1838 map of Spain and Portugal produced by the Society for the Diffusion of Useful Knowledge. Thanks to David Rumsey for permission to use his digital copy of the map in the illustration. http://www.davidrumsey.com/

The text of this book is revision 2009.01

∞ The paper used in this publication meets the minimum requirements of the American National Standard for Information Sciences—Permanence of Paper for Printed Library Materials, ANSI Z39.48-1992. The paper is acid-free and lignin-free.

This is a 'Print-On-Demand' book by Durrant Publishing http://www.durrantpublishing.co.uk/
It may be ordered on-line at Amazon, or obtained through special order at most bookshops.

For Palmyra and Yasin

Contents

IV Summaries

List of Illustrations

Acknowledgements

MANY THANKS are due to those who, over the years, helped out in one way or another with the writing and publication of this study.

First and foremost among these is, of course, Dr. Ann Ridler, Chairman of the George Borrow Society and of the George Borrow Trust, and Editor of the George Borrow Bulletin, whose knowledge of Borrovian affairs is only outdone by her willingness to help others at every step and in every imaginable way. Dr. Ridler was one of the self-sacrificing people who close-read the earlier drafts of the study so as to clean it of my many silly mistakes and barbarous spellings. Moreover, she and the fellow trustees of the George Borrow Trust, Clive Wilkins-Jones and Andrew Dakyns, showed their unflagging dedication to the Borrovian Cause by generously financing the publication of so modest and uncommercial a work.

The inimitable Ms Kathleen Cann, former keeper of the archive of the British and Foreign Bible Society, made Borrow's unpublished expense accounts available to me. Without these, the calculations in this study could never have been made, and this book would never have been written. That aside, Ms Cann proved an inexhaustible source of valuable background information on the doings and workings of the Bible Society, and must have spent close to a full-time working week checking and correcting the final drafts.

Antonio Giménez Cruz, grand ol' man of Spanish Borroviana and doyen of us all, as always went out of *his* way to help me along on *mine*, sharing many documents from his impressive archive and personally shooting pictures of the present location of Borrow's *Dispacho*.

David Mount from Bury St Edmunds, who owns one of the finest private collections of Borrow material I know, provided essential data on the physical aspects of the Scio New Testament.

Graham York, the unstoppable bookseller from Honiton, Dorset, checked and corrected my fault-prone bibliographical statements with his outstanding expertise.

Ken Barrett from Alcalá de Henares, in many ways one of George Borrow's most dedicated successors in the missionary cause, helped out with the more intricate aspects of Scripture and patiently explained the ups and downs of Protestant missionary work of the last 150 years to me.

Basha and CuChullaine O'Reilly, who hold the reins of the marvellous Long Riders Guild, shared their incomparable knowledge of equine affairs with an author who had not been close to a horse for over 35 years, thus preserving him from many a kick, stumble and fall.

Ms Concha Varela, then of the Biblioteca Xeral of Santiago de Compostela, alerted me to several priceless and unknown documents in Spanish archives concerning the sales of the Scio New Testament in the Rey Romero bookshop.

The authors and fellow Borrovians Thomas Bean, Juan Campos Calvo-Sotelo, Michael Collie, David Fernández de Castro, Richard Hitchcock, M.B. Mencher and Ian Robertson at various times shared their expert knowledge, stimulated research, and offered their critical views of the happy nonsense which I had penned, weeding out many a gross mistake of mine in the process. Of these, my good friend M.B. Mencher deserves special mention for introducing me to my agile and efficient publisher Paul Durrant. Without the two of them, this study surely would never have seen the light.

Finally, Ronald Lamars, of Cedar Ceres Website Productions, Houten, The Netherlands, helped out with his sense of humour, his irony, and his knowledge of Scripture, type-setting, elegant style and the remedies for hangovers.

Author's introduction

THIS STUDY concentrates on the sales figures, the finances and the surrounding circumstances of George Borrow's Bible-peddling activities in Spain between the years 1836 and 1840. It pretends to be an *exhaustive* study, and therefore its true title ought perhaps to be: *'Everything You Never Cared To Know About George Borrow's 1837 Spanish New Testaments'*. It would, however, be a trifle too frivolous to dismiss one's own best intentions and several months of steady toil so rudely in the very first words of a serious book. Hence the somewhat shorter title which adorns the cover; a quotation lifted from one of George Borrow's own letters, which has the additional value of describing the adventurous nature of Borrow's operations quite adequately.

There are always advantages and disadvantages to an abundance of source material. The good news about George Borrow's 1837 Scio New Testament in Spanish is that we can bring to light just about everything there is to know about the edition. It is merely a matter of wringing the facts and figures from the documents. This will be done in the pages below, with the aim, first and foremost, to establish *how many* copies of this New Testament were sold where, at what moment, in what manner, and to whom. It is high time this be done, because in the 170 years which have passed since publication, the sales figures for the Scio New Testament have never been determined with certainty, with the predictable result that one finds the wildest and sometimes most fantastic guesswork in later biographies and historical studies.

But inevitably, such a study contains quite a lot in the way of numerical calculation and a sometimes voluminous discussion of petty problems. This cannot be helped if one wants to reach more or less reliable figures from which to draw reasonably safe conclusions. Yet it makes for lengthy, stringy texts which cannot always carry away the reader's full interest. I have therefore chosen a structure which anticipates the public's possible wish for instant satisfaction. In the first parts, each sales-method and each sales-period will be minutely examined and hard data will be separated rigorously from those we must assume or can only guess at. Then, in the latter part, all these data, certain and conjectured, will be brought together in the *Summaries*, so as to draw justified conclusions. Those who are willing to accept my numerical conjectures without more ado, may move immediately to this section (part IV). The others, who prefer to subject my suppositions to their critical judgement, may start at the beginning and work their way through. They are still advised, however, to select the juicier bits which interest them most, and to ignore the rest of the chewy grub.

Estar, Brion (Spain), May 1ˢᵗ, 2008.

A note on references, money and place names

THE MANNER of reference to documents, consulted books and other source material will be fully explained in the first paragraphs of the section 'Bibliography and sources' at the end of this book.

Due to the confusing nature of Spain's monetary system in the 1830s, and the additional complications brought on by the exchange rates with the old duodecimal system of British money, I thought it best to reduce all prices and financial data to the *real vellum*, Spain's unit of currency in the 1830s. Only occasionally a direct quotation from a letter or a bill may retain the original figure in pounds sterling; in all those cases, however, its equivalent in *reales* will also be noted between brackets. An explanation of the coinage, the rate of exchange and the purchasing power of Spanish money will be found in Appendix 1 at the end of this book.

Borrow's spellings of place names are sometimes wildly different from modern usage, either because he uses archaic or translated versions (e.g. *St. Jago* for *Santiago* and *Corunna* for *Coruña*); or because, in the absence of accurate maps and road-signs, he wrote down the names of minor towns and villages by ear (for some of the odd forms Borrow used, see Knapp, *Life*, I : 388f). Where possible, geographical names have been modernized and standardized throughout the text, except in direct quotations from contemporary writers. Only in those cases where identification is impossible or unsure, I maintain Borrow's enigmatic spellings. Thus 'Cobeña', whose identification is certain, will always be used instead of Borrow's 'Cobenna'; but 'Villallos', which can only tentatively be identified as the modern village of Velayos, will remain 'Villallos' throughout the text.

Abbreviations

THE FOLLOWING abbreviations are used in references throughout the following text, and are provided here in alphabetical order to serve as a quick reference.

Acc *n*	Borrow's *n*th Expense Account, as listed in Appendix 3
APP	*Account of Proceedings in the Peninsula*
BiBo *n*	Borrow's *n*th bill from Borrego's *Compañia Tipográfica*
BiOSh	Bill from the Bible Society's Madrid Banker, O'Shea
BiS	*The Bible in Spain*
L *date*	Letter of *date*, from Borrow to the Bible Society
ROS	*Report on Past and Future Operations in Spain*

THE ABBREVIATIONS used to refer to consulted literature can be found in the list of Secondary Sources, on pages 186–189.

I

Preliminary

I.1 The story of the Scio New Testament

E ARLY IN 1836, George Borrow was sent to Spain by the British and Foreign Bible Society to see what might be done there in the way of distribution of Bible texts printed in a vernacular translation. Spain had recently passed through profound socio-political changes, which made such an initiative feasible for the first time in centuries. A new liberal regime, which followed on the archaic absolutist system kept in place for 20 years by the late king Fernando VII, had granted the country a – still limited – freedom of the press, which might perhaps be stretched just enough to allow for the distribution and sale of Spanish language, Protestant Scripture.

Borrow looked around and made inquiries, and soon after he had reported back his findings, it was decided that, rather than import – illegally – large stocks of books from abroad at high costs and high risks, it would be better to print a fresh edition of a Spanish language New Testament in the country itself. To this purpose, the Bible Society agent sought formal permission from the Madrid government first to print and then to distribute such an edition. The Spanish government was most unwilling to grant this, because there were two rather formidable obstacles to such a project. First of all: the law quite simply forbade this kind of publication, unless the publisher received a formal licence from the all-powerful Catholic church. And secondly: the Catholic church was rigorously opposed to any such vernacular edition of Holy Writ, unless it answered to the conditions formulated by the Holy See in 1756,

1

namely: that all the books considered canonical by the Catholic Church be included[1], and that the text be accompanied by the copious explicatory notes which guided the reader towards the correct theological interpretation of each and every delicate passage[2]. Since this latter addition would necessarily have turned the New Testament into a *Catholic* publication, the Bible Society, a Protestant organisation at heart, refused to do so. Its projected New Testament had to be published 'without note or comment', according to the Society's fundamental law; and would consequently be incomplete in Catholic eyes.

This ought to have been the end of it. Except that Borrow had the backing of Sir George Villiers, the British Ambassador to Spain, and that Villiers had tremendous leverage over the Spanish government, because Britain lent the liberal regime essential diplomatic and military aid in its civil war against the Carlist rebellion in the north – a rebellion which throughout these years always stood on the verge of winning and of replacing the liberal experiment with a repetition of Fernando VII's anachronistic autocracy. Thus, caught between a rock and a hard place, the Spanish government first stalled, then wavered, and finally caved in. They could not, of course, grant an illegal formal permission; but they went so far as to give a covert *verbal* go-ahead to the printing of the New Testament, under the condition that it would be done in a most private, discreet and unobtrusive manner; in other words: completely on the sly and in such a way that the offence could never be laid at the government's

---

1 This divergent view of Scriptural matters only concerned half a dozen Old Testament books considered canonical by Catholics and unauthentic by Protestants (see Appendix 2). Since Borrow only published the New Testament, where no difference of opinion existed as to what books ought to make up the text, the absence of the so-called *Apocrypha* played no role in the ups and downs of his enterprise.

2 It is sometimes suggested in Borrow's defence that he was not fully aware of the legal position, or that the legal position was not altogether clear. This is not borne out by the facts. From the very first Borrow knew that his publication broke the law. As early as mid 1836 he wrote unequivocally to his employers: 'though by the law of Spain the publishing of the Scripture in the vulgar tongue without notes is forbidden, measures have been taken by which the rigor of the law can be eluded and the printer be protected, until such time as it shall be deemed prudent to repeal the law made, as is now generally confessed, in a time of ignorance and superstitious darkness' [L 30.6.1836]. Borrow simply decided to disregard the laws of his host country. As we shall see, it was not the only time he did so.

doorstep[3]. This astonishing, not to say absurd, policy already contained the doom of Borrow's mission; but the prospective Bible-salesman nevertheless jumped at the chance. Much as he always derided and ridiculed Spain's lawlessness and the blatant ease with which even the authorities themselves ignored their own most rigorous legislation, he gladly made use of this practical 'flexibility' when it was convenient for his purpose[4].

As will be told below, Borrow's Spanish language gospel was printed in early 1837 and some 1,100 copies were distributed in various, sometimes adventurous ways over the following year. Then things changed drastically. First of all, a new, more conservative cabinet under Count Ofalia was appointed in December 1837. Additionally, Borrow's successful distribution became known to the ecclesiastical powers, who balked at the sheer audacity of the thing. And thirdly, one of Borrow's missionary colleagues, Lieutenant James Graydon, began to cause scandal and uproar in Valencia and Malaga by aggressive sales-policies and the distribution of Protestant tracts which rashly insulted the Catholic Church and its holiest tenets [Giménez, *Graydon*, 247 footnote 32]. Consequently the government decided to crack down on all foreign Bible-selling activities in the land. Borrow received an order to stop selling his New Testament; his shop in Madrid was raided and books confiscated; he himself was jailed for a week and a half when he threw an obnoxious police-officer out of his apartments; and on 19 May 1838, the Queen Regent signed a formal Royal Decree (published 25 May) prohibiting the sale, possession, and distribution of all vernacular Scripture. All extant copies were to be confiscated and only returned to Borrow under the solemn pledge to export them from the land.

This, once again, ought to have been the end of it. Only: due to a silly blunder, it once again was not. Borrow's arrest and imprisonment, executed by an overzealous lower official, had been very much against the

---

3 This was no mere slip of the tongue, but policy. James Graydon, the Bible Society's agent on the East coast, received a perfectly identical 'verbal permission' at this exact same time. See Giménez, *Graydon*, 229f.

4 Nor was he the only one. Once, in a private letter to Palmerston, Ambassador Villiers typically scoffed that 'legality is the last thing ever thought of in Spain' [*Palmerston: Private Correspondence with Sir George Villiers 1833–1837* (1985), 493]. Yet he wholeheartedly supported, not to say *caused*, this deplorable breach of the law. One might well say that Spanish indifference to legality was contagious!

Spanish laws in regard to foreigners. This enabled Ambassador Villiers to 'talk big' in defence of the rights of an English subject [Fraser, *Sleeping*, 38], and make the government tone down its position to such an extent, that George Borrow and his books were left in a legal limbo all of their own. The half-hearted orders which the government issued to the lower authorities were formulated in such a way that it was now strictly forbidden to own, transport, or sell the 1837 New Testament; and whenever a mayor or police-officer discovered such books being offered for sale, he was under strict obligation to detain them and place them under embargo. Yet these orders also specified that people found to be engaged in such forbidden trade, should not be bothered or detained under any circumstances. Nothing muddier than such a strict prohibition of commodities, combined with outspoken impunity for those who trafficked in them, can possibly be imagined; it only compares with a prohibition of automatic weapons but not of their everyday use. It needs no saying that Borrow was quick to make the most of that ambiguous situation.

Between July 1838 and November 1839 he mounted his greatest sales-efforts ever, effectively disposing of some 3,100 more copies of the New Testament in the surroundings of Madrid and the plains of Andalusia. Only by late 1839, when the government showed unmistakable signs that they were tired of this shameless game and were getting ready to imprison him for real, no matter what the British Ambassador might think or say, did he draw the line and stop selling Testaments. By that time, however, only some 800 copies of the original 5,000 remained unsold; and he could retire to England in missionary satisfaction.

I.2 The Printing of the Scio New Testament
I.2.a Preparation, printing and binding

Having consulted with his Employers in London in the autumn of 1836, Borrow returned to Madrid on 26 December 1836 with the assignment of printing a New Testament in Spanish, for which he had received his 'verbal permission' from the Spanish government in the first week of the previous July. He set briskly about the task.

The first two weeks of January 1837 were spent in preparation of the printing process; and it may be said that Borrow left nothing to chance.

On the recommendation of such an impressive collection of worthies as Prime Minister Isturitz, Henry O'Shea (the Bible Society's Madrid banker), and Sir George Villiers (the English Ambassador) he chose to entrust the work to the *Compañia Tipográfica*, a print-shop located in Madrid's Calle de Leon n° 21 and owned by the formidable Andrés Borrego [L 14.1.1837; APP; BiBo 2 verso][5]. It was, without a doubt, the best choice. Borrego, who worked with hyper-modern, state-of-the-art, steam-driven printing presses which he had personally imported from England [L 14.1.1837; BiBo 2 verso], was not only the 'most fashionable printer at Madrid' [APP], but also by far the safest for the job in hand. A militant liberal of old and proven loyalties (he had begun his political career at age 17 helping out in the 1820 Riego rising, and had spent most of the next 15 years in French and English exile), Borrego counted as one of the most prominent supporters of the present regime, was the government's official and 'confidential' printer, and could therefore be trusted 'to keep the matter secret', as Prime Minister Isturitz himself brazenly stated to Borrow during an interview [L 7.7.1836]. On top of that, the hyper-active *entrepreneur* was willing to keep his prices low [L 14.1.1837], work fast, and take upon himself a major part of the distribution to booksellers in the country at large [BiBo 1; BiBo 2]. To this effect, a regular contract containing seven articles was drawn up and signed by the two parties on 14 January 1837 [Knapp, *Life*, I : 266], after approval by O'Shea [Acc 4].

For the printing, Borrow had been authorised by the Bible Society to purchase 600 reams of paper at 60 *reales* per ream, i.e. to a total cost of 36,000 *reales* [L 14.1.1837][6]. However, having learned a good deal about

---

5 The original arrangement of July 1836 had been made with Charles Wood, an English printer settled in Madrid and then working for Borrego [L 25.7.1836]. But when Borrow returned to Spain in November, he 'found that during my absence from Madrid Mr. Wood had quitted Mr. Borrego, and had accepted a situation in another printing establishment'. Borrow stuck to the original agreement because Borrego possessed the only modern English machinery in Madrid [L 14.1.1837; Knapp, *Life*, I : 263].

6 The paper necessarily had to be acquired locally, because 'the importation of this article from foreign countries is forbidden', as the Barcelona printer Antonio Bergnes (*Anthony* for English friends) informed Graydon on 17 October 1835 (original letter in Bible Society Archive, Foreign Correspondence Inwards 1835, volume 4, p. 51).

logistics and acquisition from his previous assignment in St Petersburg (where under very adverse circumstances he printed a New Testament in Manchu), he decided to look around for a better deal. Knowing that his banker, Henry O'Shea had in the past 'been connected with the paper-manufactories of the south' and to the paper-mills of Catalonia, he asked that gentleman if he could not perhaps get him better paper at a lower price. O'Shea was glad to be of service to a good customer, and a few days later showed Borrow 'paper at 45 *reals*, better than what I could have purchased at 70'. Borrow jumped at the chance, so that he could triumphantly report to his employers that 'in paper alone 9000 *reals* will have been saved to the funds of the Society, and at the same time a superior article have been procured' [L 31.12.1836; L 14.1.1837]. In the end, this turned out to be something of an overstatement, since not 600 but 670 reams were ultimately used in the printing, with an additional 3 reams spoiled, so that the total cost of paper came to 673 x 45 = 30,285 *reales*, saving the Society 5,715 *reales* [Acc 4].

Back in England, Borrow had been given an example book, most probably the 1826 London version of the New Testament printed by T.C. Hansard [Knapp, *Life*, I : 255 and 263]. Once in Madrid he resolved to print his own edition in practically the same shape and size, except that he used a single column of text instead of the customary double one[7] [L 14.1.1837; L 27.2.1837]. As a copy-text, he kept to the Spanish translation made from the Vulgate by Father Phelipe Scio de San Miguel, first published in 1793, and at the time the standard text for all Scriptural editions in Spanish [Collie & Fraser, *Bibliography*, 110; Knapp. *Life*, I : 247]. This use of a translation from the Latin was already something of a concession for the British and Foreign Bible Society to make, since they

---

7 Why he did so is a mystery. The choice was all at once unprecedented for Bible Society publications and terribly paper-consuming. Due to the vast blank spaces left at the end of verses, single column Scripture is often 1.5 times longer than double-column editions (see illustration 1 and 2 below). For sake of comparison: the London 1826 and 1828 editions of the Scio New Testament, printing the very same text in double columns on a page of identical size, count 366 and 450 pages respectively. Borrow's edition, using a *smaller* lettertype, has 534! Graydon's roughly comparable 1837 edition in Catalan even makes do with only 252 pages, a great advantage for travel, postage and distribution. (Personal communication from Kathleen Cann, 19 February 2008.)

108   EVANGELIO   *Cap.* 14. 15.

vean, comiencen á hacer burla de él.

30 Diciendo: ¿ éste hombre comenzó á edificar, y no ha podido acabar?

31 ¿O qué Rey queriendo salir á pelear contra otro Rey, no considera ántes, de asiento, si podra salir con diez mil hombres á hacer frente al que viene contra él con veinte mil?

32 De otra manera, aun quando el otro está léjos, envia su embaxada, pidiéndole tratados de paz.

33 Pues así qualquiera de vosotros, que no renuncia á todo lo que posee; no puede ser mi discípulo.

34 Buena es la sal. Mas si la sal perdiere su sabor, ¿con qué será sazonada?

35 No es buena, ni para la tierra, ni para el muladar: mas la echarán fuera: Quién tiene orejas de oir, oiga.

CAP. XV.

Los Escribas, y Pharisèos murmuran del Señor, porque recibe á los pecadores. Les responde proponiéndoles tres parábolas, la de la oveja perdida; la de la drachma que perdió, y halló la muger; y la del hijo pródigo.

1 Y se acercaban á él los Publicanos, y pecadores, para oirle.

2 Y los Pharisèos, y los Escribas murmuraban, diciendo: Este recibe pecadores, y come con ellos.

3 Y les propuso ésta parábola, diciendo:

4 ¿Quién de vosotros es el hombre, que tiene cien ovejas y si perdiere una de ellas, no dexa las noventa y nueve en el desierto, y va á buscar la que se había perdido, hasta que la hálle?

5 Y quando la hallàre, la pone sobre sus hombros gozoso:

6 Y viniendo á casa, llama á sus amigos, y vecinos, diciéndoles: Dadme el parabien, porque he hallado mi oveja, que se había perdido.

7 Os digo, que así habrá mas gózo en el Cielo sobre un pecador que hiciere penitencia, que sobre noventa y nueve justos, que no han menester penitencia.

8 ¿O qué muger que tiene diez drachmas, si perdiere una drachma, no enciende el candil, y barre la casa, y la busca con cuidado hasta hallarla.

9 Y despues que la ha hallado, junta las amigas, y vecinas, y dice: Dadme el parabien, porque he hallado la drachma, que había perdido.

10 Así os digo, que habrá gózo delante de los Angeles de Dios por un pecador que hace penitencia.

11 Mas dixo: Un hombre tuvo dos hijos:

12 Y dixo el menor de ellos á su padre: Padre, dame la parte de la hacienda, que me toca. Y él les repartió la hacienda.

13 Y no muchos dias despues, juntado todo lo suyo, el hijo menor se fué léjos á un pais muy distante, y allí malrotó todo su haber, viviendo disolutamente.

14 Y quando todo lo hubo gastado, vino una grande hambre en aquella tierra, y él comenzó á padecer necesidad.

15 Y fué, y se arrimó á uno de los ciudadanos de aquella tierra: el qual lo envió á su cortijo á guardar puercos.

16 Y deseaba enchir su vientre de las mondaduras que los puercos comian: y ninguno se las daba.

17 Mas volviendo sobre sí, dixo: ¡Quántos jornaleros en la casa de mi padre tienen el pan de

---

Cap. 15.   SEGUN S. LUCAS.   159

CAPITULO XV.

Los Escribas, y Pharisèos murmuran del Señor, porque recibe á los pecadores. Les responde proponiéndoles tres parábolas, la de la oveja perdida; la de la drachma que perdió, y halló la muger; y la del hijo pródigo.

1 Y se acercaban á él los Publicanos, y pecadores, para oirle.

2 Y los Pharisèos, y los Escribas murmuraban, diciendo: Este recibe pecadores, y come con ellos.

3 Y les propuso ésta parábola, diciendo:

4 ¿Quién de vosotros es el hombre, que tiene cien ovejas, y si perdiere una de ellas, no dexa las noventa y nueve en el desierto, y va á buscar la que se había perdido, hasta que la hálle?

5 Y quando la hallàre, la pone sobre sus hombros gozoso:

6 Y viniendo á casa, llama á sus amigos, y vecinos, diciéndoles: Dadme el parabien, porque he hallado mi oveja, que se había perdido.

7 Os digo, que así habrá mas gózo en el Cielo sobre un pecador que hiciere penitencia, que sobre noventa y nueve justos, que no han menester penitencia.

8 ¿O qué muger que tiene diez drachmas, si perdiere una drachma, no enciende el candil, y barre la casa, y la busca con cuidado hasta hallarla?

9 Y despues que la ha hallado, junta las amigas, y vecinas, y dice: Dadme el parabien, porque he hallado la drachma, que había perdido.

10 Así os digo, que habrá gózo delante de los Angeles de Dios por un pecador que hace penitencia.

11 Mas dixo: Un hombre tuvo dos hijos:

12 Y dixo el menor de ellos á su padre: Padre, dame la parte de la hacienda, que me toca. Y él les repartió la hacienda.

13 Y no muchos dias despues, juntando todo lo suyo, el hijo menor, se fué léjos á un pais muy distante, y allí malrotó todo su haber, viviendo disolutamente.

14 Y quando todo lo hubo gastado, vino una grande hambre en aquella tierra, y él comenzó á padecer necesidad.

15 Y fué, y se arrimó á uno de los ciudadanos de aquella tierra: el qual lo envió á su cortijo á guardar puercos.

16 Y deseaba enchir su vientre de las mondaduras que los puercos comian; y ninguno se las daba.

17 Mas volviendo sobre sí, dixo: ¡Quántos jornaleros en la casa

Illustration 1: A page of the Scio New Testament (London 1826), Borrow's example book with double column

Illustration 2: A page of George Borrow's own Scio New Testament (Madrid 1837), with its single column

much preferred to print faithful renderings from the original Hebrew and Greek. The choice was inspired by the hope that printing the translation by an uncontroversial Spanish scholar – and a Roman Catholic bishop at that – would dispose the ruling hierarchy somewhat in favour of the edition. This was however a forlorn hope, since Borrow, in order to bring the publication into line with Bible Society criteria, left out all of Father Scio's many explicatory notes, thus rendering the work absolutely unacceptable to the Catholic Church.

To ensure the greatest possible accuracy of the text and avoid typographical errors, Borrow next engaged the services of the great Hebraist Doctor Luis Usoz y Rio, 'the first scholar in Spain' as Borrow styled him [APP], who for a modest remuneration of 732 *reales* [Acc 4] agreed to proofread each page once Borrow himself had done so first [L 14.1.1837; L 16.3.1837; APP].

Printing started a few days after the 14th of January 1837, and was to last some ten weeks [L 14.1.1837]. This planning was kept beautifully, for on March 16, a mere eight weeks later, Borrow informed his employers 'that the New Testament in Castilian will be ready in a few days' [L 16.3.1837; L 27.2.1837].

Borrego printed the whole of the edition in two batches: a first lot of 1,000 copies, in whose price were to be included the costs for the type-setting of the sheets; and a second lot of 4,000 copies at less than half the earlier price [Acc 4]. Each of the 5,000 copies of the Scio New Testament needed 67 sheets of paper to print its 534 pages of text, plus a blank front- and end-paper [Acc 4]. From this we learn not only that the reams delivered to Borrow counted a 'modern' 500 sheets of paper each (67 sheets x 5,000 copies being equal to 670 reams x 500 sheets), but also that the sheets in question were of rather small size and modest weight. Nowadays, the Scio New Testament is always entered in the library catalogues as a large 'octavo', due to its dimensions of 18.5 x 11 cm[8]. Yet, in purely *technical* terms, it was produced in 'quarto', since each sheet was folded only twice, to produce 4 leaves and hence 8 pages (67 x 8 = 536 pages). Consequently, the sheet in question measured around 2 x 18.5 = 37 cm by 2 x 11 = 22 cm (not counting the margin cut off from the top or bottom of the gatherings to separate the pages[9], and the small loss of width caused by the stitching). For comparison: a modern standard A4 page measures 29.7 x 21.0 cm.

---

8 Modern libraries typically catalogue the book as an '8º (19 cm)' or '8º (20 cm)', while a knowledgeable canon of the Santiago cathedral described it as an '8º (*mayor*)' in June 1838 (see II.4 below), and Luis Usoz, in an advertisement of 21 October 1837 in *La España*, describes it as an '*octavo prolongado*'.

9 This side of the binding process has given rise to some confusion. Thomas Wise, who published a first bibliography (*A Bibliography of the writings in Prose and Verse of George Henry Borrow*, London 1914) wrote on page 62 concerning the Gypsy *Luke* that 'I have never seen a copy of the First Edition (…) in the original binding. No doubt the book (which was printed in Madrid) was put up in paper wrappers, with untrimmed edges, in accordance with the usual Continental custom.' In fact, nobody has ever seen such an untrimmed copy in paper wrappers (Collie & Fraser, *Bibliography*, 113); which shows that the reasoning ought to be the other way around: despite the fact that these books were printed in Madrid, Borrego — who had learned much of his trade in England and had purchased his machinery there — produced an English style book for his English customer, i.e. properly bound and with the pages trimmed.

A finished copy of the Scio New Testament – *including* its binding and covers! – weighs 472.3 grams. This means that each of the 67 sheets used weighed in the neighbourhood of 7 grams (this without subtracting the weight of the covers, which cannot be established without tearing a valuable old book to pieces). The sheet having a surface of some 814 cm² (37 x 22 cm), Borrow's 'superior article' of paper can be calculated to have weighed, in modern terms, around 75–85 grams per m², which is not uncommon in Bible printing.

Already in February, Borrow arranged for the *Compañia Tipográfica* also to bind the books, since Borrego was 'about to unite bookbinding with printing' [L 27.2.1837]. The original 'very reasonable terms' for this job, 3 *reales* a volume bound in calf [L 27.2.1837], ultimately were not maintained, since the bill over the process states explicitly that each copy was bound for 4.5 *reales* [Acc 4]. The covers consist of 'leather covered boards which are fairly substantial', each some 4 mm thick [personal message from David Mount, 4 January 2008]. The entire book, with covers, is 3.6 cm thick.

A few obscure sides of the printing and binding may here be mentioned. First of all, two copies received a special '*encuadernacion de lujo*', or luxury binding, for the considerable sum of 80 *reales* each [BiBo 1]. What these show-pieces were, and where they ended up, is unknown. Since the Committee of the Bible Society frowned on extravagance, it is unlikely that they were meant for them. What is more: no such specially bound copy is at present found in the library of the British and Foreign Bible Society (deposited with the Cambridge University Library), which only contains two Scio New Testaments in simple, plain binding[10]. Possibly these were special 'memorial' copies for Borrow and Borrego himself? Until they are located we shall not know.

Then, sources also occasionally mention 'gilded copies', to the number of 800 [BiBo 1]. It is none too clear whether this means that the pages of these copies were gilt-edged or if perhaps the lettering on the binding was in gold-leaf. Next to their appearance in a bill of Borrego's, in

---

10 Either, or both, of these copies Borrow presented to his employers when he visited London for consultations in November 1838 [APP]. Why he did not send them one at an earlier time is unknown. Since they footed the hefty bill, they must have been interested.

which Borrow gets charged an extra 1 *real* a piece for the '*esceso de precio*' over this operation [BiBo 1], such gilded volumes only pop up twice in expense accounts, where 2 and 14 copies respectively are being sold for 11 *reales* a piece, i.e. 1 *real* more than the customary price of ordinary copies at this time [Acc 7; Acc 8]. Since they are never seen again beyond these three occasions, and were clearly treated just like ordinary, ungilded copies from an early moment on, their existence may and must be ignored for the present study.[11]

In late March or early April 1837, the edition was ready, and Borrow was justly proud of it. On various occasions, when he got to speak of it, he pointed out that it 'was printed on excellent English paper and well bound' [APP], that it was an 'exceedingly favourable specimen of typography' [L 25.12.1837]; that it would have been 'utterly impossible to bring out a work of the size of the New Testament, handsomely and creditably in Spain' at a cheaper price [L 27.2.1837]; but 'principally and above' all this, that it was 'one of the most correct works that have ever issued from the press in Spain' [L 25.12.1837], since 'no pains have been spared, at least on my part, to render it as correct as possible' [L 16.3.1837], so that it showed 'scarcely one typographical error, every proof having been read thrice by myself and once or more times by' Usoz [APP][12].

---

11 It cannot be excluded that these gilded copies made up the first batch of 1,000 copies printed by Borrego, with their considerably higher price [Acc 4]. In that case, however, the missing 200 ought to be somehow explained. Note, however, that the surcharge of 800 *reales* over these special copies was never paid. The sum is crossed out heavily in the original bill [BiBo 1]; when speaking in a letter to Brandram [L 9.7.1838] about the debt owed to Borrego according to the printer' statement of current account [BiBo 2], where it reads 3,884 *reales*, Borrow mentions clearly that it concerns only 3,084; and that latter figure appears as such in his expense account of 9 July 1838 [Acc 9]. Could it be that most or all of these 800 gilded copies were simply never gilded?

12 Four or five meticulous corrections by two well-paid proof readers may seem excessive, but wasn't. The worst thing one could do was to gain eternal notoriety through silly typos in printed Scripture. Cobham Brewer's famous *Dictionary of Phrase and Fable*, under 'Bible', records a few amusing *gaffes* of this kind, such as the 'Affinity Bible' of 1923, which held that 'a man may not marry his grandmother's wife'; the 'Wicked Bible' of 1631, which by failing to include the word 'not' in the seventh commandment, prescribed that 'Thou shalt commit adultery'; and the first Irish Bible of 1716, which by a subtle hopscotch of the n and the o, summoned readers to 'Sin on more'! Reading such typos, one begins to suspect that the complaint

The full title given to the book was: '*El Nuevo Testamento, traducido al Español de la Vulgata Latina, por el Rmo. P. Phelipe Scio de S. Miguel, de las escuelas pias, obispo electo de Segovia. Madrid: Imprenta a cargo de D. Joaquin de la Barrera. 1837.*' The last line shows how very aware Borrow and Borrego must have been that they were playing with legal fire; for the ascription of the printing to a fictitious publisher[13] must have been one of the 'measures' which could be taken to protect the printer from consequences [L 30.6.1836]. This act was an outright and shameless snubbing of the law, which prescribed unconditionally that works of a religious or political nature carry the full and precise name of the printer on their title page. One of Borrow's later biographers made fun of the fact that his adversaries, in May 1838, produced documents demonstrating 'that the imprint on the title-page of the Scio New Testament was false, as at the time it was printed no such printer as Andreas Borrego (who by the way was the Government printer and at one time a candidate for cabinet rank) lived in Madrid' [Jenkins, *Life*, ch 16]. But as the above shows: Borrow's adversaries were perfectly right, for the title page made no mention of *Borrego* at all; and no such person as Don Joaquin de la Barrera could be located, in spite of the fact that the Civil Governor of Madrid himself ordered that person to come forward by formal summons in the *Diario de Madrid* of May 1838 [Giménez, *Prensa*, 377, nº 22]. Borrow, quite simply, printed a lie on the title-page; and it would be silly not to admit so.

---

in Psalm 119 of the 1702 'Printer's Bible', where line 166 reads that not *princes*, but '*printers* have persecuted me without cause', may have been inspired by On High. (For some other examples see chapter 6 of Henry Wheatley's '*Literary Blunders, a chapter in the History of Human Error*' and chapter 10 of P.H. Ditchfield's '*Books Fatal to Their Authors*')

13 This printer's pseudonym may carry more significance than appears at first sight. By the looks of it, the name was deliberately coined to resemble that of the famous late-18th century publisher Joaquin Ibarra and his successors, who had brought out various licenced editions of Scripture which were still on the market in 1837. If it was indeed meant to confuse and throw the authorities off track, the plan seems to have worked occasionally (see III.3.3 below).

EL

NUEVO TESTAMENTO,

TRADUCIDO AL ESPAÑOL

DE LA VULGATA LATINA,

POR EL

RMO. P. PHELIPE SCIO DE S. MIGUEL,

DE LAS ESCUELAS PIAS, OBISPO ELECTO DE SEGOVIA.

———

MADRID:
IMPRENTA A CARGO DE D. JOAQUIN DE LA BARRERA.
1837.

Illustration 3: The title page of Borrow's Scio New Testament

I.2.b Costs of production

THE COSTS of the production of the Scio New Testament are enumerated in Borrow's expense account of 5 April 1837 [Acc 4], which – in a slightly different order – enumerates the following items:

	Reales
Composition and printing of 1000 copies at 180 *reales* per sheet, say 67 sheets (= 1 x 67 x 180)	12,060
Printing of 4,000 copies of the said 67 sheets at 85 *reales* per 1000 (= 4 x 67 x 85)	22,780
Binding in calf of 5,000 copies at 4.5 *reales* per copy	22,500
Subtotal printing and binding:	**57,340**
Costs of 673 reams of paper (incl. 3 reams spoiled)	30,285
Salary of Dr. Usoz for assistance	732
Total	**88,357**

These costs should still be augmented with the 160 *reales* charged for the luxury bindings of two copies [BiBo 1], bringing the total to 88,517 *reales*, a not inconsiderable sum at the time, seeing that it represented some *sixty yearly wages* of the average bread-winner (see Appendix 1).

Borrow always maintained that the cost price of each copy of the Scio New Testament was 15 *reales*. This was based on a very early estimate [L 27.2.1837] which was never recalculated. In reality, the cost price of each copy was nearly 18 *reales*, and that without counting Borrow's own substantial salary (200 Pounds Sterling or some 20,000 *reales* yearly) and his no less impressive travelling expenses. Possibly he took these latter into account as well when later, in his explicatory Memorial to Prime Minister Ofalia of early 1838, he mentioned that 'the Society had subjected itself to an expense of more than 100,000 *reals*' to produce and distribute the edition [L 17.3.1838]. See, however, IV.8 Finances below for a more complete estimate of costs.

I.3 Price policy

WHEN DECIDING the price for which the New Testament would be offered for sale, Borrow was not at all led by the cost price of the books, but
exclusively by considerations of speedy distribution and of Bible Society
prestige. This policy was in keeping with the guiding principles of his
employers. The British and Foreign Bible Society was no commercial
enterprise, but a spiritual charity, or what we might nowadays call a
religious NGO. Its stated aim was to make Scripture available the world
over in vernacular language; hence the Society was willing, and could afford, to lose money on these idealistic activities, as long as such financial
losses might be justified in the eyes of its sponsors by tangible results. It
was therefore quite customary to sell the books at cost price, or half cost
price, or even, at times, to distribute them gratis to the very poor, as, for
instance, Borrow's colleague and rival Lieutenant Graydon did on the
Levantine coast [Giménez, *Graydon*, 230 and 234][14].

Only the propagandistic use which the Bible Society's enemies might
make of such policies put a limit to the underpricing of the books. Thus
we hear, time and time again in the dispute which was subsequently
unleashed in Spain about the British Bible-selling effort – and almost
with the frequency and regularity of a mantra – that the missionaries sold
their infamous heretical works '*por un precio infimo*', i.e. 'for a miniscule
price'[15]; a phrase which almost suggests a conspiracy of obscure money-

---

14 This article by Antonio Giménez Cruz is the best available text on Graydon. A
much larger study, on which we mainly depend for the facts of Graydon's activities,
was written forty years ago by Tine Barrass in her Ph.D. thesis *The Catalan New
Testament and the British and Foreign Bible Society, 1820–1888* (Cambridge, April
1968); but this work unfortunately remains unpublished.

15 The expression is used, to name but a few instances, by Prime Minister Ofalia
to Ambassador Villiers [Giménez, *Graydon*, 242]; by the Justice Ministry official
Ventura González [Missler, *RRT*, 27 and 36], and by the Bishop of Tuy, in his 1838
pastoral letter [Missler, *RRT*, 31]. Note, however, that the phrase may have originated
with Graydon himself. It first appears in an advertisement of the *Diario Mercantil*
of June 1837 [Giménez, *Graydon*, 233] where it is said that the Bible Society offers
Scripture '*a todas las clases a precios infimos y hasta de balde a los menestrales*'. Borrow
himself, meanwhile, induced Madrid-based British journalists to use a comparable
expression in their reporting on his imprisonment in May 1838. On page 6 of the
Morning Herald of 16 May 1838, one 'J.W.W.' writes that Borrow established a

interests to undermine the political stability of the Spanish Kingdom, and in any case belittles the value and appeal of such works by stressing that they had to be subsidised in order to find customers. Other critics went even further, and – as Borrow himself observed in his letters with the writings of Dr. Wiseman especially in mind – 'the enemies of the Bible Society have stated in several publications that it has no vent for the Bibles and Testaments which it publishes in many foreign languages but by sending them to the various countries, and there distributing them gratis or selling them by auction, when they are bought for waste paper' [L 20.7.1837] because the Bible Society supposedly 'cannot dispose of its books at any price, nor indeed get rid of them gratis!' [L 12.6.1839].

Borrow was determined not to hand his religious adversaries such ready sticks with which to beat the Bible Society. 'My conduct in this point has been principally influenced by a desire to give, in the case of Spain at least, the direct lie to this assertion, and this conduct I shall pursue until I receive direct orders to abandon it' [L 20.7.1837]. Consequently he decided early on to sell the books for a considerable sum of money, and never to give any books away, even though he was regularly pestered for free copies by people who had heard rumours that such books could be had gratis [L 25.12.1837]. 'I wish it to be distinctly understood,' he wrote during his first great book-peddling expedition in the North, 'that throughout my journey I have given away none of the books, having invariably received money for them, viz., from 10 to 12 *reals*' [L 20.7.1837]. This indeed was the standard price he applied from April 1837, when the New Testament appeared, to May 1838, when its sale was forbidden. The booksellers whom he franchised were expected to sell the books for 10 to 12 *reales*; in his own Madrid shop he asked 10 *reales* [L 25.12.1837]; and it was the sum which he invariably received when selling single copies to individuals he met during his extensive travels in the summer of 1837.

Obviously, 10 *reales*, almost half of cost price, was 'unaccountably cheap' for the value which the customer received [L 25.12.1837]. And yet this price policy did limit the volume of his sales considerably. At

---

shop for the sale 'of the New Testament at so reduced a price that persons in the humblest circumstances might purchase it at a trifling sacrifice' [reproduced in Fraser, *Sleeping*, p. 44, Annex 2].

10 *reales*, over twice the daily wage of an unskilled worker in the 1830s, the books were practically out of reach of common folk, who had more pressing needs than spiritual literature at a time of economic crisis and civil war (compare Appendix 1). Consequently Borrow, selling to city folk at a city price, sold relatively few copies of his New Testament in the first period: only 1,100 copies at the outside, a fifth of the edition, in little over a year (see IV.6 Total Sales below).

Then, after his imprisonment of May 1838 and the diplomatic crisis that ensued, Borrow quite suddenly cuts his prices drastically: 4, 3, and sometimes even 2 *reales*, and sets off on horseback into the rough countryside, to peddle his wares to the peasantry. The reasons behind this abrupt change of heart and price policy are various. First of all, he was in a hurry to get rid of the edition. The sale of New Testaments was now formally forbidden and he played indeed a 'daring game' by selling them at all [L 14.7.1838]. Any moment, he might be ordered out of the land as a *persona non grata*, or his hidden, central stock in Madrid might be discovered and confiscated *en masse*.

Yet, as I have shown elsewhere [Missler, *Underpriced*, 19f], there were also rather more personal motives at work. During the crisis in May, as he was putting pressure on his employers to recall 'the madman' Graydon who by his overzealous doings had endangered the whole Bible Society effort in Spain, his employers had taunted him rather roughly with the fact that they considered him a lousy salesman[16], hinting somewhat obliquely at Graydon's sales figures being so much higher than his own. Graydon, however, famously sold his books for 4 or 5 *reales*, and even gave them away, which went a long way to explain his success. Hence, in the interest of his job, Borrow needed to prove – before he could be recalled to England for 'consultation'[17] – that he was just as good at

---

16 See Andrew Brandram's letter to Borrow of 29 June 1838 (quoted in Jenkins, *Life*, 264f), in which the good Reverend writes 'We shall not easily forget your services in St Petersburg, but suffer me to remind you that when you came to the point of distribution your success ended'. This was an ugly taunt, since Borrow had not been sent to Russia to distribute, only to print a New Testament in Manchu, and when he did want to go and distribute it in China, the Russian government had refused him a travelling visa!

17 There is no doubt that the Bible Society was planning to recall Borrow at the same time as Graydon, in June 1838. The intention even made it somewhat

distribution as his colleague. This meant first of all lowering his price radically, so that common folk, who were fascinated by cheap books, could afford to buy them; and then going into the hamlets and villages of the countryside as a travelling salesman, to make sure the books would come within their reach. These tactics did indeed work, for over the next year and a half, Borrow sold an additional 3,100 copies, mainly to the poor, until the edition was nearly sold out.

I.4 Methods of distribution

ONCE THE edition of the New Testament was ready, Borrow dedicated himself to its distribution. This was no easy task in a land like Spain, where for many centuries all manner of reading, printing, publishing and book-selling, except the most innocent and academic, had been curbed and kept under strict control by the Inquisition, and where the book trade had always suffered from the dismally low levels of literacy (but see III.1 for the situation in the 1830s).

Consequently, Borrow needed to bring into play every feasible way to market his wares [L 14.1.1837; L 1.11.1837], and, being an energetic and inventive agent, he employed the following methods:

1. First of all, he sold the books himself, to private people whom he met on the road, in the towns and in the villages, during his long Northern Journey of mid 1837 and other travels.

2. Secondly, he sold through the booksellers of the major cities of Spain, where he established 'depots' of books.

3. Thirdly, for little over half a year in 1837–1838, he ran his own book-shop in Madrid, where practically nothing was sold except the 1837 Scio New Testament.

4. Fourthly, in Madrid and Seville, he employed a variety of colporteurs that went around the streets of these cities with books, to sell them house to house, or to colleagues and friends.

---

prematurely into official reports. Knapp, *Life*, I : 296 quotes from the 35th Report of March 1839: 'Very shortly after the last Anniversary [May 1838], circumstances occurred which obliged the Committee to withdraw their two zealous and indefatigable friends from Spain.' Yet in March 1839 Borrow was still peddling their books quite zealously in Madrid and its surroundings.

5. Lastly, in the later period when the sale of the Scio New Testament was forbidden, he himself went around on horseback, together with collaborators, as a travelling book-peddler in the countryside, bringing his wares to the peasantry.

Each of these methods will be illustrated in the following pages. However, in order to reach a semblance of clarity in this quite confusing narrative, it will be necessary to present the different sales-methods in a mixed thematic, topographical and chronological manner, treating first of the period April 1837 to May 1838, when sales of the New Testament were still tolerated, and subsequently of his various sales methods after the formal prohibition was in place (May 1838 to November 1839) in Madrid itself, in the countryside around it, and in Andalusia and Morocco.

II

Sales in the 'tolerated period' (April 1837 – May 1838)

II.1 The Northern Journey (May – October 1837)

No sooner had the edition of the New Testament come off the press, than Borrow set out on horseback for the North-Western regions of Spain. The object of this long and dangerous journey through Spain's poorest provinces, regions swarming with common bandits and Carlist rebels, and populated by people who had barely escaped from the stone-age, was to scout the land and become familiar with its conditions [APP]; to establish depots of books with the booksellers in the principal towns and cities [L 27.2.1837]; and to sell as many copies as he could to 'the wild people of the wild regions' which he visited [L 14.1.1837][18].

The journey lasted some five and a half months, from mid May to 31 October 1837, and took him from Madrid to Salamanca, from there to Valladolid, Leon and Astorga; then to the Galician cities of Lugo, Coruña, and Santiago de Compostela; and after a swift excursion to the southern cities of Vigo and Pontevedra and to remote Cape Finisterre, out of Galicia again by Ferrol to Oviedo, the capital of Asturias. From

---

18 Borrow's Northern Journey is described in chapter 10 to 35 of *The Bible in Spain*, and was studied at length by Ian Robertson, *Tour*, 62–84. For the stunning Finisterre episode, where Borrow was nearly shot as a spy, see Juan Campos, *Naufragos*, 38ff.

here he travelled on to Santander, where he discovered that it was impossible to pass through the Basque Countries, as his original plan had been [L 7.6.1837; L 15.9.1837], because these regions were the smoking battlefield of the Carlist Civil War. Consequently, he returned to Madrid by Burgos and Valladolid, having covered some 3,000 kilometres over tremendously rough ground.

II.1.1 Packing the horses

Ever ambitious, Borrow originally planned to distribute no less than a quarter of the edition in the Northern provinces. 'I will take with me 1200 copies,' he wrote in his letter of 14 January 1837, 'which I will engage to dispose of' to the booksellers and individual clients of the north. This plan turned out to be too optimistic. At the end of the ride he only 'moved' 900 copies of the New Testament to the north, and only 'disposed' of some 700, either through direct sale to clients or by giving them in franchise to booksellers. The missing 200 copies had been dispatched from Madrid to Santander too late to reach him, and were ultimately returned to him (see II.2.2.x below).

Naturally Borrow did not transport all these 900 copies himself. His means of travelling did not allow this. The whole expedition consisted of only two riders (Borrow and his bizarre but extremely useful Greek man-servant Antonio Buchino[19]) and their two horses; and this constellation considerably limited the cargo which could be taken along. Although we may assume that Borrow and his companion packed only a bare minimum of personal belongings since they were planning to sleep and eat in the inns and taverns on the road, their mounts could barely be expected to carry much more than the riders themselves, the saddles, and the saddle-bags containing those personal belongings. Copies of the Scio New Testaments, at 472 grams apiece, were a heavy load to add.

Both considerations of travelling speed and of animal health compelled a 19th century horseman to keep cargoes as light as possible. Just as a chain is only as strong as its weakest link, an animal team is only as fast as the slowest horse, and any overloaded animal inevitably holds up the advance of the group. We see the problem illustrated on several occasions

---

19 On Buchino (or Buchini, as Borrow called him) see Robertson, *Tour*, 64

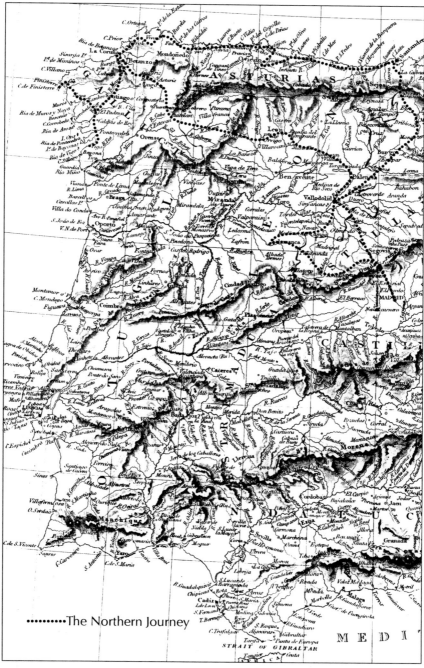

·········The Northern Journey

Illustration 4:
Map of Western Spain, showing the route of Borrow's Northern Journey

in *The Bible in Spain*, when Borrow, growing impatient, somewhat cal-
lously rides ahead of Antonio, whose horse apparently was slower [e.g.
BiS ch 24 and 26].

Even more importantly, however, a badly packed horse would soon fall
sick and become an encumbrance. Especially when travelling over the
sort of broken ground and bridle paths that made up Spain's transport
network in the 1830s, it was of supreme importance not to overcharge the
beasts, because – as Long Rider Jean-Louis Gouraud once put it – 'it is
not the *kilometres* that hurt the horse, but the *kilograms*.' A horse made
to carry more than its share, or one whose load was packed unbalanced,
would soon become exhausted or develop a saddle sore which injured
the withers. This implied visits to the vet (if there was one) and lengthy
periods of recuperation, spent in places where one did not wish to stay
at all.

Today's modern horse-travellers out on a long or difficult journey tend
to limit the load of the 'road horse' (as the rider's own mount used to be
called in the 19th century) to the absolute minimum, one rule of thumb
saying that a horse should never be made to carry more than ⅓ of its own
weight, the rider included. When more weight must be transported, or in
cases of doubt, they prefer to use an additional pack-animal which gets to
carry up to some 45 kilos, although for short weekend trips the cargo may
be increased to double that weight. Travelling at a speed of 7 or 8 km per
hour, a team will then travel some 35 to 40 km a day over normal ground,
and between 15 and 25 km over rough or mountainous country.

In former days, however, when times were less sentimental, horses a
little sturdier, and worn-down pack-animals easier to replace, the limits
seem to have been pushed a bit higher. Professional Spanish transporters
of the early 19th century typically loaded the '*caballería menor*' (probably
donkeys and ponies) with some 60 to 75 kilos to negotiate between 40
or 45 kilometres daily; while what was called '*caballería mayor*' (horses
and mules) might get to carry from 90 to 115 kilograms to cover the same
daily distance. Perhaps more illustrative for the present context, however,
are the Asturian *arrieros*, who transported commodities the whole 450
kilometres from the north coast of the Peninsula to Madrid, over the
often steep Cantabrian mountain range, very much comparable ground
to that which Borrow and Antonio had to cover. In order to perform this
journey successfully in some 12 to 20 days (between 37.5 and 22.5 km

daily), these men would load a male pack-horse with only 70 to 80 kilos, or some two-thirds of the above weights[20].

Borrow, who was an expert horseman, planned his Northern Journey with great care and much in advance. Originally, he had wanted to purchase mules for the journey, but he had a change of heart due to their high price in these times of war and the logistical trouble they caused. As he wrote to his employers at an early date: 'I confess I would sooner provide myself with mules, but they are very expensive creatures. In the first place, the original cost of a tolerable one amounts to 30 pounds [about 3,000 *reales* – PM]; and they, moreover, consume a vast quantity of fodder, at least two pecks of barley in the twenty-four hours with straw in proportion, and if they are stinted in their food they are of no manner of service; the attendance which they require is likewise very irksome, as they must be fed once every four hours night and day' [L 14.1.1837]. A month later he still reported that 'I wished to purchase a mule, according to my instructions, but though I offered 30 pounds for a sorry one, I could not obtain her' [L 27.2.1837]. So in the end he decided to make do without pack-animals, and instead to purchase for a mere 3,000 *reales* in total, two well-picked, sturdy road horses, which might be able to make the trip despite the difficult going and the heavy load they'd have to carry.

The first of these, which cost him only 900 *reales* [Acc 5; L 14.1.1837] was the sturdy bay horse of an Andalusian smuggler with whom he had travelled from Córdoba to Madrid in December 1836 [*BiS* ch 18]. It must have been quite an animal, for Borrow boasted of it – with perhaps just a touch of hyperbole – that it was 'an exceedingly strong, useful animal,' able to go 'twelve leagues a day with ease, and carry three hundred-weight on its back' [L 14.1.1837], i.e. cover 65 km daily while carrying 150 kilos. Outdoing himself still a little more, he wrote a month later to his Danish friend Hasfeld, that the animal 'will go 12 leagues a day and carry 200 pounds weight besides its rider' [Fraser, *Hasfeld*, 22]! We can only assume this was a horse the like of which has not been seen since!

The other animal, a splendid black Andalusian steed which he planned to ride himself, he got by chance for a most reasonable 2,100 *reales* [Acc 5].

---

20 For these numbers see: José I. Uriol, 'Los Transportes de mercancías por carretera en el siglo XIX', in: *Revista de Obras Publicas*, February 1984, pp. 109–118.

As he explained to his employers in late February: 'about a fortnight since I purchased another horse, for these animals are at present exceedingly cheap. A royal requisition is about to be issued for 5,000, and the consequence is that an immense number are for sale; for by virtue of this requisition the horses of any person not a foreigner can be seized for the benefit of the service. (…) He is a black Andalusian stallion of great size and strength, and capable of performing a journey of 100 leagues in a week's time [i.e. 560 km or 80 km daily! – PM], but he is unbroke, savage and furious. However, a cargo of Bibles which I hope shortly to put on his back will, I have no doubt, thoroughly tame him, especially when labouring up the flinty hills of the north of Spain' [L 27.2.1837].

Since we do not know how much either Antonio or Borrow weighed we cannot determine exactly what additional cargo these two animals could be expected to carry. Antonio, who was 'somewhat above the middle stature' [*BiS* ch 19] may have come to 65 or 70 kilos; while Borrow himself, with his 1 m 85 and his (later) tendency to obesity, must have weighed well over 80[21]. Supposing that Borrow's boasts about the two horses did indeed come near the truth, Antonio's grey bay horse might have carried another 70 kilos, while Borrow's Andalusian could perhaps have been loaded with an extra 60. This estimate would, in principle, open the possibility that the two men transported the whole necessary cargo of New Testaments themselves; for it can be calculated that Borrow, when riding forth from Madrid, took along 200 copies of the book, i.e. some 95 kilos in total, or 47.5 kilos per horse.

This number of 200 copies is a conjecture; but it squares up well with what we know of Borrow's private sales during the first leg of the trip (see II.1.2.a below); and is in perfect keeping with his later, well-documented habit of taking along, or sending before him, batches of 200 Testaments when setting out on Bible-peddling expeditions. Thus, when going to the Sagra region in July 1838 (see III.2.1), he sent before him 200 copies, and when these were all sold off, ordered a new batch of 200 to be brought

---

21 Up to the year 1843, Borrow was still admired for his athletic figure, only growing more stout towards the latter half of the 1840s. Yet he certainly was not skinny at the time he left for Northern Spain. In a letter to Hasfeld of 20 December 1838 [Fraser, *Hasfeld*, 33] he mentions that he weighs 'considerably more than two stone' (12.5 kg) above his weight during his Russian period of 1833–1835, and that it took three men to haul him up by rope from the vaults of the Villalengua Castle.

to him from Madrid. On the next excursion to Ocaña in early August 1838 (see III.2.2), he sent a servant ahead of him with slightly more than 250 New Testaments. To distribute in the regions north-west of Madrid in September 1839 (see III.2.4) he had a chest with 200 Testaments delivered to him in Segovia, which he then moved into the countryside on the backs of three donkeys. Likewise he sold 'nearly 200 testaments' to the east of Madrid in early 1839 (see III.3.3). And finally, when, towards the end of his mission, circumstances forced him to smuggle an illegal stock of Testaments into Seville so as to be able to distribute at all, it consisted, once again, of slightly over 200 copies (see III.4.1)[22].

The total weight of rider, personal luggage and books, put on the horses' backs, would then amount to some 120 to 130 kilos, a load which a truly good road horse might perhaps just be able to carry for a few days at the outset of the journey, even over the difficult Sierra de Guadarrama mountains which they had to negotiate to reach Salamanca, the first important city on their route. However, to put this strain on any horse is so very devoid of wisdom that it becomes nearly unthinkable that a fine horseman like Borrow would have chosen to do so. Not only the sheer weight would exhaust the animals within a few days; but the bulk of the cargo of books, lifted on top of the saddlebags, would make it extremely difficult for the rider to swing his leg over the burden, and would trap him dangerously in the saddle. Furthermore, there was a vast chance that such a load would become unbalanced, which quickly would inflict injury on the very sensitive loins and kidneys of the animal[23].

---

22 And it might be added that even long before his Spanish stint, Borrow had already made up his mind as to the 'perfect' number of Gospels to be carried on expeditions. In a letter of 13 October 1834 (O.S.), i.e. 25 October (N.S.), to Jowett from St Petersburg, while discussing a possible attempt to distribute the New Testament in Manchu which he had seen through the press in Northern China, he wrote: 'Far be it from me to advise that the entire stock of Testaments be hazarded in such an enterprise; 200 is the extreme number which should be ventured (...) for a seizure upon the agent and his books would be no improbable event.' However, this looks like a smaller cargo than it really was, for every copy of the Manchu New Testament consisted of 8 volumes in 4°, with a total of 1,000 pages [Knapp, *Life*, I : 178].

23 This verdict is based on the personal communications from CuChullaine O'Reilly of the Long Riders Guild, 17 January and 22 January 2008. Mister O'Reilly points out to me that 'in modern travel, we hoist each pannier [of the pack-animal] on a scale, never allowing them to vary more than a few ounces. If you don't do

Consequently, it makes sense to consider alternative ways in which the cargo of books may have been transported; and as it happens there is one vague indication that on Borrow's Northern Journey the books were transported in a chest and sent before him from town to town by courier. This indication is a chat which Borrow had with a sullen Maragato, or inhabitant of Astorga [*BiS* ch 23], where the muleteer is made to say: 'Tomorrow I set out for Lugo, whither I am told yourself are going. If you wish to send your chest, I have no objection to take it at so much (naming an extravagant price).' One may of course doubt the relevance of this remark; but Borrow had no real reason to put an unrealistic or nonsensical word into the mouth of one of his characters, and as already observed above: he often sent larger batches of books ahead of him on his later expeditions, so that he would not have to transport them himself. At the same time, he may have carried a small number of New Testaments along with him on horseback, so as to be able to sell them in the villages which he passed, something which then explains his assurance that 'a cargo of Bibles which I hope shortly to put on his back' would 'thoroughly tame' his wild Andalusian steed [L 27.2.1837].

Although we cannot tell how many books the horses were then called upon to carry next to the rider and his personal luggage, there is no doubt that the effort did 'tame' the Andalusian, for he was dead before the year was out. The poor animal fell sick after only two months of travelling, so that Borrow decided to sell him in Coruña, where soon after he 'glandered and died' [*BiS* ch 26 and 31]. Antonio's bay horse, by the looks of it, made it all the way to Galicia and back, but suffered terribly as well [*BiS* ch 31; L 29.9.1837]. Most tellingly, Borrow commented with his final expense account on the Northern Journey that 'I have been subjected to many expenses which I have not specified in the account (...) particularly farriers' bills, as the poor horses were continually ailing from over-work, bad provender and falls received amongst the mountains' [L 20.11.1837].

---

this, the off-balance load will cut your animal into hamburger before nightfall.' As to the notion that Borrow would have made his animals carry so much, O'Reilly qualifies this without more ado as a 'guaranteed recipe for equestrian travel disaster.' Note also that in his expense account of 10 May 1837 [Acc 5], which details various preparatory purchases for the Northern Journey such as saddles and bridles, there is no mention of special saddlebags or panniers which would have been necessary to carry 100 books each.

As I have argued elsewhere[24], Borrow cared deeply for his animals and treated them well; but even he could not avoid the terrible wear and tear of travel in Spain in the 1830s.

II.1.2 Private sales during the Northern Journey

II.1.2.a The first leg
(Madrid mid May – Coruña 20 July 1837)

Distribution during the Northern Journey of mid 1837 took place in two ways: franchise or sale to booksellers in the cities visited (see II.2 below), and sales or gifts to individual clients Borrow met on the road.

To start with the latter: according to his own expense account of late November 1837, Borrow personally sold 118 New Testaments to individual clients during the whole of his expedition [Acc 6]. This was a correction upward, by two copies, of the number he reported to his employers the day after his return to Madrid, when he wrote: 'I have, moreover, by private sale disposed of 116 Testaments to individuals entirely of the lower classes, namely, muleteers, *carmen, contrabandistas*, etc.' [L 1.11.1837]. The total proceeds of these transactions came down to 1224 *reales*; which shows that he sold most of these copies for 10 *reales*, and a small number for 11 or 12, as was indeed his stated practice [L 20.7.1837; and I.3 above].

Two further remarks of his allow us, furthermore, to reconstruct the size of the stock of New Testaments which he carried with him from Madrid, and the chronological order in which he distributed these. First of all, we know that this entire first stock was exhausted by the time he left Lugo in mid July 1837, all copies having either been handed over to booksellers or sold privately to clients; for he writes a week later that he brought 30 Testaments to Lugo, which were all sold in a day and that 'I was much grieved that my stock of these holy books was exhausted, for there was a great demand for them' [L 20.7.1837]. Furthermore, in the same letter he mentions that 'since my departure from the capital I have myself disposed of 65, without including those sold at Lugo and other places by means of the advertisements, on which I principally rely, as they speak at all times whether I am present or absent' [L 20.7.1837].

---

24 'George Borrow: the Rider in the Storm', preface to *The Bible in Spain*, Long Riders Guild, USA 2006.

The outlay of this first stock may partly be pieced together from the different sources:

On the road Madrid-Salamanca (May 1837)	5	L 7.6.1837; BiS ch 20
Franchise to Salamanca bookseller	?	L 5.7.1837; BiS ch 20; II.2.2.ii
Gift to the Cura of Pitiegua	1	BiS ch 21
Franchise to Valladolid bookseller	40	II.2.2.iii
Estimated 'satchel sale' Valladolid	15	see Satchel Sales, II.1.3
Franchise to Leon bookseller	40	L 20.11.1837; II.2.2.iv
Sold to Astorga Maragato	3	BiS ch 23
Arreiro in Bembribe Valley	1	BiS ch 24
Franchise to Lugo bookseller	30	L 20.7.1837: II.2.2.v

These numbers are, of course, the result of Borrow's random notations. In his writings, he did not record each and every New Testament he ever sold; and the data are therefore not complete. What is more, some of the information is notoriously uncertain, particularly the size of the 'satchel sale' near Valladolid [APP; ROS], a spurious little affair of such confusing dimensions that its treatment must be relegated to a separate chapter (see II.1.3 below). Nevertheless, some conclusions may be wrung out of these numbers.

First of all: the total number of copies attested with any measure of certainty is 135, to which the unknown 'certain number' to the Salamanca bookseller should still be added. Of these 135, however, 10 copies were sold or given away to individual clients, and these Borrow would have counted among the 65 'private sold copies' as mentioned above. This means that 55 privately sold copies are not contained in the above list. These 55 must be added to the 135, reaching a total of attested copies of 190. From here on, anything said is mere speculation; but it is obvious that these 190 come perfectly close to the 200 copies of Testaments which Borrow was always in the habit of taking along when on Bible-peddling expeditions (see above II.1.1).

The remaining 10 copies needed to reach a full 200 would then be, or be part of, the 'certain number' given in franchise to the Salamanca bookseller. Since Borrow himself mentions specifically seeing 3 sold, and elsewhere that 'several' of the stock were purchased by clients during his own stay in Salamanca, 10 copies seem rather few to be left in franchise with a promising bookseller. There are, however, good reasons to be extremely cautious in our speculations. As the final reckonings of stock (IV.5) and total sales (IV.6) at the end of this study will show, there are extremely few copies – a few dozen at best – whose whereabouts we ignore once all the certain data over the full 3.5 years of selling activity are assembled. Hence the margin for speculation is equally thin, and it is the wisest course always to assign, here as well as in every other instance of uncertainty, the lowest possible number of copies sold, left in franchise, confiscated or otherwise removed from the central reserve. For this reason I maintain these 10 copies as a first supply left in franchise in Salamanca; well aware that this may be too low an estimate and that Borrow conceivably carried slightly over 200 New Testaments with him when he set out from Madrid, perhaps 205 or 210, which would have enabled him to leave 15 or 20 copies with the Salamanca bookseller.

II.1.2.b The second leg
(Coruña 20 July – Madrid 31 October 1837)

THE CALCULATION of Borrow's private sales during the second leg of his Northern Journey serves two purposes only: to determine the stock he left behind with the Coruña bookseller when he departed from Galicia, and to determine how many of the remaining 53 privately sold copies (i.e. the 118 minus 65) he may have sold in Galicia, and how many of them in Asturias on the way to Oviedo. The first number can be calculated with reasonable certainty. At the second we can only guess.

At Coruña, a fresh stock of 500 copies, sent over for the purpose by Borrego's Compañia Tipográfica [BiBo 1[25]; BiBo 2], was waiting for him in the storeroom of the Perez bookshop [L 20.7.1837]. From this stock he sent two new batches to Lugo as fresh supply [L 15.9.1837 and II.2.2.v below]. Another large lot – quite possibly yet one more batch of 200 books – he carried with him when he travelled to Santiago de

---

25 I.e. Borrego's bill of 28 November 1837. Note that this bill is a little messy, both in the description of services lent and in the calculation of money owed. One of its many mistakes is to describe the shipment to Coruña as '*el cajon y embalaje para los cuatrocientos ejemplares de la Biblia embiados a la Coruña*', i.e. mistaking both the number and the nature of the books. As we shall see below, it is most unlikely that the batch would have contained only 400 copies, since more than that number were probably distributed from here on by Borrow himself.

Compostela, where he left 150 copies in the hands of the bookseller Rey Romero (see below II.2.2.vii). Next, he visited the southern Galician towns, during which excursion – according to the information that has come down to us – he disposed by sale or gift of 13 copies.

By mid September 1837, when he returned to Coruña, the Coruña stock had therefore been depleted with the following numbers:

Sold by Coruña bookseller	58	L 15.9.1837; see II.2.2.vi
2nd franchise to Lugo bookseller	50	L 15.9.1837; see II.2.2.v
Franchise to Santiago bookseller	150	see II.2.2.vii
Satchel sale near Santiago	15	see Satchel Sales II.1.3
Private sales in Pontevedra	8	L 15.9.1837; *BiS* ch 28
Private sales in Vigo	3	L 15.9.1837; *BiS* ch 28
Gift to Jewish Moroccan Merchant in Vigo	1	*BiS* ch 28
Gift to Antonio da Traba in Finisterre	1	L 15.9.1837; *BiS* ch 30
3rd franchise to Lugo bookseller	'more'	L 15.9.1837; see II.2.2.v

The certain total is 286 copies. However, we must still add to this the 3rd shipment to Lugo, which – seeing that all Borrow's supplies sent by mail to booksellers went in units of 50 copies – we may assume to have been 50 as well. The total then comes to 336 copies.

On his way out of the province of Galicia, Borrow certainly carried along with him 60 copies, of which he supplied 20 to a bookseller in Ferrol (see II.2.2.viii) and 40 to the bookseller in Oviedo (see II.2.2.ix), at which time he states explicitly that he was out of stock again [L 29.9.1837]. This brings the total of copies disposed of to 396.

However, in this inventory there is still missing a part of the 53 copies which were 'privately sold' during the second leg of the journey. Above, only 13 are attested (8 in Pontevedra, 4 in Vigo, 1 in Finisterre). Consequently, at some time between Coruña in July and Oviedo in late September, 53-13 = 40 copies must have been sold without leaving trace in Borrow's writings.

The stock left behind with the Coruña bookseller may therefore be calculated as follows:

Original stock	500
Disposed of while in Galicia	-336
Carried out for Ferrol and Oviedo booksellers	-60
Further private sales	-40
Remainder left with Coruña bookseller	**64**

Which – much as it has a certain margin of error due to the insecurity of the 3rd supply to Lugo and the size of the 'satchel sale' near Santiago (see II.1.3 below) – is a reasonable number for Borrow to have left behind in as important a town as Coruña.

How many of the 40 still remaining 'privately sold' copies Borrow sold in Galicia, and how many in the Asturias as he travelled to Oviedo, cannot be wrung out of the available information. We simply have no inkling. Purely for reasons of convenience, I chop the total in half, ascribing 20 to Galicia and 20 to Asturias, in whose wild mountains Borrow had, on the whole, few opportunities to sell books. This is however a complete guess.

II.1.3 The mysterious satchel sales

THE MOST mysterious episodes in the whole of Borrow's sales-efforts concern the 'Satchel Sales' which he says he performed in a village near Valladolid and another one near Santiago de Compostela during the Northern Journey. Nothing is ever seen or heard of these two events until nearly a year and a half later, when he wrote up a report for his employers on his recent doings in Spain and was trying to justify his later decision of selling books to the peasantry for nearly absurd rock bottom prices, rather than sell them to educated city folks at the approved price of 10 *reales* or more. There are two nearly identical versions of the story: one from the report he withdrew soon after writing it, because its wording was too bold [APP]; the other from the report which he did submit, and which was formally endorsed by his employers on 28 November 1838 [ROS]. The paragraph in question runs as follows:

'I twice sallied forth (…) alone and on horseback, and proceeded to a distant village, bearing behind me a satchel of books. On my arrival (…) I proceeded in both instances to the market-place, where I spread a horse-cloth on the ground, on which I deposited

my books. I then commenced crying with a loud voice: 'Peasants, peasants, I bring you the Word of God at a cheap price. I know you have but little money, but I bring it to you at whatever you can command, at four or three reals according to your means.' I thus went on till a crowd gathered round me, who examined the book with attention, many of them reading it aloud. But I had not long to tarry; in both instances I disposed of my cargo almost instantaneously, and then mounted my horse without a question having been asked me, and returned to my temporary residence lighter than I left it. This occurred in Castile and Galicia, near the towns of Santiago and Valladolid.'

At first glance, there seems to be nothing wrong with this tale. On two occasions in the summer of 1837, Borrow simply grabbed a bag of books and sold them off, by way of experiment, in a rural village, for a pretty low price. Except that these books sold at 3 or 4 *reales* apiece do not seem to pop up *anywhere* in his accounts, which for this entire period only show copies sold at 10 to 12 *reales*. A quick glance at his numbers for private sales will clarify this.

As noted above: during the whole of his Northern Journey, Borrow disposed of 118 Testaments 'by private sale' to individual customers, which brought him the total sum of 1,224 *reales* [Acc 6]. This means that all of these books must have been sold for 10 *reales* or more, for if we multiply 118 Testaments by Borrow's 'standard price' of 10 *reales*, the outcome is 1,180 *reales*, i.e. 44 *reales* short of what he really received. The conclusion must be that he sold the bulk of his Testaments for 10 *reales*, and a few of them for a slightly higher price, perhaps 44 of the 118 for 11 *reales*, or 22 for 12, or any other combination of prices which results in the sum total of 1,224. What he can hardly have done, however, is sell many copies at 3 or 4 *reales*; because every book sold for so low a sum, necessarily had to be compensated for by the sale of 6 or 7 copies at the price of 11, in order still to reach the final total. As long as those 'satchels' remain very small indeed, this is not completely unthinkable; but anything beyond 10 copies leads immediately to mathematical impossibilities.

Just to visualise this, let us suppose he sold 10 copies in that first village near Valladolid at the price of 4 *reales*. This brought him 40 *reales*. The remaining 108 Testaments sold in the north (118 − 10) then had to bring

1,224 – 40 = 1,184 *reales*. That means Borrow must have sold no fewer than 104 of the 108 for 11 *reales* each, and the remaining 4 at 10. Of course, this is not totally impossible, but the margins here are extremely narrow. Selling 10 copies at 3 *reales*, or 11 at 4, immediately implies that *not one of the remaining copies was sold for 10 reales*, but the bulk of them for 11, and some at least for 12. All that is in plain contradiction to his firm assurance that 'throughout my journey I have (…) invariably received money for them, viz., from 10 to 12 *reals*' [L 20.7.1837]; and worse still: it is counting without a second 'satchel' near Santiago!

The conclusion must therefore be that – unless these two famous 'satchels' of rock bottom price books were so absurdly small that it made no sense to mention them – they were not included in the 118 copies of the New Testament which Borrow recorded as having sold privately in his expense accounts.

Because, at this particular period, Borrow justified all his sales in his expense accounts one way or the other, the question presents itself where those copies disposed of by 'satchel sales' may be hidden in the records. And this leads us to an uncommon and inexplicable item in his expense account of November 1837 [Acc 6] which mentions income of 300 *reales* generated 'by sale of 30 at Valladolid'. At first glance, this seems a crystal clear affair. Borrow, when in Valladolid, cashed in the money over 30 copies which the Valladolid bookseller had sold while he was in the city, by way of a partial reckoning. Only, there is some trouble with that scenario. First of all: Borrow never did such a thing, with the exception of Oviedo, where the whole stock of books which he had left with the bookseller was sold off while he was in town (see below, II.2.2.ix), and in Toledo, where the sales were so dismal that he did not bother to leave books in franchise (II.2.2.xii). In all other cases he was glad to leave the money with the booksellers, until the final reckoning many months later [L 20.11.1837; L 18.7.1839; see also II.2.3].

Secondly, not 30, but only 20 books were sold while Borrow was in Valladolid [L 5.7.1837]; while the total stock which he left in franchise there came to 40 copies, which were sold off by mid July 1837 [L 20.7.1837]. In that context, it would amount to an absurdity – and a needless bookkeeping complication – to cash in on only 30 copies. Twenty might have made sense; 40 as well; but 30 would be neither fish nor fowl at the bottom line.

I suspect, therefore, that these 30 copies 'by sale at Valladolid' in reality represent the copies sold by 'satchel sale' at Valladolid *and Santiago*, recorded in such a way that they would not attract undue attention. As is proven by his own later writings, Borrow tried to be extremely discreet about these experiments. They were only, he wrote in November of 1838, 'incidents which I have hitherto kept within the privacy of my own bosom and which I have confided to none; they were but experiments, which at that time I had no wish to repeat, nor to be requested so to do' [APP]. That is to say: he did not wish the Bible Society to know of these trials. And if not through his letters, then naturally neither through his expense accounts.

That said, we ought to establish if 30 copies would be a reasonable number for sales in two villages. In other words: how big was 'a satchel' full of books in the parlance of the Bible-peddling trade of the 1830s? Here, I must move into the murky realms of semantic conjecture. Borrow, who was rather constant in his vocabulary when writing, normally uses the word 'satchel' for a small bag which got slung over the back of the rider's own horse, pony or donkey, and fastened there with a strap or a rope [L 4.3.1839; *BiS* ch 46]. The essence here seems to be that a 'satchel' was used for day-trips and short distances, when no pack-animal was available, and the mount had to carry both the rider and the load. On one occasion [L 4.3.1839] that cargo, strapped on top of the saddle-bags, consisted of a rather large lot of 61 books (i.e. nearly 30 kilos), meant to be distributed in several villages at some distance from base. But another instance, which took place during Borrow's expedition in the Sagra [*BiS* ch 43; L 14.7.1838; see also see III.2.1] probably teaches us something more revealing to the present question. There, Juan Lopez typically tosses 20 Testaments into his 'satchel', jumps onto his donkey, and sells the whole lot in a single village within a few hours. Since Borrow explicitly calls this batch 'a large bundle of Testaments', the number may reasonably be taken as the maximum (some 9.5 kilos) that should be transported in a satchel while on such a flashing day-trip.

Yet, I doubt very much that Borrow could have sold even that many in so short a time in his two experimental hamlets. Galician villages, for one, were tiny, primitive and dirt-poor in these wayward times; and even later, when he had been selling in villages for many months and had built up a considerable know-how how to go about it, his average village sales, as we shall see (IV.2) did not rise above 25. And those sales took place in well-chosen, pre-selected townships of some size, not random hamlets near larger cities. For the sake of comparison, one may quote the testimony of a young man from Vigo, who once, in the 1840s, helped two English missionaries to peddle gospels in nearby Leon. In one village, they managed to sell 15 copies, which they deemed an exceptionally successful result[26]. Consequently, if I were called upon to make an educated guess, I would say that the two villages near Valladolid and Compostela might well have taken 15 copies each, but not more; which is in fine keeping with the 30 mysterious copies mentioned in the expense account.

Of course, this is and remains a guess; but it is an elegant one. Seeing that we have, on the one hand, 30 sold copies recorded in an expense account whose sales-history we perfectly ignore; and, on the other one, the sales-history of an estimated 30 copies, whose proceeds we fail to find in the expense accounts, it is only logical to put one and one together, and identify the '30 copies sold at Valladolid' as the books dispatched during Borrow's experimental Satchel Sales near Valladolid *and Santiago*, camouflaged in such a way that they would not attract attention or cause inconvenient questions.

If this conjecture is correct, then the most remarkable side of this 'camouflage' is surely that Borrow not only tucked the 30 copies away under some vague heading, but that he also disguised them *financially*, i.e. that he himself shouldered the difference between the actual 3 or 4 *reales* for which he sold the 30 copies, and the 10 *reales* a piece which he allowed for them in his expense account, losing nearly 200 *reales* in the process. Borrow was a man who did not like losing money; but then again, the feeble financial probity which the Bible Society's accountants demanded from him, offered him ample opportunities to compensate himself for the loss. For as Sherlock Holmes discovered with his infallible eye for fishy things: Borrow was allowed, in his final expense account over the Northern Journey, to claim some 20 days of travelling expenses more than he had actually been on the road, at '*70 reales per diem*' bringing him the interesting little windfall of some 1,400 *reales* [Missler, *Underpriced*, 25 & 30; Collie, *Eccentric*, 159ff]. Borrow was an honest man, and one

---

26 See Ortiz Armengol, P., 'Borrow in Galicia', in: *George Borrow Bulletin* n° 12 (Autumn 1996), 87.

who certainly earned his keep; but we must also recognize that he never lost a nickel even through his wildest actions!²⁷

II.2 Sales through bookshops (April 1837 – May 1838)

II.2.1 Bookshop distribution and marketing

As LONG as the sale of the New Testament was tolerated by the authorities, Borrow's best hope of a wide distribution was by selling them through the principal booksellers of Spain [L 27.2.1837]. These were actually rather few in number. Due to the low level of literacy (see III.1 below) and the times of war, there was rarely more than one bookshop left in any major town. It was therefore easy to contact them, particularly

---

27 The fascinating subject of Borrow's attitude to money still awaits its student. So much may however be said, that Borrow – who had known dire poverty when young – deeply feared the prospect of falling back into penury, and therefore developed a definite 'acquisitive trait'. As he put it in his letter to Hasfeld of 20 November 1838 [Fraser, *Hasfeld*, 30]: 'Not to know the value of money is the most unpardonable ignorance. Let it be once known that you are in need of pecuniary assistance and your best friends (…) will flee from you as if you had the plague sore on your shoulder (…). Money is by far too precious a thing to be cast out of the windows by handfuls into the streets' (compare also his remarks to the young runaway Spaniard in *BiS* ch 7). In this context, Borrow was really *most fortunate* in his Bible Society situation, for his employers showered undeserved money on him at nearly every step of the way (or, as Collie, *Eccentric*, 159, put it with an understatement: 'the officers of the Society preferred to err on the side of generosity'). Not only did they allow him the above surplus in travelling expenses, but – contrary to the terms of his contract - they also picked up half the bill of his 1836 living expenses in Madrid – nearly £ 64 – 'on account of peculiar circumstances' [Acc 1]; allowed him to pocket the proceeds from all 400-plus New Testaments and hundreds of Gypsy *Lukes* sold in the summer and autumn of 1839 (see IV.8 below); and duly continued his salary from November 1839 to 11 June 1840 [Bible Society Archive, Foreign Account Current, nᵒ 5, p 79], even though by that time he was no longer performing any discernible task for them. Added up, these four items alone (and there are more!) brought him an unearned boon of over £ 200, a full year's salary. One begins to see why his old friend Santa Coloma could remark many years later that 'at the period Borrow spent a good deal of money and lived very freely (i.e. luxuriously) in Spain' [Jenkins, *Life*, 195].

with the help of Borrego, who already had a running relationship with many of these establishments. In early March of 1837, while the printing process was still in full swing, Borrow decided to inform the bookshops of the imminent appearance of the Scio New Testament. He wrote to his employers: 'Within a few days I shall despatch letters circular to all the principal booksellers in Spain, specifying the nature, size and quality of the work, and inviting them to subscribe at 15 *reals* per copy, the prime cost; for if anything will tempt them to a speculation of the kind, it will be the hope and prospect of making a very handsome profit. Yet they are so short-sighted and, like all their countrymen, so utterly unacquainted with the rudiments of business, that it is by no means improbable that they, one and all, take no notice of this proposal, which is however the only plan which at present appears available for promoting the *general* circulation of the Scriptures' [L 27.2.1837]. By the looks of it, some orders were received in reaction to this written offer, particularly from the east coast and the south [BiBo 1; BiBo 2; see II.2.2.xiii–xvi below].

Never one to sit on his haunches and wait passively for things to happen by themselves, Borrow then decided to ride forth and personally visit the booksellers of western and Northern Spain, so as to persuade them to take a stock of New Testaments in hand and sell them in franchise. As we have already seen, he did this during his Northern Journey of mid 1837. Since the whole operation was meant to establish stable depots in the country, which might function over a longer period of time, Borrow made sure to offer the most attractive sales conditions possible. Where he did not carry the supply to the threshold of the shop himself, he shouldered all the costs of transport, postage and gate-dues necessary to make the books reach their destination. He dropped his asking price to 10 *reales*, and sometimes lower still (see II.2.3 below), which enabled the bookseller to make a handsome profit out of the recommended retail price of 10 or 11 *reales*. He postponed reimbursement over books sold – even those which were purchased during his presence in town – until many months later, thereby minimizing financial risk to the bookshop [L 20.11.1837; L 18.7.1839]. And perhaps most importantly: he ensured that sales were brisk while he was in town himself, placing advertisements in the local press, holding stimulating sales-chats with the local population, and printing and posting announcements which informed the public that the New Testament was for sale at the local bookshop.

LIBROS.

—

EL NUEVO TESTAMENTO.

TRADUCIDO AL CASTETLANO

POR EL

RMO. P. PHELIPE SCIO DE S. MIGUEL.

Hace poco tiempo se ha verificado en Madrid una bellísima edicion de esta porcion interesante de la Sagrada Escritura, sin las notas y comentarios que hasta ahora han acompañado à las varias ediciones publicadas en Español, dando al tomo un volúmen escesivo, y por consiguiente aumento en el precio, poniéndole fuera del alcance de la clase pobre y mas numerosa de la sociedad. Esta obra preciosísima està ahora al de todas las clases. En el despacho de la sociedad bíblica de Lóndres, núm. 25 calle del Príncipe, se hallan de venta algunos ejemplares en octavo mayor, hermosamente encuadernados en pasta à 10 reales cada uno, siendo la mitad del gasto que ha espendido la sociedad, la cual trayendo en memoria el mandamiento del Salvador, procura en todas ocasiones propagar su santa palabra entre las gentes del mundo.   1

Illustration 5: One of George Borrow's advertisements for the Scio New Testament in the Spanish press (from the *Diario de Madrid* of 22 December 1837)

This last initiative – a somewhat unusual method of sales-promotion for Spain in the 1830s – was first conceived and executed at Salamanca, the first major town where Borrow stopped on his way to the North. As it happened, Vicente Blanco, the local bookseller, owned a small printing-press, on which he printed the official government bulletin of the province. With a fine eye for publicity, Borrow inserted a 'mild yet expressive advertisement' [APP] in this periodical, giving notice to the public that the vernacular New Testament could be purchased at Blanco's shop. Next, he had the printer strike off a large number of these advertisements in the shape of posters, which were put up all over the town [L 7.6.1837]. 'I shall repeat this experiment in Valladolid, Leon, St. Jago [i.e. Santiago de Compostela – PM], and all the principal towns which it is my intention to visit in my wanderings,' he wrote shortly afterwards to his employers, 'and I shall likewise distribute them as I ride along' [L 7.6.1837]. Both these things he did. On his way from Salamanca to Valladolid, for instance, he spontaneously affixed an advertisement to the church porch of the hostile village of Pedroso [*BiS* ch 21]. This advertisement spoke explicitly of the New Testament being available at Salamanca, which shows that somewhere, some time, he must have had other advertisements printed for the subsequent towns where they were used. We cannot tell where or at what costs [L 20.11.1837]. Borrego was asked to print and dispatch such posters for various towns which Borrow did not visit himself: Cádiz, Seville, Málaga and Valencia [BiBo 1[28]]; but there is no sign of such a batch of posters printed for and sent to Borrow on the road. We do have positive evidence for posters being used in Valladolid [L 5.7.1837], Leon [L 5.7.1837], Lugo [L 20.7.1837], Coruña [L 20.7.1837] and Oviedo [L 29.9.1837]. In the last-named town he handed a bundle of posters to the bookseller on the very day after his arrival, which suggests that – other than his Salamanca announcement – in its new shape the poster was multi-applicable (a small blank space may have been left open where the bookseller could write his name and address by hand).

All other booksellers, those in parts of Spain which Borrow did not visit, and the ones who needed extra stock once he had passed by, were

---

28 The same bill of Borrego [BiBo 1] mentions posters printed for and sent to Valladolid, but from the context it would seem that this is a writing mistake – one of several in this bill – for 'Valencia'.

supplied and dealt with by Borrego's *Compañia Tipográfica*, which not only printed Borrow's books and advertisements, but – on Borrow's request – packed the books, sent them off by mail, cashed the money over copies sold and administered the costs of taxes, dues, postage etc. This side of the enterprise deserves separate treatment at the end of this chapter (see below II.2.3).

Both the booksellers whom Borrow visited himself, and those handled by Borrego, received, on average, supplies which were multiples of 50 copies, possibly because the books were best packed in such batches or because the resultant 24 kilos represented the least troublesome weight for transport.

When the final Prohibition of 19 May 1838 was proclaimed, the government immediately ensured, by a circular letter to local authorities, that all copies which lay unsold in the bookshops would be seized, sealed up, and deposited in a safe place; from where Borrow could only recover them under formal promise to export them from the land. Where known, the numbers of such confiscated copies will be noted in the text below, to be summarized in the chapter IV.4 on Confiscated copies.

II.2.2 Bookshop sales per city

So as to keep things halfway comprehensible, the order of cities first follows the itinerary of Borrow's Northern Journey; and then treats of the towns he did not visit himself, whose booksellers were supplied by Borrego. Unfortunately for modern scholarship, Borrow did not visit the Spanish cities in alphabetical order.

II.2.2.i Madrid

Before riding off to the north, Borrow deposited stock with some of the Madrid booksellers, asking Luis Usoz to take care of the logistics, administration and finances over these books while he was away [Acc 8]. We do not know how many Madrid booksellers were involved exactly. At first there is only mention of a single one, when Borrow writes to his employers that 'some hundreds of our books have been placed in the hands of a bookseller at Madrid, and I have ordered them to be advertised, once a week, in the principal journals. Dr. Usoz and another friend will do what they can in my absence' [L 29.4.1837]. After his return from the north, however, Borrow speaks explicitly of 'the Madrid *booksellers* entrusted with the Testaments' [L 20.11.1837], so it seems that while he was gone Usoz managed to increase the number of outlets. We know from Usoz's advertisement in the Madrid newspaper *La España* of 21 October 1837 (see illustration 6 below) that the book could be bought at the bookshops of Cuesta and of Paz, who sold the work for 12 reales a piece; while Borrow himself elsewhere mentions the small establishment of Razola [APP]. Possibly no more than these three were ever involved.

ANUNCIO.

EL NUEVO TESTAMENTO

DE N. S. J. C.

traducido por el reverendísimo padre Felipe Scio de S. Miguel: un volúmen en octavo prolongado, de 534 páginas de impresion, en pasta. Se ha impreso este importantísimo libro con buen carácter de letra, papel escelente y sumo cuidado en la correccion; de modo que puede competir, bajo estos aspectos, con las mejores ediciones de Ibarra. Se ha conservado la misma ortografía del tiempo del traductor. El precio á que se ha puesto este libro, facilita su adquisicion á todas las clases de la sociedad: y el único objeto que se ha tenido en imprimirle, es el de propagar mas y mas cada vez la santa palabra del Salvador.

Véndese á 12 rs. vn. en las librerias de Cuesta y de Paz, frente á las gradas de S. Felipe.

Illustration 6: Usoz's advertisement in La España of 21 October 1837

What is certain, however, is that the number of shops made no difference at all. In the entire 6 months of Borrow's absence, only 52 copies were ever sold in the whole of Madrid [L 1.11.1837; Acc 8], and some of them not even through the booksellers, but by Usoz himself during the great autumn fair of late September and early October [Knapp, *Life*, I : 358]. This tiny number was most disappointing, and made Borrow write bitterly that the booksellers 'gave themselves no manner of trouble to secure the sale, and even withheld advertisements from the public with which they were supplied' [L 20.11.1837], that they 'refused to sell my work' [L 15.1.1838], and that they were 'averse to undertake the sale of the New Testament, with the exception of Razola, a man of no importance' [APP]. Usoz himself, with perhaps a slight touch of embarrassment, blamed the dismal sales-figures on the political circumstances and the poverty of the times [L 1.11.1837][29].

Never a man to throw in the towel, the inertia of the Madrid booksellers was Borrow's main reason to open a shop of his own in late November 1837 (see below II.3.2).

II.2.2.ii   Salamanca

SALES-FIGURES AT Salamanca cannot be computed. Borrow visited the city shortly after 15 May 1837, and deposited a 'certain number' of Testaments with 'the principal bookseller of the town', a well-to-do gentleman of the Calle de la Rua called Vicente Blanco [L 7.6.1837; *BiS* ch 20][30]. Since this was the first Spanish bookseller whom he supplied while on the road and the stock he carried was small, Borrow may have been rather cautious in the number of copies left behind in franchise, possibly no more than 10 (see II.1.2.a above for this modest estimate). While Borrow remained in town, 'several' copies were sold, three of them while he stood in the bookshop [L 5.7.1837].

---

29 Usoz wrote a report about his Madrid sales-efforts in mid 1837, which Knapp possessed and mentions [*Life*, I : 359] but which has not been seen since (it may be among his papers in the Hispanic Society of New York). The only other information we have on Usoz's activities is the line in Borrow's expense account of 26 April 1838 [Acc 8], where he states that he paid Usoz 372 *reales* for 'various expenses defrayed (…) during my absence in 1837, namely porterage at various times of Madrid edition of the New Testament, advertizements [sic] in newspapers, percentage to Booksellers, and 4 months hire of room for general depot.' Unfortunately this total is not specified further.

30 See Ruben Lugilde Yepes, *George Borrow y el inicio de la presencia Protestante en Salamanca*, p.14, lecture given on 25 October 2007 during the series '*Nociones históricas y literarias sobre el protestantismo en la sociedas española*' of Salamanca University.

The small stock which he left behind must have been sold off soon after, because on his return to Madrid he wrote 'I am expecting every day a fresh order from Salamanca' [L 20.11.1837]. And since a batch of copies of equally unknown size was confiscated from Blanco shortly before 25 May 1838, a second shipment must indeed have been dispatched and received some time between late November 37 and May 38 [L 25.5.1838; L 23.7.1838]. The size of this second shipment is once again unknown (solely for purposes of computation, I suppose it below to have been Borrow's standard batch of 50 copies, coming on top of an original 10; but this is and remains a conjecture). Consequently we do not even have sufficient data to make a wild guess at sales in Salamanca. They must, however, have been very small, since the margins for stock and total sales are too narrow to allow great sales in any city for which we have no hard data (see IV.5 and IV.6).

II.2.2.iii   Valladolid

THE TALE of Borrow's doings in Valladolid is messy; a mess which already starts with the simple dates of his visit. It can be calculated that the Bible salesman reached the city more or less on 12 June 1837; but from there on things become murky. In his letter of 5 July 1837 – written only a fortnight after the visit – he states explicitly that he stayed only 5 days. Yet in *BiS* chapter 21, this short period gets stretched to become a visit of 'a week'. And next, in the opening sentence of the following chapter, Borrow writes that he departed after 'a sojourn of about ten days'[31]. With Borrow's chronological memory in such shambles, it comes as no surprise that the data he offers on the sales in the city are no clearer. We can only make the best of a bad thing.

Within a few days of his arrival, Borrow engaged the local bookseller, a 'kind-hearted simple man' [*BiS* ch 21] by the name of Julian Pastor, whose shop was in the Calle de Cantarranas nº 31[32], to 'undertake the charge of vending the Testaments' [*BiS* ch 21]. The delivery was made

31 Although this example is extreme, time is always elastic in *The Bible in Spain*. Knapp [*Life*, I : 235] already observed that 'we constantly discover that [Borrow's] "fortnight" signifies four days, and his "three weeks" ten or eleven.'

32 The identification of Pastor is based on the 'receipt for Bibles' recorded in Knapp, *Life*, I : 266. The address comes from Madoz, *DG*, vol. xv (1849), 571. Note however that Madoz's information was gathered 10 years later, so it is not altogether certain that the shop was located there in June 1837.

on June 15 [Knapp, *Life*, I : 266]. Sales were brisk, in spite of the fact
that Valladolid was not the most liberal-minded town [*BiS* ch 21]. 'My
labours were so far favoured,' Borrow wrote two weeks later, 'that 20
copies were disposed of, and a fair prospect opened that many more
would be demanded' [L 5.7.1837]. And so it turned out. Another two
weeks later, he reported to his employers to have 'received advice from
my agent at Valladolid that the 40 copies which I deposited in his hands
have been sold, and that he was anxious for a fresh supply. I have accordingly ordered 50 more to be sent him from Madrid' [L 20.7.1837].
This Borrego did, even though it is none too clear what he sent where
at what time, the bill in question [BiBo 1] being rather unreliable in its
description of services lent.

Of this second lot of 50, very few were sold, for Borrow passed through
Valladolid again in October 1837, on his way back from the north to
Madrid, and – having just engaged a bookseller in Burgos to sell the
New Testament, but having no stock available himself – he 'ordered all
the copies which remained unsold of the second supply [of Valladolid]
to be sent to Burgos' [L 1.11.1837]. By later evidence, this lot involved 40
copies [L 17.5.1838; also II.2.2.xi below]. Once back in Madrid, Borrow
then assured his employers that he was 'now going to despatch a third 50'
to Valladolid to make up for the lost stock [L 1.11.1837].

Consequently, we may say that Julian Pastor received in franchise 140
copies (the 'first 50' being in reality a 40), of which, however, 40 were passed
on to the Burgos bookseller, making an effective supply of 100. Of these 100,
50 were sold for sure (40 plus 10), and an unknown number of the third
supply of 50. As we shall see in the conclusions below (particularly IV.5 and
IV.6) there are good reasons to believe that the further sales in Valladolid,
as elsewhere, were very few; and as in all such cases I assume them to have
been a mere 5 copies. The remaining stock of unsold books was confiscated
and placed in embargo by the summer of 1838 [L 23.7.1838].

One complicating factor in the relative clarity of these numbers is the
occurrence, in one of Borrow's expense accounts [Acc 7] of 30 copies sold
'at Valladolid' to the tune of 300 *reales* in cash. I have argued above (in
chapter II.1.3) why I consider these copies not to be part of the franchise
of Pastor, but the reflection of so-called 'satchel sales' which Borrow
later said he performed in villages near Valladolid and Santiago. Of
course, other, and perhaps no less 'creative', scenarios may be drawn up

to explain the entry in the expense account and the origin of the books sold by 'satchel'. Yet the one I propose is, to my taste, at once the most elegant and the least damaging to the accuracy of the overall sales-results computed at the end of this study.

II.2.2.iv   Leon

THE CITY of Leon, in the depth of conservative Old Castile, was one of the hotbeds of the Carlist rebellion. Led by its bishop, Don Joaquin Abarca, it had been the first city to declare for the absolutist Pretender Don Carlos when civil war broke out in September 1833. And much as the town had soon been re-conquered by the government army, and the bishop made to fly to the rebel court, the general opinion in the city was still much averse to all liberal freedoms and innovations; something which naturally included perfidious foreign missionaries selling infidel Bibles in a decent Catholic town. Borrow himself notes this hostility, when he tells of the adventures of his sales-efforts: 'Scarcely had the advertisements appeared, when the clergy were in motion. They went from house to house, banning and cursing, and denouncing misery to whomsoever should either purchase or read "the accursed books," which had been sent into the country by heretics for the purpose of perverting the innocent minds of the population' [BiS ch 22].

In spite of such opposition, and the risks it entailed, Borrow found a 'bold and determined' bookseller willing to undertake the sale of his Testaments [L 5.7.1837]. The name of this courageous tradesman, who in order to defy the local clergy actually 'went so far as to affix an advertisement to the gate of the very cathedral' [BiS ch 22], has not yet been unearthed. 'Notwithstanding the cry raised against the work', however, some 15 copies were sold in the city during the week of Borrow's stay in mid-June 1837, including four copies picked up by ex-friars and parish priests from the neighbourhood [L 5.7.1837; BiS ch 22].

For once, the distribution and total sales of a city can be neatly reconstructed. Borrow left 40 copies with the bookseller in Leon, which were all sold by the following November [L 20.11.1837]. Consequently, he dispatched a fresh supply of 50 copies here [L 20.11.1837], of which an additional 16 were sold, seeing that in July of 1839 Borrow computed the total sales in Leon as 56 copies [L 18.7.1839.] The fate of the remaining 34 copies is unknown.

II.2.2.v   Lugo

THE TOWN of Lugo, in eastern Galicia, makes a most confusing case. Although of great antiquity and the see of a bishop, it was a very small city, counting only 6 or 7,000 inhabitants at this time. And yet Lugo turned out to be one of the big buyers of Borrow's New Testaments; so much so, in fact, that its sales become rather suspicious (see IV.3 below).

Borrow reached Lugo in the 2nd week of July 1837 and stayed there some three or four days [*BiS* ch 25–26]. An as yet unidentified Madrid acquaintance (Borrego or O'Shea) had given him a letter of introduction to the bookseller of the town [*BiS* ch 26; L 27.2.1838], Pedro Pujol Macia, whose bookshop stood on the Plaza Mayor[33]. Borrow handed Pujol all the remaining copies of the New Testament in his luggage. Then, as he writes himself, 'The Lord deigned to favour my feeble exertions in his cause at Lugo. I brought thither 30 Testaments, all of which were disposed of in one day, the Bishop of the place[34] purchasing two copies for himself, whilst several priests and ex-friars, instead of following the example of their brethren at Leon, by persecuting the work, spoke well of it and recommended its perusal. I was much grieved that my stock of these holy books was exhausted, for there was a great demand for them; and had I been able to supply them, quadruple the quantity might have been sold during the few days that I continued at Lugo' [L 20.7.1837].

By the looks of it, this last remark was no exaggeration, for a second supply of 50 copies, which Borrow despatched from Coruña to Lugo in early August from his new stock, sold with equal speed [L 15.9.1837]. 'This second supply being almost exhausted' as well, he sent 'more' in the first half of the following September [L 15.9.1837]. Unfortunately, the size of the third supply is unknown; but its precise volume is perhaps

---

33 So Fernández de la Vega, C., 'Dous escritores ingleses na Praza Maior de Lugo', in: *Galicia desde Londres*, Coruña 1994. The identification is probably correct, but note that it has not yet been verified by truly authentic sources such as bills from Borrego or Borrow's correspondence.

34 This bishop, Don Hipólito Sanchez Rangel, was the only Galician prelate of liberal opinions and loyalty to the Madrid regime. His Episcopal Governor, Don José Maria Padilla y Aguila, who ran the diocese during his superior's frequent absences as MP in Madrid, was possibly an even more active and outspoken supporter of the liberal cause [Barreiro, *Carlismo*, 128 and 161f]. But see also IV.3 below.

immaterial, since none of its copies seem to have been sold. Two years later, when drawing up final sales-figures for his employers, Borrow stated, perhaps a little cooler now, that '64 copies, it appears, were also sold in the small town of Lugo' [L 18.7.1839]. This would mean that even of the 2nd supply of 50, only 34 copies were ever purchased, unless one wants to interpret the remark as meaning that 64 copies were sold *on top of* the initial 30 which changed hands when Borrow was in Lugo. This, however, would not only be a most untypical way for Borrow to put it, but would also bring total sales to 94 copies, which is rather beyond belief for so very small a town (see IV.3 below). Faced with the choice, I prefer to err on the cautious side.

II.2.2.vi   Coruña

BORROW REACHED Coruña roughly on 14 July 1837 and put up in a posada of the Calle Real, run by a taciturn Genovese and a swarm of cheerful chatty Basque sisters, possibly the *Fonda del Comercio* [*BiS* ch 26; Robertson, *Tour*, 69; Ford, *Handbook*, 971]. A fresh stock of 500 copies of the New Testament was awaiting him here at the bookshop of José Maria Perez, likewise in the Calle Real, at n⁰ 43[35] [L 20.7.1837; BiBo 1; BiBo 2].

Sales in Coruña were not particularly good. While six days after his arrival Borrow could still write that 'I have as usual published my advertisements, and the work enjoys a tolerable sale – 7 or 8 copies per day on the average' [L 20.7.1837], by mid-September he already complained that 'only 58 copies have hitherto been sold at Corunna' [L 15.9.1837]. Borrow blamed these lukewarm sales on the inhabitants being 'too much engrossed by party politics to entertain much relish for heavenly manna' [L 15.9.1837], but it is probably better to say that the Coruñese, being convinced liberals and rather worldly in their life-style, were simply not much interested in religious literature. After September, some more copies may have been sold here, but the documents provide no data on the subject. In any case they must have been very few.

Once he had supplied various cities in Galicia and Castilla-Leon from Coruña, and taken out a further lot of perhaps 80 copies to carry away

---

35 Odriazola, A., and Barreiro Fernández, X.R., *Historia de la Imprenta en Galicia*, Coruña 1992, 211ff.

with him to the Asturias, some 64 copies were left with Perez (see II.1.2.b above). Nothing more is heard of them. It is unknown whether they were sold, used to supply other booksellers, confiscated at the time of the Prohibition, or if they are still gathering dust in the attic of an antiquarian bookshop today.

II.2.2.vii Santiago de Compostela and Pontevedra

THE CALCULATION of sales in the city of Santiago de Compostela gets complicated by the fact that the sales-figures for Pontevedra got mixed up with those of the old pilgrimage-town itself, since José Manuel Garcia, the Public Notary who took care of New Testament sales in Pontevedra, functioned as a franchise of Francisco Rey Romero, the Santiago bookseller. Both cities must therefore be treated together.

What is beyond question, is that Santiago, at the time an extremely conservative and even Carlist town, was one of George Borrow's greatest sales-successes. Rey Romero was not a very good businessman (having inherited a large fortune from his parents, he died bankrupt), but he did do everything in his power not to go under in these times of civil war and economic slump [Missler, *Considerable*, 32–45; Missler, *RRT*, 22ff]. As the only bookseller still in business in the city, he was offered a windfall monopoly on Borrow's New Testaments, and made the most of it. Only about a week after reaching the town, Borrow wrote to his employers that 'since my arrival in Santiago between 30 and 40 copies of the New Testament have been despatched' [L 19.8.1837], and this promising result

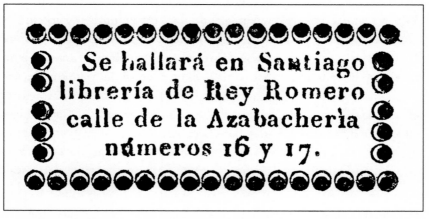

Se hallará en Santiago
librería de Rey Romero
calle de la Azabacheria
números 16 y 17.

Illustration 7: Bookplate of the Rey Romero bookshop from the 1830s was such that Borrow left the greatest part of the stock he had carried along from Coruña in the hands of the old and venerable bookseller. 'About one hundred Testaments have been disposed of at Saint James of Compostella,' he wrote a month later, 'and there is at present a steady regular demand for them' [L 15.9.1837].

The latter sentence shows how very careful one must be with George Borrow's casual remarks in his correspondence. For when he says 'disposed of', he means – for once – not 'sold' but 'left in franchise', and with 'about one hundred Testaments' he designates the number of copies left behind *on top of those* that were sold while he was in Santiago. We know this for a fact, because a few weeks after the definite Prohibition of May 1838, when the bookshop was raided by a task-force of cathedral canons looking for Scio New Testaments to confiscate, Rey Romero's wife and son stated under circumstances which did not allow for frivolities, that exactly 125 copies had originally been received in franchise from George Borrow (for the full story of this raid and the sources involved, see II.4 below). Of these 125 copies, 27 remained unsold on 12 June 1838, and were duly placed in embargo; which means that 98 copies were sold in Compostela between August 1837 and June 1838.

It seems a crystal-clear case; but the reader will by now have learned that things are never that unequivocal when it comes to the sales of the Scio New Testament. Santiago is no exception to the rule, for a year later, Borrow wrote to his employers that 'a few days since I received a communication from (…) old Rey Romero (…). The good old man has sent me in his account, by which it appears that 115 copies of the New Testament were sold at Saint James between the months of August 1837 and May 1838, at which time the further sale of the work was forbidden, and 35 copies, which remained unsold, placed in embargo. The balance of the account in our favour is 950 *reals* after deducting all expenses' [L 18.7.1839].

Where, one may ask, does the difference come from? Now: although all sorts of other scenarios may be imagined (Rey Romero's wife and son were not fully acquainted with the exact number of books left in franchise, and they overlooked a hidden lot of 8 unsold copies stacked away under the dust-bin etc.) the more probable solution is that the extra 17 copies sold, and the extra 8 copies placed in embargo, derived from the sales effort of José Garcia in Pontevedra. Borrow visited that town in late

August 1837 [*BiS* ch 28], and handed 8 copies to the Public Notary, to see what the man could do. The man did well. 'Three days subsequent, on my return,' Borrow wrote shortly afterwards, 'I found that he had disposed of them, and I have since sent him a fresh supply' [L 15.9.1837] Due to the vagueness of this statement, it is a little difficult to decide where to place these first 8 copies; but seeing that this was a direct deal between Garcia and Borrow, and that no money received from the sale pops up separately anywhere in the expense account, I prefer to believe that Borrow counted these 8 among the 118 New Testaments sold 'by private sale' which he reported for the Northern Journey [Acc 6; see II.1.2.b above].

Things are however different when it comes to that 'fresh supply' which Garcia received. Much as Borrow writes that *he* sent this supply, Garcia received these copies from, and in franchise of the Santiago bookshop, for in Rey Romero's letter of 22 June 1839 to Borrow, (the 'account' mentioned above) the old bookseller states that 'pursuant to your instructions, I wrote to Don José Manuel Garcia of Pontevedra to make up the account of the New Testaments I sent him to sell. I enclose his statement with mine, whereby you will see that 35 copies remain on hand here and in Pontevedra, and 950 rs. vn. in money for which you can draw on me at sight' [Fraser, *Mol*, 80][36]. This way of going about the business made perfect sense, because ever since the mid 1820s Garcia, who only dabbled in bookselling on the side, had functioned as the Pontevedra outlet for Rey Romero's Santiago bookshop, as I have shown elsewhere [Missler, *Considerable*, 37].

Seeing the complete similarity in terms and numbers, it is obvious that, when Borrow speaks in his letter of 18 July 1839 of 35 copies left unsold and a credit in his favour of 950 *reales*, he is merely echoing Rey Romero's letter of a month earlier, and hence that both the 115 copies sold and the 35 confiscated concerned those of Santiago and Pontevedra combined. Of course, since he was still trying to impress his employers – from whom at the time he hoped to receive a commission to sail to China – Borrow,

---

36 This somewhat pompous translation is William Knapp's, and – much as Borrow's first biographer was a professor of Spanish and an excellent linguist – not necessarily trustworthy (Knapp famously adapted his facts to fit his idol). Unfortunately I have not been able to see the Spanish original. The whole translation may be seen in Knapp, *Life*, II : 293f.

never one to miss an opportunity at subtle boasting, took the opportunity to pen: 'Who has not heard of Saint James of Compostella, the
temple of the great image of the patron of Spain, and the most favourite
resort in the world of benighted Popish pilgrims? Nevertheless 115 copies
of the pure unadulterated Word of God were purchased there in a few
months at the high price of ten *reals* each' [L 18.7.1839]. But these were
only the peacock's puffed-up feathers. In reality only 98 copies of those
115 were sold in the old Catholic bulwark itself.

To wrap it all up: Borrow carried a large stock of New Testaments
(quite possibly 200 again) from Coruña to Santiago in early August 1837,
and left 150 of these in the hands of Rey Romero. Rey Romero, on
Borrow's request, passed on 25 copies to Garcia in September 1837. He
himself sold a most respectable 98 copies up to the time that sales were
forbidden, and the remaining 27 were confiscated in his shop, on 12
June 1838, by the cathedral canons. Garcia, in Pontevedra, sold 17 copies,
which, together with the 8 sold which he received from Borrow himself,
makes a no less respectable 25 copies in a city of little more than 4,000
inhabitants [Madoz, *DG*, vol. xiii, 151]. The remaining 8 copies were
confiscated there, sometime before 23 July 1838 [L 23.7.1838].

For the 'satchel sale' which Borrow says he performed in a village near
Santiago, and which has no bearing whatsoever on the booksellers' sales,
see chapter II.1.3 above.

II.2.2.viii Ferrol

Passing by the little harbour town of Ferrol on his way out of Galicia
in late September 1837 [*BiS* ch 31], Borrow left 20 New Testaments
'in the hands of a person who has just established a small bookshop'
[L 29.9.1837]. They are never heard of again. We do not know if they
were sold, confiscated or returned to him; and if they were sold, we do
not know what happened to the money. The small margins in the total
numbers for sales and stock (which will be seen in IV.5 and IV.6) allow,
however, for only very few sales in spots like these.

II.2.2.ix Oviedo

Borrow reached Oviedo in the last days of September 1837 after an
extremely exhausting journey over the Peninsula's roughest ground [*BiS*
ch 31–32]. He put up in a posada on the central city square, established in

the gloomy Gothic Palace of the Marques de Santa Cruz. In the morning of the 29th he paid a visit to 'the petty bookseller of the place', Nicolas Longoria in the Calle de la Herreria nº 4 [Robertson, *Tour*, 72], and in the evening of that same day handed this bookseller the last 40 copies of the New Testament in his possession with a number of advertisements [L 29.9.1837; *BiS* ch 33].

Sales were excellent and immediate. Within hours, 10 copies were sold to what appears to be a reading-club of wealthy gentlemen [Ford, *Handbook*, 1039], the famous 'ten gentlemen in cloaks', who visited Borrow in his hotel room that same rainy evening to thank him for bringing such choice books to Oviedo [L 29.9.1837; *BiS* ch 33]. On the morning of the 30th, another 20 copies had been sold [L 29.9.1837, postscript]; and before Borrow left, each and every copy of the stock had been picked up by customers [L 1.11.1837]. For some unexplained reason, and against his habit during the Northern Journey, Borrow then

Illustration 8: Borrow's Oviedo posada, where the 'ten gentlemen in cloaks' and Benedict Mol visited him [*BiS* ch 33]

immediately cashed in the money (400 *reales* for 40 books at 10 *reales* each) due to him from the bookseller [Acc 6][37].

Once back in Madrid in November 1837, Borrow dispatched a new stock to Longoria, whose size he himself described as 'a still larger quantity' than 50 [L 1.11.1837]. Seeing his habit of supplying booksellers in multiples of 50, it probably concerned 100 copies.

If this number is correct, then sales were a little less brisk from there on, for shortly after the definite Prohibition of 19 May 1838, 97 copies were seized and confiscated in Oviedo, and strict orders issued to export them out of the country [L 23.7.1838]. This seizure, and the issuing of orders to export the books, originated with Spain's central government, and were communicated by the very Prime Minister of the land to the very British Ambassador in a letter of 1 June 1838, who, in his turn, passed the information on to Borrow by 4 July [Fraser, *Sleeping*, 41f].

These were obviously orders which one ignored at one's peril; and in that context, it is rather surprising to read the following passage in the memoirs of Samuel Widdrington[38], a travelling navy captain with an impressive knowledge of Spain, who passed through the town some five years later: 'In a shop at Oviedo, where I was in search of old books, I saw one lot of a rather unusual appearance, and on inquiry the people told me they were Bibles left in consignment by mister Borrow, but that they were totally unsaleable, being imperfect from want of the Apocrypha, and that even if asked for, they durst not dispose of them' (note the splendid exercise in self-evidence: nobody wanted the books, but if they wanted them they were not allowed to buy them; hence the books were totally unsaleable!)

---

37 One reason may have been that Borrow needed cash for his further travels, but was unable – in spite of O'Shea's general letter of credit [L 10.5.1837] – to draw on a bank. Without bills, his cash flow 'on the road' is difficult to compute. Note, however, that he carried 15,000 *reales* with him from Madrid, and acquired 3,000 from the sale of his horse, plus perhaps 1,700 from New Testaments sold. His total expenses came to some 17,000 plus unclaimed costs [Acc 6; L 20.11.1837]. In that constellation, it is not unthinkable that he preferred to replenish his flat purse when in Oviedo.

38 Samuel Widdrington (called Cook until 1840, when he changed his name), *Spain and the Spaniards in 1843*, London 1844, vol. 2, ch. 14; quoted in the *George Borrow Bulletin* 31 (2005), 47.

It is a little difficult to decide what books these may have been. One does not wish to suggest that a 'meticulous and well-informed' expert on Spain (as Richard Ford once qualified Widdrington) was telling an untruth, or that he invented a tall tale just to score a Borrow-bashing point. But as the above shows: it is impossible that these books could have been copies of the 1837 Scio New Testament, since those were all confiscated, and it is most unlikely that they could have remained in Oviedo, only to be returned to the bookshop so as to be offered for sale a second time. Consequently I prefer to think that this was a so far undocumented shipment of full Bibles, sent over directly from England to Spain's north coast on Borrow's request, corresponding to the passage in his letter to Brandram of 29 September 1837 and in chapter 33 of *The Bible in Spain* where the leader of the 'ten gentlemen in cloaks' expressed the wish:

> *'I hope you can furnish us with the Old Testament also.'*
> *I replied that I was sorry to inform him that at present it was entirely out of my power to comply with his wish, as I had no Old Testaments in my possession, but did not despair of procuring some speedily from England.'*

If Widdrington's mysterious books were indeed full Bibles, it would explain why in the above quotation he makes such an issue of the *Apocrypha*. Since there exists no difference of opinion between Catholics and Protestants as to the books which ought to make up the New Testament, it is most unlikely that the Oviedo bookseller would have complained of New Testaments 'being imperfect from want of [them]'[39]. But, alternatively, Widdrington's books may of course have been a handful of copies – New Testaments or complete Bibles – sold to a second hand bookshop by their first owners. We shall probably never know.

II.2.2.x   Santander

Feeling a need to leave a somewhat large stock of Testaments in Coruña, from which adjacent cities could be supplied if the need arose, Borrow carried with him only the bare minimum of copies – some 80 – to supply

---

39 For the nature of and the disagreement over the *Apocrypha*, see Appendix 2.

Ferrol and Oviedo and do some selling on the road (see II.1.2.b and II.2.2.vi). But since he had great plans to visit and supply the rest of the North-coast of the Peninsula, he made arrangements for a fresh stock to be sent ahead of him to Riesgo, his Santander bookseller [BiBo 1]. Just before leaving Coruña, he wrote home: 'Santander, being a large and flourishing town, affords me a tolerable prospect of success, and I have accordingly directed my agent at Madrid to despatch thither forthwith 150 Testaments' [L 15.9.1837]. It seems that Borrow soon afterwards corrected this Coruña order of 150 copies to one for 200 (the actual number received in Santander), probably by the letter from Ferrol to Borrego 'for NT's' of 20 September 1837 which Knapp records in *Life*, I : 266.

Unfortunately, all these plans failed awfully. Borrow, travelling at an irksome pace through one of the most inaccessible areas of the Peninsula, and feeling ever more sickly after his difficult journeys through Galicia and Asturias, reached Santander around 9 October 1837, only to discover 'to my great sorrow that the 200 Testaments which I had ordered to be sent from Madrid were not come; and I supposed that they had either been seized on the way by the Carlists or that my letter had miscarried' [L 1.11.1837]. Neither was the case. In reality, Borrego had received the order, but for some reason did not dispatch the shipment of the 200 copies until 31 October, one day before Borrow's return to Madrid [BiBo 1; L 1.11.1837, footnote].

Borrow did not rightly know what to do. He had no books to sell and it would take weeks to order new ones; Santander, on the edge of the battlefields and full of lavishly spending soldiers and sailors, was a most expensive place; he himself felt ever worse, and due to the warfare there was no chance to travel on to Pamplona, as his original plan had been [L 1.11.1837]. Consequently he decided to throw in the towel and return to Madrid. Before setting out, however, he did what he could to guarantee future sales in the city. 'I of course entered into conference with the booksellers as to what they should do in the event of my finding an opportunity of sending them a stock of Testaments from Madrid' [L 1.11.1837]. What they did cannot in any manner have been what they agreed to. Riesgo received Borrego's shipment in perfect order a little while later, and duly charged the printer – hence Borrow – with the costs of shipment [BiBo 1]. Next, however, he did nothing at all. The 200 copies of the New Testament were laid up in a store-room and never touched, until they got placed in embargo by the authorities soon after the Prohibition of May 1838 [L 18.7.1939]. In March or April 1839, Borrow recovered these 200 copies and added them to his central stock in Madrid [L 18.7.1839]. There were, in short, no sales in Santander.

II.2.2.xi Burgos

Borrow stopped over in Burgos on his way back to Madrid from Santander in mid October 1837, and located a bookseller who was willing to undertake the sales of New Testaments. But since he himself did not have a single book left to supply the shop, and since the Burgos bookseller apparently preferred to sell in franchise of a colleague, Borrow asked Julian Pastor, the bookseller of Valladolid, to forward all his unsold stock to Burgos [L 1.11.1837; also II.2.2.iii above]. This was done, and the Burgos bookseller sold 40 copies of the New Testament between October 1837 and mid May 1838 [L 17.5.1838].

II.2.2.xii Toledo

A month after his return to Madrid, in the early days of December 1837, Borrow made a quick book-selling excursion to Toledo, the ancient capital of Visigoth Spain, See of the Primate of Spain, and traditionally one of the most Catholic cities of the country. To have a sufficient stock of books, he sent a muleteer ahead with 100 New Testaments [L 28.11.1837; *BiS* ch 36]. Once in Toledo, he contacted the local bookseller, who turned out to be a radical liberal, and therefore gladly took charge of selling the work [*BiS* ch 36]. It was surely well-meant, but futile. During the whole of Borrow's ten days' stay in Toledo, only 13 copies were sold at 10 *reales* apiece, which turned the endeavour not only into a commercial failure, but also into a financial bleeding [Acc 7]. There are no indications that any books were left in franchise with the Toledo bookseller.

II.2.2.xiii Seville

While in the northern provinces, Borrow ordered Borrego's print shop to send stock of New Testaments to booksellers in various important cities of Spain's southern and eastern provinces. One hundred copies, plus a hundred advertisements, were consequently dispatched to a Seville bookshop [L 1.11.1837; L 30.3.1838; L 12.1.1839; BiBo 1] called 'Caro y Cartaya' [BiBo 2].

From this shop, 76 copies were confiscated before 25 May 1838 [L 25.5.1838; L 23.7.1838; L 12.1.1839; *BiS* ch 45], which implies that 24 copies were sold. Of these 24, Borrego settled the proceeds of 10 copies, and credited the resulting 80 *reales* to Borrow in his bill of 11 May 1838 [BiBo 2]. Since this is one day before Borrow was released from jail, and only a week before the definite Prohibition of his gospels was proclaimed, these 10 copies will have been the last ones sold by the Seville bookseller.

The copies confiscated in Seville were entrusted to the office of the Ecclesiastical Governor of Seville. Borrow, stopping over in the city when on his way from Cadiz to Madrid in January 1839, paid that gentleman a visit to see if he could retrieve his books. The somewhat hilarious scene that resulted gets told in his letter of 12 January 1839 and in *BiS* chapter 45. The venerable and highly aged ecclesiastic turned out to be a 'fierce persecuting Papist', of the sort whom Borrow just loved to present to the world in all their inquisitorial splendour. When hearing who Borrow was and on what business he came, the old man, 'with a stammering tongue, and with eyes flashing fire like hot coals', expressed his indignation that 'being once lodged in the prison of Madrid, I had ever been permitted to quit it', and thundered on that 'he should not deliver up the books on any condition, save by a positive order of the Government'.

This Borrow then set out to achieve, through the mediation of his friend Henry Southern of the British Embassy, who, interceding energetically with the Madrid government, managed to have the confiscated copies put 'at the disposal of the Society' again six months later, under the condition that they be exported from the land [L 21.9.1839; Knapp, *Life*, II : 294]. On Borrow's request where to send this batch of books, G. Browne, one of his contacts at the Bible Society, suggested that they be sent to Gibraltar [Letter from Browne to Borrow of 9 October 1839, quoted in Shorter, *Circle*, ch 18]. Whether this was actually done is not known; but seeing the final and total sales-figures as they stand, it becomes rather unlikely that Borrow exported these copies from Spain (see IV.5 and IV.6 below).

II.2.2.xiv Valencia

ANOTHER 100 copies of the New Testament were sent to the bookshop of Juan B. Jimeno in Valencia in the summer of 1837 [L 1.11.1837; BiBo 1; BiBo 2]. Jimeno sold 24 copies up to 11 March 1838, and credited their proceeds (220 *reales* and 24 *maravedís*) to Borrego, who in turn credited them to Borrow in his 11 May 1838 bill [BiBo 2]. Since this settlement was performed only a week before the final Prohibition of Borrow's books, the number may reasonably be taken as the total sales of New Testaments through the Valencia bookshop.

II.2.2.xv Cadiz

ANOTHER 100 copies of the New Testament, with 100 advertisements, were sent to a so far nameless bookshop in Cadiz [L 1.11.1837; BiBo 1][40]. Nothing is known of sales or the final fate of these books; yet once again the computations of stock and total sales below (see IV.5 and IV.6) do not allow sales to have been anything but extremely small, in the way of 5 rather than 10 copies.

II.2.2.xvi Malaga

ANOTHER BATCH of unknown size was dispatched, likewise in the summer of 1837, to a Malaga bookshop owned by a gentleman called Medina [BiBo 1; BiBo 2]. The size of this stock is not mentioned anywhere, but we may assume it to be yet another 100 copies, first of all because this was the standard supply which Borrow asked Borrego to dispatch to bookshops he did not visit himself; and secondly because the costs of transport – which depended on the weight of the box, the distance it was carried, and the sort of roads that needed to be negotiated – came to 146 *reales* [BiBo 2], i.e. even 36 *reales* higher than the postage for 100 copies sent to Seville, which lay at the identical distance of 520 km from Madrid [BiBo 1].

There are no indications as to sales in Malaga. The bookseller's stock was seized sometime before 25 May 1838 [L 25.5.1838; L 23.7.1838], and is never heard of again. As in the above cases, sale must have been very small.

II.2.3 Prices, costs and bookseller commission.

WE KNOW less than we would like about the wholesale price which the franchised booksellers paid for Borrow's Scio New Testament, the retail

---

40 Possibly the bookshop of Meraleda, the only one which Richard Ford (*Handbook*, 313) mentions in Cádiz. Giménez, *Prensa*, 375, entry n° 7 records an advertisement for the Scio New Testament placed in the Cádiz newspaper *El Tiempo* on 8 December 1837. Possibly it offers the bookshop's name.

price for which they sold the book to their customers, and the profit or 'percentage' [Acc 8] which they realized on the sales. Only in the case of Madrid do we get any clarity on the subject. There Borrow cashed in 520 *reales* for the 52 copies sold in half a year by all the bookshops he employed [Acc 8; II.2.2.i]; and we know that at least two of these (Cuesta and Paz) sold the book to their customers at a retail price of 12 *reales* apiece (see Illustration 6 in II.2.2.i). These numbers translate into a net profit for the bookseller of 2 *reales*, or a rather hefty 20 % over the retail price. Wealthy, cosmopolitan Madrid cannot, however, be taken as the norm for the country as a whole, and the situation in the smaller provincial cities was different.

Unfortunately, the only available information on the situation in the provincial towns comes from half a dozen rather haphazard annotations sprinkled throughout the sources, each of which is of difficult interpretation. On two occasions, we see that Borrow received an identical 10 *reales* per copy in cash from his booksellers over the entire stock supplied. This happened in Oviedo, where the whole batch of 40 copies he had brought to town was sold off during his own presence [Acc 6; II.2.2.ix], and in Toledo, where after the disappointing sales of a week he decided to call it a day and leave no franchise [Acc 7; II.2.2.xii]. This asking price obviously implies that both bookshops sold their copies to clients for more than 10 *reales* apiece so as to realize any sort of profit; and Borrow's own standard price of 11 or 12 *reales* naturally suggests itself. Yet the sources are mute on the subject, so that we have no clue as to the profit these two bookshops made.

Borrow immediately cashed in the proceeds in Madrid, Oviedo and Toledo because sales in these cities were – each in its own way - completed. In all other cases, however, he was happy to leave town without calling in the money for sold copies, postponing payment until many months later. On his return from the Northern Journey, he stipulated to his employers as he sent in his financial statement, that 'in the account of Testaments sold you will observe that I make no mention of by far the greater number, namely those disposed of at Lugo, Saint James, etc., as I have not yet received the money from the booksellers' [L 20.11.1837]. In fact, in several known cases, he was not to call in the sums due until *more than a year* after the Prohibition of May 1838, when he made a final effort to wrap up his franchises and figure out the definite sales-figures of his booksellers [L 18.7.1839]⁴¹. His was clearly not a *commercial* enterprise.

The only instance where the numbers of this final settlement have come down to us is Santiago de Compostela, which included those for Pontevedra (see II.2.2.vii above). Some time in early 1839, Rey Romero, Borrow's Santiago contact, was asked to draw up the definitive sales-figures for Compostela and Pontevedra. In his turn, the old bookseller contacted José Garcia in Pontevedra, and once he had received the necessary information from the book-peddling notary, sent Borrow a final statement for each town on 22 June 1839, 'whereby you will see that 35 copies remain on hand here and in Pontevedra, and 950 *rs. vn.* in money for which you can draw on me at sight' [Fraser, *Mol*, 80]. These proceeds, which came from the total sale of 115 copies in both cities, translate into a wholesale price of 8.25 *reales* per copy. This is far short of the customary 10, but that difference can be explained, because Borrow states explicitly that the 950 *reales* were the balance in his favour 'after deducting all expenses', and that the Santiago bookseller sold the books 'at the high price of ten *reals* each' [L 18.7.1839]. Since this retail price is absolutely certain⁴², the 'expenses' – a sum which contains the bookseller's commission as well as various costs - came to 200 *reales* (115 x 10 – 950), nearly 17.5 % of the total amount. This in itself was perhaps not excessive, for it is in keeping with the estimate of costs which Antonio Bergnes, the Barcelona printer, once mentioned in a tender to Lieutenant Graydon, Borrow's colleague on the Levantine coast, when he wrote that 'you may calculate (and I judge from my own experience) that all [charges] included agents' commission amount from 15 to 20 per Cent'⁴³. And yet there is a small problem with Rey Romero's 'expenses',

---

41 When precisely Borrow staged his general 'wrapping up' operation is not known, but it is surely no coincidence that he recovered the 200 unsold copies from Santander just before his move to Seville in April 1839; that he received Rey Romero's final answer in late June 1839; and that he could communicate definite sales-figures for places like Leon and Lugo in his letter of 18 July 1839. This late date of settling outstanding debts has another unfortunate side-effect, namely that we never learn what sums Borrow cashed in over copies sold by his booksellers; the last expense account which mentions income being the one of 9 March 1839 [Acc 11].

42 It is borne out by the statement of Ramona Perez and Juan Rey Romero Alcocer at the time of the confiscation of these books; see II.4 below.

43 Letter from Bergnes to Graydon of 17 October 1835, in Bible Society Archive, Foreign Correspondence Inwards 1835, vol. 4, p. 51.

for most of the possible costs that the sale of the New Testament might have generated had already been picked up by Borrow himself when he personally brought the supply to the door of the Santiago bookshop. One is therefore left to wonder of what sort and how large the true 'expenses' may have been which encroached on the bookseller's commission.

Unfortunately no more clarity as to the size of such costs is gained from the last two sources at our disposal: two settlements concerning small batches of books sold by the booksellers of Valencia and Seville, who were supplied and administered by Borrego's *Compañía Tipográfica* since Borrow himself did not visit these cities[44]. Both appear in Borrego's bill of 11 May 1838 [BiBo 2]. There Borrego credits Borrow with the '*liquido producto de venta de 24 ejemplares, hecha por Jimeno de Valencia*', i.e. income from 24 copies sold by the Valencia bookseller. Those proceeds come to 220 *reales* and 24 *maravedís*, which – with the *maravedí* at its impossible rate of 34 to the *real* – comes down to a weird 9 *reales* plus 6⅔ *maravedí*, or roughly 9⅕ *real*, per copy. The item following concerns the credit to Borrow from 10 copies sold by Caro y Cartaya of Seville, amounting to 80 *reales*, i.e. a straight but very low wholesale price of 8 *reales* per book.

Put into a simple summary, we possess the following data:

	Asking price	Asking price – costs	Retail price
Madrid	10		12
Oviedo	10		10+
Toledo	10		10+
Santiago		8.25	10
Seville		8	
Valencia		9.20	

---

44 Unfortunately only two of Borrego's bills to Borrow have survived [BiBo 1 and BiBo 2]. Hence it is impossible to tell for how many of the 16 provincial booksellers the Madrid printer performed this service. One imagines that the system mainly suggested itself where Borrego already had a running account with the bookshop in question, i.e. old and regular customers of his. Incidentally, we have no information on the commission which Borrego charged for such services, but it is possible that he did so for free. His Barcelona colleague Antonio Bergnes typically wrote to Graydon in the letter already quoted: 'as for my commission for the sale – whole sale and retail – I charge none when the work has been printed and bound at house'.

Obviously, very few conclusions can be wrung from these numbers, because no regular pattern emerges from them. By the looks of it, Borrow left the retail-price of the Scio New Testament pretty much to the discretion of his booksellers; and was even willing to lower his customary asking price of 10 *reales* still more[45], so as to enable his outlets to sell as cheaply as they liked (as the Santiago retail price proves). But we cannot reconstruct his wholesale price in half the cases, since he also allowed his booksellers to subtract expenses in their final settlements. As said: what expenses those may have been is anybody's guess. Costs of logistics and marketing were very few in number, and most of them would not need to be advanced by the bookseller. In fact we only find four such items in the available sources: the packing of the books for transport; postage and carriage; gate-dues; and local publicity.

The first of these is typically something which Borrego's company took care of as long as it functioned as distributing house for the edition during the tolerated period. Whenever Borrow gave Borrego an order to supply a certain bookseller with a specific number of books, the *Compañía Tipográfica* would pack that batch into a '*cajon y embalaje*' (i.e. a box and casing) and send the package off by mail. One of Borrego's bills [BiBo 1] spells out the costs of this, but the numbers are of such variety that comparison becomes difficult. The 500 New Testaments sent to Coruña (see II.1.2b and II.2.2.vi) went into a box worth 50 *reales*; while for the box dispatched to Santander with no more than 200 copies (see II.2.2.x) Borrego charged a rather pricey 40 *reales*. The four boxes for 100 copies each to Cadiz, Seville, Malaga and Valencia (see II.2.2.xiii-xvi), packed together with 100 advertisements, came to 30 *reales* apiece; yet a box to Valladolid, which contained 50 copies, was only 5 *reales* cheaper than that. How the costs of packing worked out precisely is therefore hard to understand; but in any case, such costs did not have any influence on the amount of the final reimbursement made by the booksellers, since Borrego charged them not to the outlets, but directly to Borrow himself.

---

45 Note that the cost price of the Scio New Testament was 18 *reales*, and that Borrow never stopped dropping his wholesale price as time went by. Originally, he had contemplated selling the book to bookseller for the 'fictitious' cost price of 15 *reales* [L 27.2.1837]; yet before setting off on the Northern Journey in the following May it had become 10; and the Seville bookseller paid no more than 8 in 1838.

Cost of transport might conceivably have had an influence, except that this seems to have been rigorously avoided. Borrego dispatched the shipments with a courier or a muleteer; but as was the custom in the 19th century: not the sender, but the recipient paid for the postage on delivery. This was indeed money advanced by the bookseller; but it never seems to have been deducted from the final reimbursement over books sold; for in several instances we see that soon afterward, the bookseller notified the *Compañia Tipográfica* of the correct delivery of the shipment and the '*portes y gastos*' disbursed; and Borrego then immediately charged Borrow for these expenses. The rate for postage depended on the weight of the shipment, the distance of the transport and also, by the looks of it, on the roads negotiated or the number of times the box had to change vehicle. Borrego's bills [BiBo 1; BiBo 2] spell out the costs of some of them, namely:

500 copies to Coruña	236 kg	604 km	403 *reales*
200 to Santander	94 kg	390 km	157 *reales*
100 to Malaga	47 kg	530 km	146 *reales*
100 to Seville	47 kg	530 km	110 *reales*
100 to Valencia	47 kg	350 km	84 *reales*

The presence in this list of both Seville and Valencia (the two bookshops already mentioned above for which Borrego took care of the settlement of sold copies) shows that these costs of transport were reimbursed to the booksellers separately, and not subtracted from the payment for sold copies (otherwise, Borrow would be paying the postage twice).

What is not altogether clear is whether the latter costs of transport did or did not contain the gate-dues disbursed for the books as well. In the 1830s, Spain's fiscal system still leaned heavily on the medieval arrangement of tolls, turn pikes, and incidental custom duties; and the liberals were only just beginning to replace this cumbersome and counter-productive system with something a little more rational. Hence at every other bridge, mountain pass, highway, provincial border, city gate and hole-in-the-wall, duties were demanded on merchandise, passengers, wagon wheels and track-animals. Borrow himself commented to the Bible Society accountant that during his Northern Journey he invariably had to come up with 'gate-dues for the books in every town where I have introduced them' [L 20.11.1837][46]. They were in fact so many and messy that he never bothered to specify them, with the one exception of his Toledo excursion, where he claimed 56 *reales* 'gate dues at Toledo for the introduction of 102 New Testaments at 8 % upon supposed value' [Acc 7; II.2.2.xii], a remark which allows us to calculate that this 'supposed value' was 7 *reales* per book. That aside, there is only one occasion on which a bookseller claims custom duties from Borrego, and hence from Borrow. This is the a-typical shipment of the 500 New Testaments to Coruña, which resulted in 120 *reales* of '*derechos de aduana*' paid by José Maria Perez [BiBo 2], whose 'supposed value' (*if* the same 8 % applied!) must have been an oddly low 3 *reales* per copy.

Finally there are the possible costs of advertisements in the press and posters on the city walls, which booksellers were supposed to place and pay for. Borrow himself left such pre-printed advertisements with many of the booksellers he visited (see II.2.1) and he had Borrego print and send bundles of 100 to Cadiz, Seville, Malaga and Valladolid or Valencia [BiBo 1; L 1.11.1837]. If the booksellers in question actually dared to take such provocative steps as hanging up posters and placing advertisements in the local press, some expenditure may have resulted. But seeing that Borrow's own ads in the prominent and expensive *Diario de Madrid* never cost him more than 10 *reales* apiece on all 26 occasions he placed them [Acc 8], and that the pay of billstickers surely did not surpass the customary minimum wage of 3 to 4 *reales* a day, the influence which such publicity may have had on the final wholesale price of the booksellers' copies can only have been minimal.

All the above leaves us guessing as to the 'costs' which provincial booksellers may have subtracted from Borrow's credit generated by sold New Testament copies; and consequently we can calculate neither the retail price which they maintained, nor the commission which they derived from their franchise.

---

46 Bergnes, the Barcelona printer, specified in his letter to Graydon of 17 October 1835 that 'in some towns books pay gate duty, and in others they do not,' but – to add to the confusion - he added that in Barcelona books also paid 1 % dues to be *exported* from the city. Note that these gate-dues to take books into and out of the city limits may well be the reason why Borrow often lodged in hotels *outside* the city walls during his Northern Journey.

II.3 Private sales in Madrid (April 1837 – May 1838)

APART FROM the scanty 52 New Testaments sold through the Madrid booksellers, which belong more properly to a previous section (II.2.2.i above), Borrow also sold a large number of copies himself, in a variety of ways, in Madrid and its immediate surroundings. These sales, stretching from April 1837 when the book came off the press, to April 1839, when Borrow moved his operations to Seville, are best separated into his sales in the tolerated period (this chapter) and those performed after the Prohibition of May 1838 was in place (III.2 and III.3 below).

II.3.1 Supply to the British ambassador

A SMALL PIECE of luck came Borrow's way as soon as his Scio New Testament was ready. In early May 1837, when his foot was already in the stirrup to ride north, Sir George Villiers, the British Ambassador, communicated to him through his assistant Henry Southern that he had decided to purchase 'a very considerable number of copies of the New Testament, and to despatch them forthwith to the various British consuls established in different parts of Spain, with strict and positive orders to employ all the means which their official situation should afford them, to circulate the books in question and to assure their being noticed' [L 7.6.1837]. It was a friendly gesture and a sign of support; but in the end it caused something of a disappointment, for, as Borrow wrote in a footnote to a letter at the end of the year: 'Mr. Villiers has hitherto taken but 50 copies, which he has distributed amongst his friends; his situation has been such lately, that more could not be reasonably expected from him.' [L 25.12.1837]. There is no sign that Villiers ever purchased additional copies.

II.3.2 Sales from the 'Despacho'

WHEN ON his return from the north, Borrow discovered that the Madrid booksellers 'gave themselves no manner of trouble to secure the sale' of his books, he decided to take matters into his own hands and establish a shop of his own, where only the Scio New Testament and a few related

publications would be offered for sale. [L 20.11.1837; L 15.1.1838; APP].
To this effect, he rented a somewhat expensive space in the fashionable
centre of Madrid, at the *Calle del Principe* nº 25, for 240 *reales* a month
[L 12.11.1837; Acc 6; Acc 8; Acc 9].

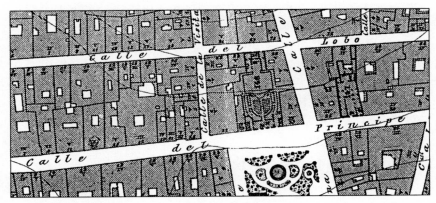

Illustration 9: Map of Central Madrid. Borrow's Despacho stood on the plot just
above the "-el" in the phrase Calle del Principe

The *Calle del Principe* runs north to south between the *Plaza Canalejas*,
past the *Plaza Santa Ana*, and beyond to the *Calle Huertas*. The prominent Spanish investigator Antonio Giménez Cruz has determined, in
his usual meticulous manner, that Borrow's *Despacho* was located at
the north-east corner of the *Calle del Principe* and the *Calle de Manuel
Fernandez y Gonzalez* (formerly the *Calle de la Visitación*). The building
itself has long since disappeared, and the house-numbers have changed.
The new, 1970s edifice that has replaced it now houses a dental clinic with
the street number 21[47].

After 'furnishing it handsomely with glass cases and chandeliers' to
the tune of 950 *reales* [*BiS* ch 36; Acc 6], and painting '*Despacho de
la Sociedad Biblica*' on the shop window, Borrow formally opened the

---

47 Shorter, *Circle*, footnote 188, already observed in 1913 that 'the Calle del Principe
is now rapidly being pulled down and new buildings taking the place of those
Borrow knew.' On p. 192a, Shorter prints a rather narrow picture of the street. This
picture, however, was taken from the north side of the street, at Plaza Canalejas,
and much as the subscript says that this is 'where Borrow opened a shop', what is
meant is the *street*, not the buildings shown, which are 100 yards away from the
actual site!

Illustration 10: The corner where Borrow's Despacho was located
(Courtesy of Antonio Giménez).

establishment on 27 November 1837 [L 28.11.1837]. From the very beginning the Madrid public did show interest, but the choice of merchandise
on offer was perhaps a trifle limited (not to say that in comparison a
Soviet supermarket was a model of diversity). 'Several Testaments have
been sold,' Borrow wrote after the first day of business, 'but three parts of
the customers departed on finding that only the New Testament was to
be obtained' and that no full Bibles were for sale [L 28.11.1837]. Borrow
did his best to remedy the situation, buying up a number of Spanish
language Bibles from a bookseller who did not dare to sell them himself
[L 25.12.1837; Acc 9] and beseeching his employers to send him a large
stock of full Bibles as soon as they possibly could [L 28.11.1837][48].

Leaving the shop in the care of a hired Gallego salesman called Pepe
Calzado [*BiS* ch 36], Borrow then made his short trip to Toledo (see
II.2.2.xii). On his return, he discovered that in spite of the attractive price
of only 10 *reales* per copy [L 25.12.1837; Acc 8], sales in the *Despacho* were
still terribly slow. Only 26 copies (two of them 'gilded' ones at 11 *reales*
each) had been sold in the two weeks between the opening of the shop and

---

48 For the history and exact numbers of Borrow's sales of complete Bibles, see
Appendix 2 below.

his return from Toledo on December 10th or 11th [Acc 7]. Blaming these low sales-figures on the public's lack of awareness, Borrow then decided to mount a major, sensational publicity-campaign. 'I printed three thousand advertisements on paper, yellow, blue, and crimson, with which I almost covered the sides of the streets,' he writes 'and besides this inserted notices in all the journals and periodicals' [L 25.12.1837; BiBo 1; *BiS* ch 36]. On top of that, to the amusement of his employers and 'the astonishment of the populace', he hired 'a man after the London fashion to parade the streets with a placard' [L 12.5.1837; *BiS* ch 36], which is the first recorded instance of such a 'sandwich man' being employed in Spain.

Due to these actions, sales did pick up in December 1837. By Christmas, Borrow could write, still without much enthusiasm, that between 70 or 80 copies had been sold since the shop was opened [L 25.12.1837]. By the end of the year, this total number (i.e. including the earlier 26) had almost risen to 100 [*BiS* ch 36; L 25.12.1837 footnote]. Then, in the first days of the new year, sales suddenly soared dramatically, and began to average some 20 copies a day [APP; L 15.1.1838]. Consequently, in the first ten days of 1838, some 200 additional New Testaments seem to have been purchased, to a total of 'nearly 300' [L 15.1.1838].

However, not only the attention of the buying public was drawn to the *Despacho* by these noisy, aggressive marketing techniques: Borrow's political and clerical foes were likewise alerted to the existence of the shop and the murky, heretical things that went on there[49]. On 11 or 12 January 1838, he received an order to send two copies of the New Testament to the office of the Civil Governor of Madrid for examination [L 15.1.1838]. This he did, and immediately afterwards, on Saturday evening 13 January 1838, 'an *alguacil* arrived at the shop with the notice prohibiting the further sale of the New Testament' [L 15.1.1838; also Borrow's Memoir to Ofalia, tagged on to L 17.3.1838]. Consequently, Borrow postponed further sales of the New Testament until he could persuade the government – with a little help from the British Ambassador – to have the ban lifted. While these negotiations were going on, he closed the shop, only opening it up

---

49 An additional provocative factor which whipped the government into action was the imminent publication of the 'Gypsy *Luke*', the gospel according to Luke in the Gypsy language Caló which Borrow printed over Christmas 1837. See Missler, *Gypsy*, 32ff.

again for a short while in April, so as to sell full Bibles and his Gospels in Caló and Basque [L 19.4.1838]. But by 24 May 1838, soon after his books were finally and formally prohibited by Royal Decree, he had no choice but to close the *Despacho* for good [Fraser, *Sleeping*, 41].

At the end of April 1838, Borrow drew up his expense account for the whole of the previous period. There, he computed the total sales of the New Testament between 12 December 1837 and 26 April 1838 as '291 copies (at 10 *reals*) of the New Testament sold at Madrid (…) partly in Society's establishment n° 25 Calle del Principe, partly by private sale' adding another '14 copies (gilded) at 11 *reals*' below, making a total of 305 copies and 3,064 *reales* [Acc 8]. Adding to this number the 26 copies sold earlier in Nov–Dec 1837 for 262 *reales* [Acc 7], and overlooking the fact that some seem to have been sold 'privately', it may be said that 331 copies of the New Testament were distributed through the Madrid *Despacho*, while total income from these sales came to 3,326 *reales*.

II.4 The confiscations after 19 May 1838

ON 19 May 1838, Queen Regent Maria Cristina signed a formal Royal Decree forbidding the printing, possession and distribution of all Spanish language scripture, and less than a week later, on the 25th, the measure was formally issued by publication in the government paper. This Royal Decree, combined with the firm resolution to curb the foreign missionary effort, automatically implied that such batches of books which were known to lie around in bookshops or depots – Borrow's own as well as those of his franchised booksellers – would be actively searched out by officials and placed in custody. 'Immediately on receiving intelligence of the scenes which had taken place at Malaga[50], the Spanish Government resolved to put an end to all Bible transactions in Spain, and forthwith gave orders for the seizure of all the Bibles and Testaments in the country wherever they might be deposited or exposed for sale', Borrow wrote two weeks after being set free from his short bout in jail [L 25.5.1838].

The government was clearly serious about the matter. Already in late

---

50 Where Lieutenant Graydon had stirred up and run into trouble by overzealous propaganda – PM.

May, Borrow learned that 'several of my depots have been seized in various
parts of Spain, for example, at Salamanca, Seville, and of course at Malaga'
[L 25.5.1838]; and by late July he reported that 'the following seizures
have already been made (…): the Society's books at Oviedo, Pontevedra,
Salamanca, Santiago, Seville, and Valladolid' [L 23.7.1838]. In the end, all
the depots which Borrow had established with so much care and trouble
in the distant corners of the Peninsula were swept up by the authorities,
with the one exception of his own central stock, containing some 3,000
New Testaments [L 26.6.18238], which he had had the foresight to hide.
'On receiving intelligence that my depots had been seized in various parts
of the country,' he wrote in July, 'I thought it advisable to place my stock
in Madrid in safety, and in consequence under cover of night removed
it from the shop, and concealed it in portions in the houses of various
friends.' [L 9.7.1838; Acc 9] From there, at a slightly later stage, the stock
was furtively removed again to a very secret storehouse, whose whereabouts we do not even know today [APP; Acc 10].

In one instance, we possess a detailed report of how the confiscations at bookshops took place. That instance is, once again, Santiago
de Compostela; and it will be instructive to reproduce its story in some
detail, since it shows both the length to which the government went to
have Borrow's edition swept up, and the trouble they had in making it
happen[51].

On 30 May 1838, Ventura González Romero, under-secretary of the
Ministry of Justice, wrote a long and confidential letter on behalf of his
superior to the ecclesiastical governors of Santiago (i.e. the canons of the
cathedral who ran the diocese in the absence of the exiled Archbishop).
Marked with a large *Reservado* ('Classified') in the margin, this letter
explained that the Queen, following a proposal of the government, had
decided to forbid henceforth all vernacular, noteless and incomplete
Scripture in the realm, and that all copies 'available for public sale' ought
to be seized and placed in embargo, later to be 'handed over to their

51 The story is based on the documents and letters kept in the Archivo Histórico
Diocesano of Santiago, Mazo 472, Ramo de Imprenta, Legajo '*Leyes, Decretos y
RR.OO. 1813–1860*', and ibid, Mazo 473, Legajo 1º, Ramo de Imprenta 1777–1894.
Additional information comes from the letter of Ventura González to the *Ministerio
de Estado* kept in the Archivo Histórico Nacional in Madrid, Legajo 5.502, nº 59,
Ingleses, Borrow y Graydon. See also Missler, *RRT*, 27–29.

owner in a wrapped and sealed package, with the obligation to remove them [from Spain] by the custom-post of a frontier or a harbour.'

The Santiago canons, who were of course perfectly aware of what was going on in their city, needed no prompting. No sooner had they received the message, on 12 June, than they swung into action. Two of their number, Doctor Fermín Álvarez de Eulate and Doctor Diego Mosquera, first established themselves by formal notarial act as some sort of legal task force which represented the central government of Spain, and then rushed over to the Azabacheria nº 16–17, where Rey Romero's shop was located, with the notary and a couple of sturdy episcopal footmen in their wake. Once inside, the two dignitaries demanded to see the bookseller, but it so happened that Rey Romero himself was out of town, and that only his wife, Ramona Perez, and his eldest son, Juan Rey Romero Alcocer, were present in the shop. The canons were however in a hurry, and decided to address the matter then and there nevertheless. They pressured Ramona and Juan to tell them 'if they sold or distributed copies of the Holy Bible; and [the two of them] answered that in commission

Illustration 11: *Calle de Azabacheria* nº 17 and 19 (formerly nº 16 and 17) where the Rey Romero bookshop used to be.

of Mr. Jorge Borrow, director of the Dependency of the Bible Society of London established in Madrid, they had received 125 copies of the New Testament, of which number they still possess 27; that the others had been sold for ten *reales* each, the price prescribed by the Commission of Madrid according to the orders of said director.' The canons then asked to be shown one of the books; and having been given one, identified it as 'a volume in 8º [*mayor*], of normal binding, whose title-page read *El Nuevo Testamento traducido al Español de la Vulgata Latina por el Rmo. P. Phelipe Scio de San Miguel de las Escuelas Pias,*

Obispo electo de Segovia: Madrid, imprenta a cargo de D. Joaquin de la Barrera: 1837'. Observing next that its title-page made no mention of a licence to print the work, the canons concluded that this publication broke the law of the church and the realm, and therefore 'instructed Doña Ramona and her son to retain [these books] under the strictest responsibility, to sell no other copy, and to keep the 27 remaining ones locked away, without allowing anyone to read them, until the pertinent decision about their fate be taken.' Ramona and Juan wisely promised to do so, and signed the official protocol drawn up during the visit as a token of their agreement.

Four days later, on 16 June, Don Fermín informed Ventura González in Madrid of the action taken. He told his Justice department friend the whole story of the successful raid, but in spite of the happy result, the canon clearly remained unsatisfied. 'We ensured,' he wrote, 'that the copies were placed in a box, which we then bound and sealed, instructing the bookseller to put them at the disposition of their owner, and to inform us when that person intends to recover them, so that we can impress upon him the obligation to remove them from the Kingdom. But,' Don Fermín fretted, 'we fail to see how we can ensure that he will really comply with this obligation, and that he will truly remove them from the realm, or how to stop the copies so lost from sight from being read and circulated. Consequently we beg of Her Majesty that she agrees to amplify her wise measures so as to avoid the serious damages, and call a halt to the baneful consequences, which her Royal Pity intends to evade.' It is quite a mouthful; but behind the remarkable arabesques of this canonical poetry one recognises that Don Fermín solicits permission to confiscate the box of books himself, and – if possible – to keep or destroy them, without having to hand them back to George Borrow.

That far, however, not even the zealous Don Ventura dared to go. A different wind had begun to blow in Madrid, particularly as a result of the vehement protests of the British Legation, and González now needed to move cautiously. First of all, on 2 July, he informed the office of the Secretary of State about the proceedings in Santiago, copying out Don Fermín's latest letter verbatim. Then, it seems, he waited patiently for instructions from on high to see how far he might go in so delicate a diplomatic matter, for it was to take him a full two weeks before, on 19 July, he finally managed to dash off an answer to Don Fermín. The decision reached was something of a compromise. He could not allow the ecclesiastical governors to confiscate the books or to destroy them; but he did give them the go-ahead to collect the box, and to place it *en depósito*, i.e. lock it away, either in some government office like that of the Civil Governor, as seems to have been the case in Madrid and Toledo [Knapp, *Life*, I : 302] , or in a building of their own, as ultimately happened in Seville (see II.2.2.xiii). So it was done. Another two weeks later, on 3 August, the ecclesiastical governors wrote back to Don Ventura, acknowledging receipt of his last message and explaining that the box had been put *en depósito*, 'until its owner, the Englishman Borrow, issues a formal promise to remove them from the Kingdom, under overall supervision of the competent authorities, proving that he has done so by a valid document of the Customs Service.'

As we have already seen (II.2.2.vii above) Borrow was notified roughly a year later by Francisco Rey Romero that these confiscated copies (plus another 8 at Pontevedra) were at his disposal; and by the looks of it, he did recover them shortly afterwards. What became of them is a matter which can only be dealt with later on, when all necessary data have been gathered and processed (see IV.4 and IV.5). Here, we should merely look quickly into the somewhat bizarre nature of the operation which we have just witnessed.

What most catches the eye in the Santiago story, is that the government – once they were determined to rake in the unsold copies of Borrow's New Testament – did not call upon their own civil or military authorities (who under the reigning martial law were omnipotent in the town), but decided to alert the ecclesiastical authorities of the Diocese, who had so little legal say in these matters that they felt the need first to register themselves, by notarial act, as the appointed and competent government representatives. The reason behind this is that the Ministers probably did not trust their own officials to execute their orders faithfully; which is rather ironic, since they themselves had deliberately appointed extremely radical governors to Compostela so as to control and combat the notorious Carlist tendencies of this ultra-Catholic town [Barreiro, *Carlismo*, 140–144]. These same officials could not now be trusted to take action against George Borrow's books; so instead the clerical adversary had to be mobilised to do the government's bidding and clean up the mess of its own making! A similar thing happened in Seville (see II.2.2.xiii above), in Barcelona[52], and surely in other places as well; and the mere fact that the books once confiscated could be 'deposited with the political governors of the said provinces *or in the hands of such persons as the chiefs have entrusted with them*', as Count Ofalia admitted to Ambassador Villiers in a letter of 7 July 1838 (my cursives – PM), shows the uncertainty of the government's sway in this matter.

Quite naturally, mobilising the Bible Society's most outspoken adversaries resulted in having to deal with somewhat unwanted attitudes. Thus, in Don Fermín's subtle suggestion as to what *really* ought to be done to Borrow's New Testaments, one clearly hears the pent-up echoes of book-battling churchmen, who thought it a scandal that such illegal heretical books[53] should be returned to their misbehaving owner at all. An identical stand was taken by the furious Ecclesiastical Governor of Seville, who refused to return Borrow's books to him unless the government positively ordered him to do so; and by the clerical authorities of Toledo, who later tried to burn 200 copies confiscated from Borrow himself (see III.2.2 below). This, in turn, handed ammunition again to the British Legation in its defence of the rights of a British citizen. And so, rather than solving all their problems in one go, the government put its head ever deeper into the lion's mouth; and it comes as no surprise that Borrow could continue to play his 'daring game' for another year and a half, until the problem had gone away by itself, namely: by almost the entire edition of the Scio New Testament having been sold to the populace.

---

52 In Barcelona, the establishment of Antonio Bergnes, Graydon's printer and collaborator, was raided in later September 1838 by an impressive episcopal task force consisting of a cathedral canon, one of the local *alcaldes*, a notary, two witnesses and an *alguazil*. Having been tipped off by a friend, Bergnes – no less cunning than Borrow in these cases – had removed the bulk of his stock of Bibles and Catalan New Testaments to the house of a friend, leaving a small lot behind in his storerooms as booty for the raiders to carry off. For his good offices, the Bible Society made the Barcelona printer a present of a precious Polyglot Bible. [Letter from Bergnes to Brandram from Barcelona of 24 September 1838, in the Bible Society Archive, brought to my attention, once again, by Ms Kathleen Cann.]

53 Elsewhere qualified rather amazingly as 'books and pamphlets against Religion and Christian morality'!!! See Missler, *RTT*, 32.

III

Sales in the 'prohibited' period (July 1838 – November 1839)

III.1 Peasant attitudes and popular literacy

In July 1838, when the diplomatic dust over Borrow's illegal imprisonment had settled and the formal Prohibition of all Biblical works in the vernacular language was firmly in place, Borrow found himself in Madrid with nothing to do. He had been forced to close his *Despacho*; the booksellers of Spain were strictly forbidden to sell his books; and some 3,000 copies of the New Testament were gathering dust, growing mildew and falling prey to nibbling rats, somewhere in a secret storehouse of the capital.

Never one to waste time in idleness or to reconcile himself meekly to set-backs, Borrow then decided to ride forth from Madrid and to peddle his New Testaments, illegally, to the peasantry in the countryside for bottom prices. Over the next year-and-a-half, he staged six major expeditions to visit the hamlets and villages around Madrid, and in between distributed books in great numbers in the poorer neighbourhoods of the capital and of Seville. His various reasons behind this decision – personal as well as commercial – have been explained above (see I.3). Here, we shall merely take a quick look into the nature of his new clients, particularly their level of education.

Borrow, it must be said, was overjoyed with his new customers. While in his first year he had been dealing mainly with the jaded and indifferent city bourgeoisie who only purchased his precious books piecemeal, the poor and the peasantry were highly enthusiastic and hungry for the 'heavenly manna' which he brought them [L 15.9.1837]. In itself this came as no surprise to him, since from an early moment onward, he had made minute enquiries with the booksellers about the feasibility of such a scheme [APP] and he had learned a lot from various experiments such as the satchel sales near Valladolid and Santiago (see II.1.3 above). Of course, Spain's petty farmers rarely set foot in the city, and even more rarely in bookshops, so selling to the peasantry implied that one had to carry the books to their dwelling places, in the style of the travelling salesman. But if such an effort were made, one could 'at any time be sure of a glorious harvest' [APP; *BiS* ch 42].

The peasants, always fascinated with the printed word, and forever deprived of all sorts of luxury goods, instruction and amusement, showed the keenest interest in books sold at the 'price adapted to their humble means' of 3 or 4 *reales* [L 17.7.1838]. They flocked to Borrow like bees to the honey pot as soon as they heard of his arrival in the area, and eagerly picked up copies, particularly in those places where the priest was well-disposed and recommended the books[54]. The only problem Borrow faced (beside an occasional furious curate threatening hell, doom and denunciation) was the lack of currency in the countryside. The dirt-poor Spanish farmers essentially lived in a barter-economy and rarely saw, or held, money. Hence he got paid with handfuls of small, nearly worthless copper coins, and sometimes even with hunted rabbits, seasonal fruits, and barley, which Borrow accepted, however, since he was eager to sell, loath to disappoint his clients, and because 'such articles are of utility either for our own consumption or that of the horses' [L 17.7.1838; L 15.2.1839].

The peasantry, in short, received his New Testaments 'with transport and with gratitude' [APP], and better still: these grateful poor folk were sure to *read* the books which they bought with their petty cash. 'One circumstance was very gratifying and cheering to me,' Borrow wrote in the summer of 1838, 'namely, the ocular proof which I possessed that the books which I disposed of were read, and with attention, by those to whom I disposed of them, and that many others participated in their benefit. In the streets of Aranjuez and beneath the mighty cedars and

---

54 So it happened, for instance, in Cobeña (see III.3.3), in Abades (III.2.4), and of course earlier in Lugo (see II.2.2.v, but also IV.3 for a cooler view).

gigantic elms and plantains which compose its noble woods, I have frequently seen groups assembled, listening to individuals who, with the New Testament in their hands, were reading aloud the comfortable words of salvation' [L 3.8.1838]. What a contrast indeed with his old urban target group, those city-dwellers among whom 'I found little desire for sober serious reading, but on the contrary a rage for stimulant narratives, and amongst too many a lust for the deistical writings of the French, especially for those of Talleyrand, which have been translated into Spanish and published by the press of Barcelona, and for which I was frequently pestered' [APP]. Nay, the difference was such that by early 1839 he barely even bothered to sell to the wealthy at all, for 'the poor of Madrid receive the Scripture with gladness: to the rich I offer it not, their hearts are hard' [L 4.3.1839].

Borrow, who, as his latest biographer observed, always felt ill-at-ease with the wealthy middle classes, but perfectly at home among the doormen and the grooms [Collie, *Eccentric*, 120], celebrated his success among plebeians as a worthy triumph of the Fisherman's religion. 'The fate of this edition has been a singular one,' he wrote jubilantly at the end of the ride, 'by far the greatest part having been dispersed among the peasantry of Spain and the remainder amongst the very poor of the towns, the artisans of Madrid and Seville, the water-carriers and porters. You will rarely find a copy of this work in the houses of the wealthy and respectable, but you will frequently light upon it in the huts of the labourers, in the garrets or cellars of the penniless, and even in the hulks and convict-garrisons. I myself saw it in the prison of Seville' [L 24.12.1839].

Peasants, artisans, muleteers and smugglers, *jailbirds* and *deported felons*...! The one thing which Borrow never seems to have realized, or was ignoring to his cost, was that his employers weren't half as enthralled with his sales to smelly peasants and unwashed donkey-drivers as he was himself. A collection of venerable parsons and wealthy benefactors who formed the backbone of an Empire which was class-conscious to its marrow, Borrow's Bible Society correspondents remained forever silent as long as he reported delightedly how he had peddled his gospels 'to individuals entirely of the lower classes: muleteers, *carmen, contrabandistas*' [L 1.11.1837] and other examples of the gutter species. But no sooner did they hear his tale of the ten Oviedo gentlemen in cloaks, who were clearly solid, civilised, upper class fellows to their liking, than they were aroused to the keenest fascination. 'We were all deeply interested in your ten gentlemen of Oviedo', Andrew Brandram wrote back in reply to the story, 'I have introduced them at several meetings!' [Jenkins, *Life*, 207].[55] Borrow's romantic outlook simply disagreed with the sedate propriety of his employers; or as Kathleen Cann once formulated it aptly: '*Wild* was one of his favourite adjectives; one of the Society's favourites was *respectable*' [Cann, *Correspondent*, 8].

Yet this attitude was based on more than moneyed prejudice. Not wholly without reason, the gentlemen of the Bible Society were somewhat sceptical as to the *usefulness* of selling heavily subsidised books to fully uneducated folk. In England itself, they did effect considerable distribution among the poor, the disadvantaged and even convicts; so they knew the dangers and the pitfalls involved. Was it worth the cost at all? Were such people able to turn it to any advantage? Worse: 'Can the people in these wilds *read*?' Brandram asked incredulously when Borrow first announced his plans to go peddle his gospels 'to the wild people of the wild regions' in the outback of the Peninsula [Jenkins, *Life*, 194]. It was a question well worth asking at the time, and one which still awaits an answer; so a small excursion into the state of Spanish literacy may not be superfluous.

Let us start with the bad news. Up until the liberal revolutions of the first quarter of the 19th century, Spanish society had of course never aimed at general education. Reading was not only seen as needless for the poor and the peasantry; it was considered a dangerous skill, because a reading man will most probably develop ideas, and ideas necessarily threatened the divinely ordained status quo between the classes of nobility, clergy and peasantry. This outlook gets reflected in the few official numbers on literacy we have available: according to an official inquest of 1803, only 5.6 % of Spaniards were literate. More than half a century later, after each of the various liberal regimes had organised its own broad educational system with various degrees of success, this percentage had

---

55 The difference in outlook was old. Already in April 1836 Borrow reported how in Madrid he mixed with common folk and told them 'who and what the Pope is, and how disastrous to Spain his influence had been'. His Bible Society's correspondent instantly told him not to pursue this course since 'our hopes are founded on the simple distribution of the Scriptures', i.e. not on religious dispute and propaganda [Ridler, *GBaaL*, 374].

improved somewhat, but still stood at a dismal 15 to 20 %. And by the census of 1877 it was established that 62.7 % of male Spaniards were totally illiterate, and 81 % of Spanish women[56].

Of course, Borrow was perfectly aware of this low literacy rate and the doom it spelled for his mission. In an early letter to the Bible Society, he writes frankly that 'few amongst the lower class of the population of the towns are acquainted with letters, and fewer still amongst the peasantry; but though compelled to acknowledge the ignorance of the Spaniards in general, I have great pleasure in being able to state that during the latter years it has been becoming less and less, and that the rising generation is by no means so illiterate as the last, which was itself superior in acquirements to the preceding one' [L 10.8.1836][57]. Two years later, when explaining his recent sales-effort in rural areas, he writes: 'True it is that the Spanish peasantry are in general not so well educated as their brethren of the cities, their opportunities of acquiring a knowledge of letters having always been inferior; nevertheless it would be difficult to enter a cottage of which at least one of the inmates could not read, more or less' [ROS].

This last remark is the crux of the matter. *Formal* literacy – i.e. the ability both to read *and* write – stood at the dismally low levels mentioned above; but *passive* literacy, the ability merely to read (which a census would not count as 'literate'), was considerably higher. And it was this passive literacy which was the vehicle of and the secret behind Borrow's rural sales-success; for among the peasantry and the poor city folk of Spain's 19th century, reading was not the silent, isolated and individual

---

56 Inquest of 1803: Barreiro, *Carlismo*, 20, footnote 14. Only 15 % (of male population) literate in 1860: García de Cortazár, F., and González Vesga, J.M., *Breve Historia de España*, Madrid 1993, 444. Only 20 % in 1860: Artola Gallego, M., *La Burguesia Revolucionaria (1808–1874)*, Madrid 1976, 80. Census of 1877: Artola Gallego, *ibid*, 281. Note, however, that there were also vast regional differences. The 1877 census reported that in Galicia, some 30 to 45 % of men were considered literate; yet in Andalusia only 15–30 %. On the literacy of woman, see also Ford, *Handbook*, 252.

57 Authorities did sometimes do their best to remedy the situation. In Oviedo, for instance, there was a special night school in the 1840s where illiterate artisans and labourers were taught the fundamentals of reading and writing, mainly with the object of keeping them out of the *tavernas*. See Madoz, *DG*, vol. xii, 472.

activity that it is today, but very much a collective event. Just as stories
were told and music was performed during the group-wise cottage industry of the winter-months, one person talking or playing while the
others laboured away, the reading of a book or a newspaper was a social
occasion of solemn importance. Helped along by the fact that people as a
rule read out loud whether there was an audience or not[58], a group often
formed around the best reader of the house, of the inn or even of the
village, which would be entertained for hours at a time by the wonders
of the printed word[59].

As seen above, Borrow himself already noticed this custom in Aranjuez,
where 'beneath the mighty cedars' of its noble woods, he often spotted
'groups assembled, listening to individuals who (...) were reading aloud'
[L 3.8.1838]. But there are many other instances of it in his own, and in
other travellers', writings. To give but a few examples: in the inn of Evora
in Portugal, Borrow handed a religious tract to the eldest of a group of
Spanish smugglers, who 'then rose from his seat, and going into the middle of the apartment, began reading it aloud, slowly and emphatically;
his companions gathered around him (...). He continued reading for upwards of an hour, until he had finished the tract' [BiS ch 3]. Another such
session Borrow witnessed in the town of Sahagún, where the local priest,

---

58 Thus, when Borrow met a peasant woman near Cobeña who asked to be allowed a glance at one of his books, 'she instantly commenced reading it with a loud
voice, and continued so for at least ten minutes, occasionally exclaiming, '*Que
lectura tan bonita, que lectura tan linda!*' ('What beautiful, what charming reading!')'
[L 15.2.1839 and BiS ch 46]. Another instance he observed in Villaseca: 'An old
peasant is reading in the portico. Eighty-four years have passed over his head, and
he is almost entirely deaf; nevertheless he is reading aloud the second of Matthew:
three days since he bespoke a Testament, but not being able to raise the money, he
has not redeemed it until the present moment.' [L 17.7.1838 and BiS ch 43]

59 It is in this context that we ought to understand the – often questioned – tale
which Borrow tells of peasants coming into Rey Romero's Santiago bookshop 'with
the intention of purchasing some of the foolish popular story-books of Spain',
whom the old bookseller persuaded, 'in lieu thereof to carry home Testaments,
assuring them that it was not only a better and more instructive, but even a far
more entertaining book than those they came in quest of' [L 19.8.1837; BiS ch 27].
These were undoubtedly the best readers of the village, who had been delegated to
purchase, with the petty savings of the whole community, a Book which would
entertain the village for many winter evenings in a row.

a staunch Carlist, read a newspaper of surely suspect political loyalties to some 50 of the town's inhabitants in a meadow [*BiS* ch 22]. Washington Irving, in his turn, describes in his Granada memoirs of the 1820s, how an invalid veteran called *El Tio Polo* was in the habit of reading aloud to his neighbours from the only book in his possession: the magnificent 7th volume of Father Benito Feijoo's *Teatro Critico Universal*, a highly intelligent but far from simple book on legends, mythology, superstitions and religion [Irving, W., *The Alhambra*, chapter 42: 'Expedition in quest of a diploma']. And Richard Ford invited his readers to 'observe the singular groups of sallow, unshorn, hungry, bandit-looking men, with fierce-flashing eyes and thread-bare shorn *capas*, which cluster like bees round the reader of some 'authentic letter" in the Madrid Puerta del Sol [Ford, *Handbook*, 1092].

Such, then was the setting into which Borrow sold his vernacular gospels; and the implications of this social custom are something to keep well in mind when judging of the relevance of bookselling missions, Borrow's own as well as others. For just as nowadays the sale of a single modern paperback represents two or three readers on the average, the sale of a Scio New Testament probably resulted in four or five *listeners* taking notice of its contents. Or in other words: selling small numbers of books to the common people of the past whom we are in the habit of deriding a little for their ignorance, was not perhaps as insignificant an action as it may appear at first sight.

III.2 Sales Madrid area (July – August 1838)
III.2.1 Trip 1 to the Sagra of Toledo (10–22 July 1838)

BORROW'S FIRST Bible-peddling expedition took him to the Sagra, a flat and arid plain just East of Toledo and North of the Tagus. In *The Bible in Spain* (ch 42) he credits his Madrid landlady[60] with suggesting this

---

60 In Madrid, Borrow lived at the Calle de Santiago n° 16, on the third floor in the years 1836–1838, and on the first in 1839 [Knapp, *Life*, II : 289]. After thorough study, Antonio Giménez Cruz has determined that the building – which has been torn down and replaced – used to stand at the location of the present n° 12. See Shorter, *Circle*, 192a for a picture of the original house.

project to him. This may well have been the case, for Maria Diaz was herself a native of the area, and could offer Borrow room and board in the house in the small town of Villaseca de la Sagra where her husband, Juan Lopez, was living with their children (there is no reliable information on the state of their marital bliss…). Borrow set out from Madrid on 19 July 1838, having sent before him, a day in advance, an *arreiro* with a stock of 200 New Testaments [L 9.7.1838; L 14.7.1838; *BiS* ch 42]. Arrived in Villaseca, he put up in the house of Lopez in the Calle Vacas[61] and started organizing his distribution.

His manner was that of all countryside peddlers of all time. He himself, Antonio, or any of his various local collaborators (Juan Lopez among them) would load a small number of books onto a horse or a donkey and ride to a nearby village. There he would spread a horsecloth on the ground in the most public place, in the central square or at the entrance of the local tavern, expose the merchandise, and stay until the stock was exhausted or the local *cura* threatened to have him arrested.

It was a successful venture. After only four days in Villaseca, Borrow wrote to his employers: 'For the last two days I have been riding in various directions. I have already disposed of about 30 Testaments, of course at exceedingly low prices' [L 14.7.1838]. And it continued this way, each village, in Borrow's own word, taking 'from 20 to 60 [copies], according to its circumstances' and rarely fewer than 30 [ROS]. These numbers may have been inflated just a little so as to impress his employers (20 to 25 seems nearer the truth as we shall see in IV.2 below), but there is no doubt that sales were brisk. The peasants carried him handfuls of small change, scraped together in a hurry, or barter goods like barley and hunted rabbits, to pay for such precious wares. They even searched him out actively, whether he was busy selling or not, knocking on the door of his lodgings, or disturbing his bath in the Tagus river [L 17.7.1838]. The rural schoolmasters, forever starved of teaching materials because

---

61 A fact unearthed by the local historian, Antonio Diaz Fernandez, and recorded by Tom Burns Marañon [*Hispanomania*, ch 5, 149]. The Calle Vacas, nowadays known as the Calle Principe, runs north from the central square behind the city hall. In 1908, A.G. Jayne published an interview with Eduardo Lopez, the (then) septuagenarian son of Maria Diaz and Juan Lopez, in which the old man described the blond *Inglés* and his grumpy servant Antonio during their stay in Villaseca [Shorter, *Circle*, ch. 19; Jenkins, *Life*, ch. 17].

Illustration 12: The central square of Villaseca de la Sagra,
which women were forbidden to cross (Bible in Spain chapter 43).
The Calle Vacas runs behind the row of houses on the right side.

the government set up schools but failed to finance them, were no less
ready to buy copies, often a dozen at a time [L 14.7.1838; L 17.7.1838; *BiS*
ch 43 and 46].

After only a week, the whole first stock was sold off, and he had to
apply to Madrid for a new supply of 200 copies [L 17.7.1838]. These
books were brought, surely for reasons of caution and to avoid large
batches being confiscated on the road now that his activities were getting
known, by a peasant who was 'continually passing and repassing between
Villa Seca and Madrid, bringing us cargoes of Testaments on a *burrico*'
[*BiS* ch 43]. The new 200 were likewise sold off, within the next six days
[L 23.7.1838], so that in less than a fortnight, Borrow sold 400 copies
of the New Testament in the villages of the Sagra [APP], 170 copies at
4 *reales* each and 230 at 3, making a total of 1,370 *reales* [Acc 10]. Since
his activities had now been denounced to the authorities in Toledo, and
interference might soon be expected, he decided to call it a day and
return to Madrid [*BiS* ch 43].

The villages which were actually supplied during this expedition are
listed in his letter of 17 July 1838 (repeated in the last lines of *BiS* ch 43)
and in a 'post-script' to the letter of 3 August 1838, where they are, however, mixed up with the names of places visited during his subsequent
expedition to Aranjuez (see III.2.2 below). If we rearrange these so as
to reflect his itineraries, and correct both Borrow's own odd spellings

and the misreadings by the letters' editor[62], we may show that he sold Testaments in Leganes, Getafe, Parla, Torrejon de la Calzada and Illescas while on the road from Madrid to the Sagra; and in Alameda de la Sagra, Añover de Tajo, 'Azaña', Cobeja, Mocejon, Magán, Olias del Rey, Bargas, Villaluenga de la Sagra, Villaseca de la Sagra and Yuncler in the Sagra itself.

Borrow mentions only a few concrete sales-figures in his writings, namely: 20 copies in Bargas, of which 12 went to the schoolmaster and 8 to harvesters drinking at a wine-shop [L 14.7.1838]; 12 copies to the schoolmaster of Villaseca [L 17.7.1838], plus 1 gift to the *alcalde's* daughter of that town [*BiS* ch 43]; and 9 copies in Mocejon [ROS].

III.2.2 Trip 2 to Aranjuez and Ocaña (late July – 3 August 1838)

AFTER a short visit to Madrid to settle current affairs, Borrow sent a large supply of books ahead of him to Aranjuez, and soon after 27 July [Shorter, *Circle*, 193] set out once again, together with his servant Antonio and Juan Lopez, in a south-easterly direction, with the object of selling books in the villages of La Mancha. 'On leaving Madrid I proceeded in the direction of Aranjuez,' he wrote, 'selling from 20 to 40 copies in every village that lay in the way or near it' [L 3.8.1838; *BiS* ch 44]. Two of these villages were Pinto and Valdemoro [L 3.8.1838, postscript]. The total sales during this stretch of road came to 102 copies at 3 *reales* each [Acc 10].

Arrived at Aranjuez, the group spent three days going from door to door and having 'visited every house in the town' [L 3.8.1838], managed

---

62 The 'P.S.' attached to the letter of 3 August 1838, is in reality a loose slip of paper, written in another hand than Borrow's (Juan Lopez's perhaps?) and in the common Spanish ortography of the age. But whoever transcribed Borrow's letters, probably T.H. Darlow himself, clearly possessed no knowledge of the area, did not have a proper map and was unfamiliar with Spanish handwriting. Thus, 'Torrejon' was rendered 'Forrejon' in Darlow's printed version; 'Getafe' became 'Zetafe'; 'Olias' turned into 'Oliar' and so on. (Most unfortunately, internet versions of Darlow's edition of Borrow's letters add to the confusion by turning the Spanish 'ñ' into a plain 'n', as when Ocaña becomes Ocana, and Añober becomes Anober!) Only in one case, the village written as 'Azaña', we cannot make a definite identification. I suspect, however, that it concerns Aceca, on the Tagus 5 km south of Villaseca, which Borrow spells 'Azeca' in *BiS* ch 43; or it could be Seseña near Aranjuez.

to sell 80 copies 'purchased entirely by the very poor people', for 4 *reales* each [L 3.8.1838; Acc 10; *BiS* ch 44]. Seeing that Aranjuez did not have more than 4,000 regular inhabitants at this time[63], these sales – with a density of 1 copy to every 50 inhabitants – were indeed an impressive accomplishment.

Aranjuez having been supplied, they next bent their course to the city of Ocaña. Juan Lopez was sent ahead in the early morning 'with between two and three hundred Testaments' [L 3.8.1838], or 259 copies to be exact, while Borrow and Antonio, travelling lighter, followed in the early evening of the same day. Just outside the city-gates of Ocaña, however, they got stopped by a man who warned them that Lopez had been arrested in the morning while he was selling his books in town, and that officials were waiting in the local posada to arrest Borrow himself as well [L 3.8.1838; *BiS* ch 44]. Consequently, Borrow and Antonio turned around and returned to Aranjuez, where Lopez, having been set free, joined them next morning. In perfect keeping with the government orders, the books – which seem to have numbered 232 copies [Knapp, *Life*, I : 320] – had been retained, sealed up and dispatched to Toledo, but the seller himself had been set free [L 3.8.1838; see also I.1 above]. Even so, in the ten minutes before his arrest, Lopez had managed to sell 27 copies at 3 *reales* each in the town [L 3.8.1838; Acc 10].

The total distribution during this 2nd expedition was therefore 102 (on the road to Aranjuez) + 80 (in Aranjuez) + 27 (in Ocaña) = 209 copies sold, with a total yield of 306 + 320 + 81 = 707 *reales* [Acc 10]; while 232 copies were confiscated at Ocaña.

A few months later, during Borrow's absence in England, the Madrid Government and the Toledo authorities, grown impatient with these goings-on, made plans to destroy the books seized at Ocaña. On 17 November 1838, the Duke of Frias (the new prime minister who had succeeded Ofalia in September) formally notified Ambassador Villiers

---

63 Madoz, *DG*, vol. ii, 444 gives 3,629 inhabitants. Note, however, that the population of this town was very unstable since the Royal Court – its only 'industry' – no longer resided regularly at Aranjuez. Richard Ford [*Handbook*, 1270] typically observed that when the court was present, the little town played host to 20,000 people living in 'crowded and expensive discomfort'; but when absent, it dwindled to 4,000 inhabitants and became 'dull as a theatre after the play is played and the spectators and actors gone.'

that '232 of Borrow's Bibles were in the possession of the Civil Governor of Toledo' and that unless these books were taken out of the kingdom, the Government 'would be compelled to proceed to their destruction' [Knapp, *Life*, I : 302]. Borrow, informed of this threat by Villiers on his return to Madrid in January 1839, remarked laconically that 'it was not our intention to take any steps towards preventing the civil or ecclesiastical authorities of Toledo from destroying the Testaments seized at Ocaña; and (...) that the only wish we ventured to express concerning the matter was that, in the event of these books, which contain the Word of God, being committed to the flames, the said authorities (...) would commit the act with all the publicity possible' [L 25.1.1839; *BiS* ch 45]. Seeing the final numbers for stock and total sales below (IV.5 and IV.6), it is *most* unlikely that it ever got that far. But the fact is that the final destiny of these books is not recorded in the sources.

III.2.3 Sales in villages near Madrid (July – August 1838)

A SOMEWHAT MYSTERIOUS '123 [copies] in villages in the vicinity of Madrid at 3 *reals*' gets mentioned in Borrow's expense account of November 1838 [Acc 10], wedged in between the sales-figures of his expedition to Aranjuez of July (III.2.2 above) and his expedition to Segovia of August 1838 (III.2.4 below)[64]. The best guess is that these are the copies which Borrow sold while travelling from Madrid to the Segovia region (and perhaps also on the way back) and which he preferred to count separately since they were not, strictly speaking, sold in his target area. In that case one does wonder why he would qualify such a large lot as 123 copies with a dismissive phrase like 'some Testaments [sold] in

---

64 The closeness of the numbers would *almost* suggest that these 123 copies 'in villages in the vicinity of Madrid', reported in November 1838, would be the same as the 122 copies sold 'in town' (i.e. Madrid) as reported in his expense account of 9 March 1839 [Acc 11] and in his personal list of finances for early 1839 [Knapp, *Life*, I : 305]; and that these were entered doubly by mistake. But – as will be noted below – those latter 122 seem to correspond with the remark that Antonio and he himself sold 'considerably upward of a hundred Testaments' in Madrid in February 1839 [L 4.3.1839]. What is more: the 122 copies in Madrid are specifically said to be sold for 4 *reales*, the 123 at 3, which makes confusion unlikely.

the villages near the roadside' [L 1.9.1838]; yet there are few alternatives to this interpretation. No other sales-event pops up anywhere in the sources: not in the correspondence, not in the major reports, and not in *The Bible in Spain*. And since Borrow himself was gone from Madrid most of this time, we would have to assume that some unknown person in Borrow's service was going around the villages near Madrid with bags of New Testaments in the summer of 1838, and silently sold these off before Borrow left for England in mid September 1838. This being unlikely, I prefer the above scenario.

III.2.4 Trip 3 to Segovia and Avila (5–29 August 1838)

Borrow's THIRD expedition, in the provinces beyond the Sierra de Guadarrama mountain-range, and the villages around Segovia and Avila, was his greatest exploit ever. The whole expedition consisted of 5 salesmen: Borrow himself, Antonio Buchino, Juan Lopez and two local peasants whom Lopez hired on the spot [*BiS* ch 44]. Furthermore, it took place at a time, August 1838, when yet one more Carlist Expedition came marching down from the north into Old Castile and turned the province into a veritable battlefield. Yet in spite of that, Borrow managed to sell over a sixth of the whole edition of the Scio New Testament during this journey, which was no mean feat!

As he tells it himself [L 1.9.1838; *BiS* ch 44[65]], Borrow was so enthralled with the idea of selling in proud, venerable Castilla-Leon that he started preparations the very day – August 4 – he returned from his expedition to Aranjuez (III.2.2 above). He dispatched several big cargoes of books to places he intended to visit in the area, and then 'sent forward Lopez with his donkey, well laden' with the understanding they would meet later either at La Granja or exactly below the 107th arch of the Segovia aqueduct [*BiS* ch 44][66].

---

65 Much as the story in *BiS* ch 44 was based on Borrow's letter of 1.9.1838, which covers exactly the same ground, the two versions differ in dates, places and details. Here, I have had to summarize and synthesize to reach a running narrative.

66 Borrow could be a little tiresome at times when it came to showing off his erudition. The arch in question is the one bordering on the south-western side of the road which used to pass beneath the famous Roman structure, right next to the three pillars which carry the niche with the statue of Virgin and Child.

A few days after Lopez left, Borrow and Antonio followed, selling 'some Testaments in the villages near the roadside' in spite of his haste (as noted in III.2.3 above, these sales probably came to 123 copies). Reaching the old royal residence of La Granja by the unfrequented and dangerous Peña Cerrada pass, he expected to meet Lopez and another helper, but they were nowhere to be found. So after a day of rest for the horses, he pushed on to Segovia, without having done any selling, since he was 'well aware that orders had been transmitted to the authorities of the place to seize all copies of the sacred writings which might be offered for sale'. At a friend's house in Segovia he received one of the chests he had sent ahead, containing 200 copies; but Lopez still did not appear. Only after two days of idleness – during which he once again refrained from selling – Borrow heard by chance from a farmer that there were men selling books in the neighbourhood of Abades village. So he instantly loaded his books onto the backs of three donkeys and set out to cover the roughly 20 km to the village.

Arriving at nightfall, he finally found Lopez, together with two peasants whom he had engaged, in the house of the local surgeon. Lopez 'had already disposed of a considerable number of Testaments in the neighbourhood, and had that day commenced selling at Abades itself'. No sooner had the good man exposed his wares, however, than he had been 'interrupted' by a couple of village *curas*, 'who with horrid curses denounced the work, threatening eternal condemnation to Lopez for selling it and to any person who should purchase it'. And notwithstanding the fact that the third, liberal, priest of Abades did all in his power to recommend the book and denounced his colleagues for being 'hypocrites and false guides', Lopez thought the better of it, and postponed sales until Borrow should arrive. This, of course, was the sort of challenge Borrow loved, and he immediately swung into provocative action. 'Upon receiving this information, I instantly sallied forth to the marketplace, and that same night succeeded in disposing of upwards of 30 Testaments'. It did have its effect. The next morning, the two hostile priests made their appearance in the surgeon's house; but Borrow, as he tells it himself, faced them down, and they were not heard from again.

In the following week, Borrow and his collaborators succeeded in selling 'from 5 to 600 Testaments amongst the villages from one to seven leagues distance from Abades.' Then, at the very time that he received

a new shipment from Madrid, some well-placed person in Segovia informed him that orders had been issued to the mayor of Abades to stop
him and to confiscate his stock. With the two hostile *curas* surely still
on the look-out and ready to surge down, it was clearly time to make
himself scarce. So that very same evening, he left Abades 'with all my
people and upwards of 300 Testaments', and after spending the night
in the open, reached and settled in the village of Labajos. Grown wiser
now, he did not sell in the town itself, but for the better part of a week
used Labajos as a base from which to supply, again with great success, the
surrounding villages and the travellers on the highway to Valladolid.

Then Armageddon swung around. 'We had not been at Labajos a
week,' Borrow wrote on 1 September 1838, 'when the Carlist chieftain
Balmaseda at the head of his wild cavalry made his desperate inroad into
the southern part of Old Castile, dashing down like an avalanche from
the pine woods of Soria. I was present at all the horrors which ensued –
the sack of Arrevalo – and the forcible entry into Martin Munoz and San
Cyrian.'[67] But how could such petty things as pillage and mass murder
stop George Borrow from what truly mattered? 'Amidst these terrible
scenes,' he writes 'we continued our labours undaunted, with the exception of my servant [Antonio], who seized with uncontrollable fear ran
away to Madrid.' There are times that one does not rightly know what
to think of George Borrow. He obviously did not lack in courage; but
if a tough survivor like Antonio Buchino lost his nerve in this situation,
one may, with some justice, wonder about the British Bible salesman's
mental health...

Next thing Borrow knew, Juan Lopez disappeared. Nothing was heard
of him for three or four days, and Borrow already imagined him to have
been caught and shot by the Carlists. Fortunately this was not the case.
He had merely been arrested, on the instigation of the local priest, in a
little village of the name Villallos (probably modern Velayos, just west
of Labajos). On 22 August 1838, the day after this news reached him,
Borrow hurried over to the hamlet, only to discover that Lopez was
already to be set free by order from the Ávila authorities, although the
books which he carried would be detained. The *alcalde* and *cura* were

---

67 I.e. modern Arévalo, Martin Muñoz de la Dehesa or Martin Muños de las
Posadas, and Sancidrian, all on the highway from Madrid to Valladolid.

unwilling to let their catch go; but, Borrow wrote later to his friend
Hervey at the British Embassy 'I deemed it my duty, as a Christian and
a gentleman, to rescue my unfortunate servant from such lawless bands,
and in consequence defying opposition I bore him off, though perfectly
unarmed, through a crowd of at least one hundred peasants' [L 23.8.1838;
BiS ch 44; both texts copy his complaint of 23 August from Labajos to
Sir William Hervey].

How many books were confiscated at Villallos is unknown. But it
is obvious that Borrow had grown more cautious and cunning since
Abades. He had taken to the habit of putting up in a larger town, where
the stock was kept but no selling was done, and then to make day-trips to
surrounding villages with small batches of books (some 20 to 30) which
he could afford to lose. Thus, the stock seized from Lopez was surely
small; and for convenience sake we may put it at 20 in the calculations
below.

With the Carlists in the region, the *curas* alerted and the *alcaldes* under
orders to intercept him, even Borrow now admitted that things were
getting too hot for Bible peddling. His stock, furthermore, was practically exhausted, and he himself was feeling the onset of a heavy fever,
which would soon confine him to his bed for a fortnight. He therefore
decided to call it a day and return to Madrid. More than enough had
been accomplished in any case. He and his men had 'in the course of
little more than a fortnight disposed of nearly 900 Testaments – not in
populous and wealthy towns but in highways and villages, not to the
spurious Spaniards of Madrid and the coasts, but to the sun-blackened
peasantry of Old Castile, the genuine descendants of those terrible men
who subjugated Mexico and Peru' [L 1.9.1838; L 29.8.1838; APP]. In a
later instance, when all was properly counted up, the number turned out
to be 884 copies exactly: 322 copies at 4 *reales*, 546 at 3, and 16 at only 2,
to a total of 1,288 + 1,638 + 32 = 2,958 *reales* [Acc 10].

III.3 Sales Madrid area (January – March 1839)

AFTER SPENDING the better part of November and December 1838 in
England for consultations with his employers, Borrow returned to Spain
once again, landing in Cadiz on the last day of the year and reaching

Madrid in the middle of January 1839 [*BiS* ch 45; L 12.1.1839; L 25.1.1839; Knapp, *Life*, I : 300]. At first he was somewhat undecided what actions to undertake 'in order to dispose of the copies of the Scriptures remaining on hand in Madrid, and in the other Depôts established by him in various parts of that Country', as his new instructions defined his remaining task[68]. As he had told his employers when in England, half the remaining 2,000 copies of the New Testament might be distributed in La Mancha, the rest perhaps in the villages between Madrid and Aragon [ROS]; yet by the looks of it, he was already toying with the idea of moving his operations to Seville. Until such a time that he could make up his mind, however, he decided to make another major sales-effort in Madrid itself and the immediate surroundings. The sales-figures for this particular place and time are difficult to determine, because, most unfortunately, Borrow stops reporting the numbers of sold Testaments in his expense accounts after the one of 9 March 1839 [Acc 11], which leaves us to calculate sales merely on the basis of the random remarks in his correspondence, which are not always as clear and unequivocal as one might wish.

III.3.1 Sales in Madrid city by Antonio (January – February 1839)

IN THE expense account of 9 March 1839 [Acc 11] there is mention of 'the sale, in town, of 122 (copies) at 4 *reals*', making 488 *reales*. This exact same phrase gets repeated in a personal summary of income and expenditure of his [Knapp, *Life*, I : 305; see below III.3.6]. As far as we can tell, these sales correspond to the remark in a letter to his employers saying that 'Antonio and myself have lately been very successful at Madrid, having sold considerably upwards of a hundred Testaments and several Bibles' [L 4.3.1839; Acc 11]. This endeavour must mostly have been the work of Antonio, who stayed in Madrid to oversee operations while Borrow rode forth to the Cobeña region [L 15.2.1839 and III.3.3 below].

---

68 So quoted in Cann, *Correspondent*, from the meeting of the BFBS General Purposes Sub-Committee of 14 December 1838, printed in Darlow p. 379.

III.3.2 In the 'purlieux' of Madrid by Vitoriano Lopez (January – February 1839)

A FOLLOWING ENTRY in the same expense account [Acc 11], mentions the sale 'in the purlieux of Madrid, vizt. (sic) at the Puente de Segovia, Embarcadero etc., of 27 at various prices', to a total of 104 *reales* (perhaps 23 at 4 and 4 at 3 *reales*). This is probably the reflection of two earlier communications in the correspondence, namely: a first one in which Borrow tells how in late January 1839 he sent his new collaborator Vitoriano Lopez to the poor neighbourhoods of Madrid, where the man 'succeeded in disposing of 12 Testaments, amongst the very poor people, in a few hours' [L 25.1.1839]; and a second one in which he mentions how immediately after his return in mid February 1839 from the area around Cobeña (III.3.3 below), he despatched Vitoriano to Caramanchel (modern Carabanchel), 'a village at the distance of half a league from Madrid, the only one towards the west which had not been visited last year. He stayed there about an hour and disposed of 12 copies, and then returned' [L 15.2.1839; *BiS* ch 46]. The stated sales, in these two quick day-trips, add up to 24 copies, which comes reasonably close to the 27 justified in the expense account of 9 March 1839 [Acc 11]. (Below, in the regional break down of IV.1.1 and IV.1.2, I will arbitrarily ascribe 14 of these copies to Madrid city and 13 to the surrounding Madrid area.)

III.3.3 Trip 4 to Cobeña and the area East of Madrid (27 January – 4 February 1839)

SOON AFTER his return to Madrid from England in mid January 1839, Borrow prepared for another expedition, this time to the region immediately east of Madrid [L 25.1.1839][69]. He summoned from the Sagra of Toledo what he called 'my largest and most useful horse'. This was the magnificent Arabian steed Sidi Habismilk, imported from Algeria, which he had purchased at some undetermined time from 'an officer of the French Legion' [*BiS* ch 45]. The animal reached him on 23 January 1839

---

69 The plan was rather ambitious: before setting out Borrow speaks of travelling as far as 30 leagues (165 km) from the capital [L 25.1.1839]. In reality he never got further than 4 (23 km) [L 15.2.1839].

[L 25.1.1839]. Deciding against summoning his 'other horse', which was stabled at Salamanca and too worn out after the 1838 expeditions to be of much service [L 25.1.1839][70], he acquired instead a *'burrico'* or donkey as a pack-animal to carry the cargo of books [L 15.2.1839]. Antonio was left in charge of operations in Madrid itself [L 15.2.1839], so that another collaborator had to be engaged. Juan Lopez, approached for the purpose, was too busy farming, but he sent over the above mentioned Vitoriano Lopez, an elderly neighbour or cousin of his from Villaseca, whom he thought fit for the job [L 25.1.1839; L 15.2.1839; *BiS* ch 45]. Together, Borrow and Vitoriano set out to the east of the capital on 27 January, each soon taking his own route [L 25.1.1839; L 15.2.1839].

Borrow himself, disguised as a peasant from the Segovia region, and driving before him the *burrico* 'with a sack of Testaments lying across its back', first made for the village of Cobeña, some 15 km North-East of Madrid. It was a good choice. The village was very poor, and money extremely scarce, but people were fascinated by such beautiful books at only 3 *reales* apiece. Already just before the town, he sold a copy to a young peasant woman who showed considerable interest in this 'soap to wash souls clean'. In the village itself, after a very lukewarm first hour, sales surged once the village priest had made his appearance, and declared the books very good books for a very good price, setting the example by buying two himself. 'The poor people no sooner heard their curate recommend the volumes,' Borrow wrote later, 'than all were eager to secure one, and hurried here and there for the purpose of procuring money, so that between 20 and 30 copies were sold almost in an instant', which showed the immense influence that the village priests had over the minds of their flock. At another village, it was the local schoolmaster who passed favourable judgement and set the example by buying no fewer than 5 copies. One woman there bought a full 4 copies, one for herself, one for her son at school, one for a brother, and one – if we may believe Borrow – for her *deceased* husband [all the above from L 15.2.1839 and *BiS* ch 46].

---

70 He writes literally about this second animal that 'my other horse is at Salamanca, in Old Castile; but he suffered so much during my late expeditions, that it will hardly answer my purpose to send for him' [L 25.1.1839]. What horse this was – perhaps the marvellous smuggler's bay horse of the Northern Journey? – and why it was ever sent to Salamanca, remains to be determined.

Naturally, not all village priests were as well-disposed to vernacular gospels as the one of Cobeña. In Vicalvaro, a very small hamlet, Vitoriano had barely made his appearance, when he got stopped by the local *curate*, who asked him what his business was, and on learning what he was selling, 'told him that unless he instantly departed, he would cause him to be imprisoned' [L 15.2.1839]. The priest likewise announced that he would denounce these goings-on to Madrid; a threat which indeed he fulfilled, for that same month, an angry letter of his was reprinted in an article of *El Nuncio de la Verdad*, as evidence that Bible Society agents were still active in Spain despite the Royal Decree of May 1838. In his letter, the priest complained about the presence in his village of 'a man dressed in the coarse clothes of a journeyman', who 'set up a stand in the village square offering for sale eight copies of the New Testament, translated into Spanish, according to its title-page, by Father Scio, and printed in Madrid in 1837, by the printing house of Ibarra.'[71]

In this manner the two salesmen proceeded, with ups and downs, depending on the place. 'In some villages the people were so poor and needy that they had literally no money;' Borrow wrote later. 'Even in these, however, we managed to dispose of a few copies in exchange for barley or refreshments' [L 15.2.1839]. But at the end of eight days, he announced triumphantly that 'all the villages within the distance of four leagues to the east of Madrid have been visited', and that, in spite of these villages rarely being more than a dozen cabins thrown together [*BiS* ch 46], 'Testaments to the number of nearly 200 have been disposed of' [L 15.2.1839].

---

71 Giménez, *Prensa*, 378, n° 31. The article may be found in 'El Nuncio de la Verdad', tomo II, cuaderno IV, febrero de 1839, pp. 202–205. 'Ibarra' may simply have been a misprint for Joaquin de la Barrera (by way, perhaps, of a handwritten 'I. Barrera'). Yet, as noted above (see the end of I.2a), the name of Borrow's fictitious printer may have been deliberately chosen to cause confusion with the well-known Madrid print shop of Joaquin Ibarra, which had brought out various licensed versions of Scripture in the past. If so, the ruse clearly worked, as this episode shows. Borrow, who followed the Spanish press closely, did notice this article, and passed on a copy to his employers with the comment: 'I beg leave to call your attention to the work I sent you, and the ferocious attack which it contains against the Bible Society, and especially to the letter of the curate (...). This publication was established and is supported by money sent by the Cardinals of Rome, and is principally directed against us. Its abuse, however, is our praise.' [L 20.3.1839].

'Nearly 200', in Borrovian parlance, invariably means 'pretty much short of 200'; and this leads us to a small problem of interpretation, since the only rural copies which we encounter in the expense account over this period, drawn up on 9 March 1839, are specified as 'By the sale, in country, of 213 Testaments at 3 rs' with a total yield of 639 *reales* [Acc 11]. Seeing that Borrow rarely if ever erred on the low side in his correspondence with the Bible Society, and that the 46 copies which Vitoriano Lopez sold shortly afterwards in the Guadalajara region (see III.3.4 below) are absent from this same expense account, I surmise that Borrow, for the sake of convenience, tossed all the sales of New Testaments at 3 *reales* together into a single figure, and that these 213 copies therefore represent 167 copies sold around Cobeña and 46 around Guadalajara. The former number, 33 short of 200, may seem a little low; but it is not inconceivable that Borrow failed to enter some of the copies disposed of for 'barley and refreshments' since these had generated no money. However that may be, we cannot do better than to retain this cautious number of 167 for the total sales in the Cobeña region.

III.3.4 Trip 5 to Guadalajara (16–28 February 1839)

Borrow's FIFTH expedition – in the latter half of February 1839 – to the countryside around Madrid was certainly his greatest failure, seeing that it never really took off. His plan was to perform a wide distribution in the area of 'Guadalajara and the villages of Alcarria' [L 15.2.1839; L 4.3.1839], where the people were honest, mild and serious [ROS]. Before setting out, however, he wished to find out what sort of demand to expect and what size of stock to bring along. With this object in mind, he sent Vitoriano Lopez ahead on a pony, with a satchel containing 61 Testaments [L 4.3.1839].

In mid February, Vitoriano set out, and once past Alcalá de Henares, began his sales, which went relatively well. In the village of 'Arganza'[72] alone, he sold 25 copies, and another 18 in several other villages on the highway towards Saragossa [L 4.3.1839]. Next, however, he turned off

---

72 A place difficult to identify. Knapp, *Life*, I : 304 and 388, hesitantly proposed Daganzo, which is as good a guess as any, since there is no village anywhere between Madrid and Guadalajara whose name corresponds better to this 'Arganza' (the only true *Arganzas* in Spain are in the North, near Leon, Oviedo and Soria). Knapp's alternative 'Arganda' [*Life*, I : 388] makes little sense, since this town, to the South-East of Madrid, lies way out of Vitoriano's route.

the highway towards 'Fuente la Higuera' (a village which answers to the
impressive modern name of Fuentelahiguera de Albatages, roughly 25
km north-west of Guadalajara), and there, after selling 3 Testaments, got
arrested by the village priest, the local barber, and some other worthies
in league. He was thrown into jail, and kept *incommunicado* for the
next week (in spite of the fact that the mayor of the town had granted
permission to sell books there). With the help of some sympathisers and
a vagrant soldier, Vitoriano managed to smuggle out a letter to Borrow
telling of his plight; and Borrow immediately dispatched his formidable
Greek servant Antonio to Fuentelahiguera. By a combination of tact and
menaces Antonio managed to get Vitoriano sent to the Civil Governor of
Guadalajara, a sympathetic official, who immediately set Vitoriano free,
even though he considered it his duty to place the remaining 15 unsold
Testaments in embargo. He added, however, that 'they should be sent to
me whenever I [i.e. Borrow – PM] chose to claim them' [L 4.3.1839].

Thus, 46 copies in total were sold north of Alcalá de Henares, and 15
copies confiscated. As argued above, the 46 copies sold are most probably
contained in the 213 copies sold in the countryside for 3 *reales* a piece
reported in the expense account of 9 March 1839 [Acc 11].

III.3.5 Trip 6 to Navalcarnero (early March 1839)

SOON AFTER Vitoriano's release and return to Madrid, Borrow set off
on the highway to the south-west of Madrid. He was accompanied by
Antonio [*BiS* ch 47] and by Vitoriano, who insisted on coming along
despite his recent calvary at Fuentelahiguera [L 4.3.1839]. Their first stop
was in the town of Navalcarnero where they stayed three days [L 4.3.1839].
Vitoriano was 'sent forth to the circumjacent hamlets with small cargoes
of Testaments' [*BiS* ch 47], where he sold 'twenty and odd Testaments' in
total [L 20.3.1839]. The original plan had been to push on to Talavera de
la Reina and distribute around there [L 4.3.1839; L 20.3.1839], and then
to move on further still, to the Portuguese border and the mysterious
Batueca valley [Knapp, *Life*, II : 288]. But it turned out that 'our proceedings, on the other side of Madrid, had caused alarm amongst the heads
of the clergy, who made a formal complaint to the Government – who
immediately sent orders to all the *alcaldes* of the villages, great and small,
in New Castile to seize the New Testament wherever it might be exposed

for sale' [L 20.3.1839]. This order was effective, as Borrow learned when on 5 March a batch of 20 Testaments was seized and confiscated in a nearby village [L 20.3.1839]. To engage in sales – with the authorities both alerted and under close government scrutiny – was simply becoming too risky. So Borrow turned around and went back to Madrid, where we find him on 9 March. The whole trip had lasted only 5 days [Acc 11] and it was to be the last of his expeditions in the Madrid neighbourhood. The rest of the month he dedicated, with remarkable success, to the sales by colporteurs in the capital itself (see next section).

The short excursion was still to have an amusing consequence of sorts. As Borrow tells it in Bible in Spain chapter 47, one box of New Testaments, sent over separately to Navalcarnero, was intercepted before it could reach him. From there it was returned to Madrid, where, as it lay in the 'waggon office', it was spotted by Antonio, who happened to be on an errand there. The savvy Greek immediately claimed it as his master's property, managed to get it released, and took it to Borrow's secret warehouse. Since it was a trifling affair among so many shipments of stock up and down, the Greek then forgot to tell his master. Borrow, however, was summoned to the office of a furious Civil Governor a little later and asked how he dared to lay hands on formally confiscated property. As he tells it himself, Borrow, always full of 'spunk', faced the great official down, although he promised to return the box, which he says he did soon after. The precise number of copies it contained is not stated. However, Borrow writes that he could 'afford to lose 50 or a 100' copies, and that the 'united value' of the box and the cargo of books 'would scarcely amount to 40 dollars', i.e. 800 *reales*. Therefore we may perhaps surmise that – with the box at a not unlikely 50 *reales* (see II.2.3 above) – it contained 50 copies at the supposed 'cost price' of 15 *reales* each, or 75 at the 'high sales-price' of 10. In the conclusions below I will maintain the fictitious number of 50 for the sake of caution.

Hence 20 copies were confiscated near Navalcarnero, another 50 to 75 at Navalcarnero itself, and '20-odd' copies were sold in the neighbourhood of Navalcarnero, at a price of 3 *reales* each [Knapp, *Life*, I : 305, see next section]. These '20-odd' copies sold are absent from Borrow's expense account of 9 March [Acc 11], drawn up just after he returned from this very trip to Navalcarnero. This is probably due to Borrow not yet having gotten around to making a proper inventory of the precise sales and the money received when he wrote that expense account (something also suggested by the vague formulation '20-odd'). They were therefore set aside to be included in a later expense account, which was never sent or has not survived. For the purpose of calculations, I will use a simple number of 20 sold copies in the conclusions.[73]

III.3.6 Sales in Madrid by 'colporteurs' (March 1839)

BORROW'S TRULY spectacular sales-effort of this period took place *after* the expense account of 9 March 1839 was written, and unfortunately cannot be verified by financial sources; something of which – seeing the magnitude of the sales – it stands rather in need. As he himself tells it, in the second week of March, on his return from his expedition to Navalcarnero he hired 5 women and 3 men 'of the most intelligent' *Madrileños* that he knew[74], gave them each a parcel of New Testaments and sent them off into the parishes, to sell door to door over the next 16 days [L 20.3.1839; Knapp, *Life*, I : 305]. Helped along by the fact that he now sold the book 'for the same low price as in the country' [*BiS* ch 47], namely 3 *reales* per copy [Knapp, *Life*, I : 305], the results were magnificent. 'Since my return from Naval Carnero,' he writes, 'nearly 600 copies (...) have been sold in the streets and alleys of Madrid' [L 20.3.1839]. He then goes on to boast that in every house of the fashionable Puerta del Sol and Calle Montera there is now a Testament, sometimes even one per inhabitant; that many more copies were sold in the wealthy streets that border the central square; and that some churches even use his Spanish language gospels for their religious education [L 20.3.1839; *BiS* ch 47].

Even Borrow was perhaps a little taken aback by the success of this new method, which cut far too fast and deep into his last available stock. Soon after he wrote: 'I have at present sold as many Testaments as I think

73 Alternatively, these 20-odd copies may also have been contained in the above mentioned figure of 213 copies sold 'in the country' mentioned by the expense account of 9 March 1839 (see III.3.3). Such an assumption would, however, lower the number of sales in the Cobeña region to less than 150 (which is a little *too* short of 200 to my taste). The difference is in any case academic, since it has no influence on final sales figures.

74 The corresponding item in Borrow's personal record of expenses [Knapp, *Life*, I : 305] speaks of *nine* people, not eight.

Madrid will bear (…). I have therefore called in the greatest part of my people, and content myself with the sale of 12 or 14 a week, for I am afraid to over-stock the market, and to bring the book into contempt by making it too common' [L 20.3.1839]. Less than three weeks later, he drew a final bottom line below the Madrid sales-effort, writing that 'I have discontinued selling Testaments in Madrid, as it appears to me that we shall have barely sufficient (…) for Andalusia and one or two other points which I wish to visit' [L 10.4.1839].

The precise number sold by the Madrid colporteurs can only be guessed at. As said, there is no formal expense account against which we can verify this remarkable number of 'nearly 600'. There is, however, a rare surviving personal summary of income and expenditure which Borrow's first biographer, William Knapp, possessed and reproduced in his 1899 *Life* (I : 304–305). This summary runs from 21 December 1838, when Borrow left London for Madrid, to 16 April 1839, when he was ready to move to Seville. It therefore covers not only the period of Borrow's expense accounts of 9 March 1839 [Acc 11], which it copies to the letter, but also the subsequent 5 or 6 weeks when the great Madrid *colportage* took place. Its data are revealing, as much in what it says as in what it leaves out. Here is a comparative rundown of the significant numbers in the Knapp summary and the expense account of 9 March 1839:

Knapp Life, I : 304–305			Acc 11 of 9 March 1839		
Description of sales	Sold	Rls	Description of sales	Sold	Rls
New Testaments in country at 3 rls.	213	639	New Testaments in country at 3 rs.	213	639
New Testaments in town at 4 rls.	122	488	Ditto in town at 4 rs.	122	488
Bibles at 10 rls.	17	170	Bibles at 10 rs.	17	170
Gypsy St. Luke at 16 rls.	3	48	St. Luke in Gipsy at 16 rs.	3	48
Basque St. Luke at 10 rls.	2	20	Ditto in Basque at 10 rs.	2	20
(Sales)		104	In the Madrid *purlieux* (various prices)	27	104
Bibles at 10 rs.	443	4430			
New Testaments in country at 3 rs.	602	1806			

The occurrence of the 443 full Bibles in the penultimate line shows that this summary was drawn up at the very end of Borrow's Madrid period. We know from his correspondence that he only began to sell full Bibles in any serious way after his return from Navalcarnero in the second week of March 1839, and that no fewer than 463 had been sold by 2 May 1839 [L 9.3.1839; L 20.3.1839; L 10.4.1839; L 2.5.1839]. This implies that the 602 New Testaments which follow immediately below were likewise the final and complete reckoning, after a more careful inventory, of the New Testament copies sold in March and April. Hence these 602 represent the '20-odd' copies sold during the Navalcarnero expedition (absent in the expense account of 9 March), the 'nearly 600' sold by the Madrid colporteurs, and all those '12 or 14 copies a week' personally sold by Borrow himself after 20 March. Since we cannot in any reliable way separate the last two items, the 582 which result if we subtract the 20 of Navalcarnero, shall be kept together as total Madrid sales in the conclusions below.

By mid April 1839, Borrow could rest content. He had done his best and had accomplished no mean feat. As he notes, once to his mother in late April [Shorter, *Circle*, ch 18] and once to his employers in early May [L 2.5.1839]: 1,000 New Testaments had been sold since his return to Spain in early January 1839, and most of his full Bibles. It was now time to move to Seville.

III.4 Sales in Andalusia and Africa (May – November 1839)

IN LATE April 1839 Borrow moved his operations from Madrid to Seville. This meant not only moving himself and his personal belongings to the Andalusian capital, but also a stock of books of sufficient size to have something to do there. To this effect he sent Antonio Buchino ahead with the two horses and two chests of books on 13 April 1839 [L 10.4.1839; *BiS* ch 48; Acc 12]: a large box which contained somewhat more than 330 Spanish New Testaments [L 12.6.1839; L 18.7.1839; L 21.9.1839] and a smaller one, with a number of gospels in Caló and Basque. Antonio, travelling slowly with a 'convoy', could not help being stopped and searched at the customs post of Seville on arrival, so that the two boxes of forbidden books were instantly retained [L 2.5.1839; *BiS* ch 48].

Borrow himself, having started later but travelling faster in the *Courier*, was already in Seville by this time [Acc 11; *BiS* ch 48; L 2.5.1839; Shorter, *Circle*, 194f]. Hearing of the seizure, which threatened to undermine all his plans, he contrived a trick to free some of his books. He paid 70 *reales* as a 'gratuity' to a corrupt official to authorise the transport *of the boxes* to the customs post of San Lucar, on the south coast, as if he were going to take all the books out of the country. On 1 May, he hired a *felouk* and an English servant called John Plant and dispatched the two boxes down the river. Somewhere midway, however, he landed the cargo surreptitiously on the river bank and removed from them '200 copies and upwards' of the New Testament [L 12.6.1839; L 18.7.1839] and some 90 copies of the Gypsy *Luke*. These 'liberated books' he deposited in the nearby village of San Juan d'Alfarache. Some of them he and Antonio smuggled back into Seville under their clothes that same rainy night. Other batches were brought in later by a muleteer. The *boxes* – still containing 130 New Testaments [L 21.9.1839] and some Caló and Basque gospels – then continued to the customs post of San Lucar, in charge of John Plant, just as Borrow had vowed to do when he took out the export licence [L 2.5.1839; Acc 12; *BiS* ch 48].

III.4.1 First sales in Seville (May – July 1839)

THE 200-ODD Testaments he had rescued in this underhand and illegal manner, were, in Borrow's own words 'all the Testaments of which I was in need' to start operations with [L 12.6.1839]. Nevertheless, it was a very limited number, so that he decided to be cautious. 'Indeed the quantity of books (…) at present remaining unsold in Spain is so small,' he wrote a little later, 'that I am almost tempted to be niggard of them' [L 12.6.1839]. Hence for the first three weeks in Seville, he did not sell at all; and only when he found the appropriate collaborators, was piecemeal distribution set in motion.

Borrow's *colporteurs* in Seville were an odd lot. There was the rather remarkable ambulant bookseller Dionysius Carriano, a Greek from Cephalonia, who was already dealing in books acquired from the libraries of the suppressed convents, and who sold the New Testament with fervour in the city itself and in the surrounding villages [L 12.6.1839; *BiS* ch 48; Ford, *Handbook*, 1087]. There was a venerable and aged 'professor

Illustration 13: A view of the Seville river harbour around 1900

of music', who sold his copies for a truly 'Christian motive' [L 12.6.1839; *BiS* ch 48]; 'two or three ladies of my acquaintance', who 'occasionally dispose of some amongst their friends' [L 28.6.1839]; and a Genovese waiter, who sold the books, sometimes by the dozen, to customers of the 'Swiss Ordinary' where he worked [L 18.7.1839]. Finally there was another Greek, the brick-layer Johannis Chrysostom, who peddled copies of the gospel to his friends and colleagues on the building sites, and who was Borrow's prime agent once he decided, in late June, to start selling his wares to the city's poor [L 28.6.1839].

Thus, 'in a quiet, satisfactory manner', sales took place, a dozen here, half a dozen elsewhere, the 'stock of Testaments waning apace' [L 28.6.1839], until nearly all the 200 copies which had been 'liberated' from the confiscated boxes had been sold. Then, almost inevitably, the authorities got wind of the affair and took action. On Sunday 7 July, a group of *alguaziles* led by the *alcalde de barrio*, raided Borrow's house and 'made a small seizure of Testaments and Gypsy Gospels which happened to be lying about' [L 18.7.1839]. Borrow's work for the season was over, 'for the very efficient reason, that I have no more Testaments to sell, somewhat more than 200 having been circulated since my arrival.'

III.4.2 Sales in San Lucar (August 1839)

Borrow had wanted to visit the north coast of Morocco for a long while already; and with his stock in Seville exhausted by mid July 1839, the time had come to put this plan into action [L 20.3.1839; L 2.5.1839; L 28.6.1839]. Making the best of a bad thing, he decided to recover the 130 New Testaments which had been carried to the customs post at San Lucar, and take these along over the Gibraltar Straits, to sell in Tangier and other cities on the North-African coast, 'to the Christian families established on the sea-coast of Barbary' [L 4.9.1839].

Setting out on 31 July 1839, he arrived at the San Lucar custom house[75] the next morning [L 4.9.1839; BiS ch 50], and here took place one of the more famous scenes of Borrow's adventurous years in the Peninsula; a scene which perhaps says more about Spain in the 1830s than many a long descriptive study. 'Whilst at the custom house of San Lucar', he wrote [L 4.9.1839; BiS ch 50], 'I was asked one or two questions respecting the books contained in the chests; this afforded me some opportunity of speaking of the New Testament and the Bible Society. What I said excited attention, and presently all the officers and dependents of the house, great and small, were gathered around me, from the governor to the porter. As it was necessary to open the boxes to inspect their contents, we all proceeded to the courtyard where, holding a Testament in my hand, I recommenced my discourse. I scarcely know what I said (...) My words however evidently made impression, and to my astonishment every person present pressed me for a copy. I sold several within the walls of the custom-house.' I.e. the very government officials who were supposed to search out, intercept, seize, confiscate and destroy forbidden merchandise, gladly acquired that same forbidden merchandise for their own pleasure and profit whenever they got the chance...

III.4.3 Sales in Tangier and Morocco (August – September 1839)

OVER THE next days, Borrow managed, with considerable help from John Brackenbury, the friendly British consul in Cádiz, to acquire the necessary papers to export his boxes of books from Spain [BiS ch 51]. By way of compensation for his great help, Brackenbury was allowed to

---

75 Only recently the spot of this *Casa de Aduanas* has been located by the Barcelona author David Fernández de Castro [*Crónicas*, 283]. It stood on the present *Plaza de los Cisnes* of Sanlúcar de Barrameda, on the site of the present ice-cream-parlour.

take out three copies each of the New Testament and the Gypsy *Luke*, for his own library and as gifts to the Captain-General, and the Civil Governor of Cádiz [Collie, *Eccentric*, 153]. The boxes, which after the sale at San Lucar and the gift to the consul, now contained perhaps 120 New Testaments, were then shipped to Gibraltar [Acc 12]. From there they went on to England [Collie, *Eccentric*, 153], minus a considerable stock which Borrow took out to sell in Tangier.

Unfortunately the precise number of sales in Morocco is not known. Borrow merely writes after his return, that after about a fortnight in Tangier he hired a Jewish youth (i.e. Hayim Ben Attar, who later was to accompany him to Spain and England as a personal servant) to offer the book for sale at the houses of the Europeans settled there [L 4.9.1839]. It was a successful venture. 'The blessed Book is now in the hands of most of the Christians of Tangier, from the lowest to the highest, from the fisherman to the consul,' Borrow concluded. 'One dozen and a half were carried to Tetuan on speculation (…); they will be offered to the Christians who reside there. Other two dozen are on their way to distant Mogadore. One individual, a tavern-keeper, has purchased Testaments to the number of 30, which he says he has no doubt he can dispose of to the foreign sailors, who stop occasionally at his house. You will be surprised to hear that several amongst the Jews have purchased copies of the New Testament, with the intention as they state of improving themselves in

Illustration 14: A view of Tangier around 1900,
showing the famous flag-poles of the European consulates.

Spanish, but I believe from curiosity' [L 4.9.1839]. These latter copies may well be the 'several Spanish New Testaments' which Borrow gave to his old friend Judah Lib to distribute when he met the man unexpectedly in Tangier [Knapp, *Life*, I : 301; Fraser, *Taylor*, 11f.].

The total of the lots specified above (18 + 24 + 30) comes to 72 copies, to which we still ought to add the sales to the Christian residents and the Jews of Tangier. It is perhaps a reasonable guess to ascribe 20 to the Christian residents and 5 to 'curious' Hebrews, which means that nearly 100 were sold in Morocco, and the remaining 20 carried to the Bible Society's library in England.

III.4.4 Later sales in Seville (October – November 1839)

ONCE RETURNED from Morocco, Borrow decided to wrap up his Spanish operations before returning to England for good. His original plan was to move once more to Villaseca de la Sagra, and from there to distribute the remaining stock of New Testaments in the villages of La Mancha, particularly at Manzanares and Valdepeñas [L 18.7.1839; L 29.9.1839]. However, previous to this journey – which would never take place since he got arrested again in November 1839 – he decided to sell some more copies in and around Seville itself, and he 'accordingly pro-cured a considerable number from Madrid' [L 25.11.1839]. Throughout October and November, he and his collaborators sold these copies 'with the utmost secrecy', until 'the entire stock which had reached me was circulated' [L 25.11.1839]. Unfortunately, the size of this stock does not get specified anywhere, and all we can do is suppose that it may have been somewhere in the neighbourhood of his standard 200 copies, or perhaps rather 150 to be on the safe side, which would have left a fair margin for his projected distribution in La Mancha. This, however, is no more than a *very* wild guess.

As said: nothing came of his plan to distribute in La Mancha in late 1839, because the government was definitely fed up with the Protestant doings, and it now had its hands free to act as it pleased. The Carlist Civil was won, having come to an effective close with the Treaty of Vergara in late August. Consequently the liberals stood less in need of British assist-ance and did not particularly need to please the British Ambassador any longer. Henry Southern of the Embassy had already warned Borrow on 13 July 1839 (only a few days after the raid on his Seville home) that 'the government has become excessively severe respecting *heretical* proceedings, and I caution you most particularly to be on your guard' [Knapp, *Life*, II : 294]. It was a good warning, which Borrow might have done well to heed, but which unwisely he ignored. In November he got summoned to the office of the Civil Governor of Seville and warned that he would be arrested if he tried to sell any more books. Word of his doings had obviously gotten around in spite of the 'utmost secrecy' observed. Then, on 25 November, when he tried to secure a passport to go to La Mancha, he got into a screaming argument with the *alcalde de barrio* who had to countersign the document; and was forthwith thrown into the Seville jail, where he stayed a day and a half [L 25.11.1839][76]. Enraged and perhaps a little out of control, Borrow set off immediately to Madrid to demand redress. He travelled over to the capital, reached Madrid around 10 December, stayed three weeks [Acc 12], filed complaints, saw diplomats, insisted on his rights, and got nowhere at all, so that, slightly disgusted, he returned to Seville on 3 January 1840 [L 2.1.1840].

The last three months of his stay in Spain, Borrow sold no more Testaments, since his doings were too well known, his stock practically exhausted, and the man tired of the job [L 24.12.1839; L 18.3.1840]. It was time to rest from his labours for a while [L 25.11.1839]. So he spent three more months in beautiful Seville, and then caught a boat for England, where, on landing, he married his fiancée Mary Clarke, with whom he settled in the little Suffolk village of Oulton, to write.

---

76 For details, see Giménez Cruz, A., 'La prision de George Borrow en Sevilla', in: *Historia* 16, Año XI, n° 120, abril 1986, p. 35–42.

IV

Summaries

IV.1 Borrow's sales per region

IV.1.1 Madrid city

By late March 1839, at the very end of his sales-efforts in the Spanish capital and just before moving his operations to Seville, Borrow wrote to his employers: 'Can that city justly be called "dark" in which 1,300 Testaments, at least, are in circulation and in daily use?' [L 20.3.1839]. The statement looks a little rhetorical, not to say theatrical, but – even if we cannot substantiate it entirely with hard data – seems to be roughly correct. Borrow's documented sales, within the city limits of Madrid, over the entire period between the printing of the Scio New Testament and his move to Seville, are as follows:

Date	Section	Sold to or by	Number
May–Oct 37	II.2.2.i	Madrid booksellers	52
May–Dec 37	II.3.1	Ambassador Villiers	50
Jan 38	II.3.2	Civil Governor	2
Nov 37–May 38	II.3.2	By *Despacho*	331
Jan–Feb 39	III.3.1	In the city by Antonio	122
Jan–Feb 39	III.3.2	In 'purlieux' by Vitoriano	14*
March 39	III.3.6	By colporteurs and private	582
Total			**1153**

* a rough estimate of half the 27 copies mentioned in [Acc 11]

The total here is 150 copies short of Borrow's estimate, but is probably closer to the truth than his own stated '1,300 Testaments'. Of course, it is quite conceivable that some sold copies may have slipped through the mazes of Borrow's notoriously feeble and faulty administration, but it is most unlikely that these could have come to a full 150 copies. The available margins of unsold stock simply do not allow for such a large extra sale (as we learn from the development of the Central Stock in IV.5 below). Consequently, keeping on the safe side, it is best said in conclusion that Madrid purchased somewhat over a fifth of the edition of the 1837 Scio New Testament.

IV.1.2 Countryside around Madrid.

IN THE course of the expeditions which Borrow staged over the summer of 1838 and the first three months of 1839 (plus the one quick trip to Toledo in December 1837), the following numbers of copies were sold in a radius of up to 75 km from Madrid:

Date	Section	Sold to	Number
Dec 37	II.2.2.xii	Toledo bookseller	13
July 38	III.2.1	In the Sagra of Toledo (trip 1)	400
July–Aug 38	III.2.2	Aranjuez and Ocaña (trip 2)	209
July–Sept 38	III.2.3	Villages near Madrid	123
Aug 38	III.2.4	Segovia and Avila (trip 3)	884
Jan–Feb 39	III.3.2	In the 'purlieux' by Vitoriano	13
Jan–Feb 39	III.3.3	Cobeña and to the east (trip 4)	167
Feb 39	III.3.4	Guadalajara region (trip 5)	46
March 39	III.3.5	Navalcarnero (trip 6)	20
Total			**1875**

All these sales figures come from hard data. Only three of the numbers are uncertain in a way: the 13 copies sold 'in the purlieux' (which – being simply half the 27 copies mentioned in the expense account of 9 March 1839 – may have been a few more or less); the 167 of the Cobeña expedition (which may have been more) and the 20 copies sold during the Navalcarnero trip (which Borrow calls '20-odd' and therefore surely were more). Consequently, the total sales figure is beyond all doubt a *minimum* number, and the countryside around Madrid must have received slightly more than 1,875 copies of the Scio New Testament, which represents well over 1/3 of the entire edition.

Counting these 1,875 copies up with the 1,153 sold in the capital itself, we see that a full 3,028 copies, or 60 % of Borrow's whole edition, ended up in the wider Madrid area. A small part, 448 copies, was distributed before the Prohibition of May 1838; over half the total, 1,616 copies, in the summer of 1838; and the remaining 964 in the first four months of 1839.

Of course, not all these copies were distributed in what is today the modern administrative region known as the 'Comunidad de Madrid'. As will be shown below (IV.1.6 Castilla-La Mancha) an approximate 361 copies of the above 1,875 were actually sold over the border of the La Mancha autonomous province; while the 884 copies sold in the area of Segovia and Avila must be counted to the autonomous province of Castilla-Leon. Consequently 3,028 − (361 + 884) = 1,783 were, strictly speaking, sold within the modern borders of the Comunidad de Madrid.

IV.1.3 Seville and Andalusia

BECAUSE **B**ORROW does not specify the numbers of copies sold in the south in his expense accounts, and does not describe his countryside expeditions in Andalusia in any sort of detail, it is not possible to separate sales in Seville city from those in the surrounding area. Consequently we can only reach a *very approximate* total of copies sold in the great southern province, and during all of his Spanish years, namely:

Date	Section	Sold to or by	Supplied	Sold	Assumed
Jul 37–May 38	II.2.2.xiii	Seville bookseller		24	
Jul 37–May 38	II.2.2.xv	Cadiz bookseller	100		5
Jul 37–May 38	II.2.2.xvi	Malaga bookseller	100		5
May–Jun 39	III.4.1	Seville by colporteurs		200	
Aug 39	III.4.2	San Lucar custom post			7
Aug 39	III.4.3	Consul Brackenbury		3	
Oct–Nov 39	III.4.4	Seville city & radius			150
Totals				**227**	**167**

It needs no saying that these numbers are only vaguely indicative and that the margin of error is very broad. For one thing, sales by the booksellers of Cadiz and Malaga are completely unknown, although they must have been very small indeed. For another, the 200 copies sold in Seville in the spring of 1839 may have been a few more or a few less, depending on how many Borrow really smuggled back into the city in early May of 1839 (he speaks of '200 copies and upward') and how many were confiscated during the raid on his house in July. Lastly, the only thing we know of the final batch of books which Borrow sold in Seville and its radius during the autumn of 1839 is that it was 'a considerable number'. It may have been anything from 50 to 300, although the number of 150 here assumed seems a reasonable guess (see III.4.4 and IV.7 for the considerations involved).

All this then leaves us with the observation that some 227 New Testaments were sold for certain in this area (3 of those being gifts to Consul Brackenbury in Cadiz); and that additional sales may have been as low as 100 or as high as 200. The safest course here is to make no definite pronouncement on total Andalusian sales.

IV.1.4 Galicia

ALTHOUGH ONLY about half of the Galician sales figures can be established with any semblance of certainty, an approximate total may be drawn up from the various sources investigated above.

Date	Section	Sold to or by	Supply	Sold	Assumed
Jul 37–May 38	II.2.2.v	Lugo bookseller		64	
Jul 37–May 38	II.2.2.vi	Coruña bookseller	122	58	5
Aug 37–May 38	II.2.2.vii	Santiago bookseller		98	
Aug 37	II.1.2.b & II.1.3	Santiago 'satchel'			15
Aug 37	II.1.2.b	Private Pontevedra		8	
Sept 37–May 38	II.2.2.vii	Pontevedra notary		17	
Aug 37	II.1.2.b	Private Vigo (1 gift)		4	
Sept 37	II.1.2.b	Private Finisterre gift		1	
Sept 37	II.2.2.viii	Ferrol bookseller	20		5
Jul–Sept 37	II.1.2.b	Additional private sales			20
Total				**250**	**45**

The total of certain and assumed sales comes to 295 copies, but great caution must be observed with this result. First of all: both in Coruña, where Borrow left an estimated 64 copies in stock (see II.2.b) and in Ferrol there may have been some additional sales between September 1837, when he left the province, and May 1838, when the Scio New Testament was forbidden. We have no data for these places in this period at all, but sales must have been very few. For both cities, I will assume the customary cautious 5 copies sold in all further calculations.

Secondly: the size of the 'satchel sale' near Santiago – if it ever took place at all – can only be wildly guessed at. It may have been 5 higher or lower, but we shall never know.

Thirdly: the 'additional private sales' of 20 is no more than a cowardly guess. We have no data concerning 40 of the 53 copies disposed of as 'private sales' during the second leg of the Northern Journey (from July 20 to September 29 of 1837). Some of these were surely sold within the borders of Galicia, and part of them in Asturias up to the time that Borrow ran out of stock in Oviedo. One must cut the Gordian knot in these cases, and the least awful way to do so is by cutting the 40 neatly in half, arbitrarily assigning 20 copies each to Galicia and Asturias.

Total sales in Galicia may therefore well have been considerably higher and somewhat lower; so that it is safe to assume that the true total ranged between 275 and 325.

IV.1.5 Castilla-Leon

ALTHOUGH, as noted in IV.1.2 above, the areas where Borrow staged his six Bible-peddling expeditions of the summer of 1838 and the first three months of 1839 really belonged *in the practical sense* to the orbit of Madrid, we may separate and rearrange the numbers in such a way that they reflect the sales within the borders of Spain's formal administrative regions. Spaniards, who have a very strong sense of geography, usually appreciate such a classification; and there is no reason why we should not oblige here.

In 'Old Castile' (modern Castilla-Leon) the sales of New Testaments were more or less these:

Date	Section	Sold to or by	Supply	Sold	Assumed
May–Jul 37	II.1.2.a	Private sales Northern Journey		65	
May 37	II.2.2.ii	Salamanca bookseller	60	3	12
Jun 37	II.2.2.iii	Valladolid bookseller	100	50	5
Jun 37	II.1.3	Satchel sale Valladolid			15
Jun 37	II.2.2.iv	Leon bookseller		56	
Oct 37	II.2.2.xi	Burgos bookseller		40	
Aug 38	III.2.4	Segovia and Avila (trip 3)		884	
Total				**1098**	**32**

The presence of the gigantic sales results in the area of Segovia and Avila almost makes it redundant to comment upon the possible oscillations of the smaller and more uncertain numbers. For the sake of completeness it may, however, be noted that 1. a few of the 65 copies sold privately during the Northern Journey will have been sold before Borrow crossed the border between Madrid proper and Old Castile, while some may also have been sold once he left Castile for Galicia (a total of 10 is perhaps already too high a guess); 2. the sales of the Salamanca bookseller were certainly higher than the 3 copies for which we have hard evidence (I will assume another 12 in all further calculations); 3. likewise, the Valladolid bookseller will have sold a number of copies more out of his third supply of 50 (I assume a further 5 in the calculations); and 4. the size of the 'satchel sale' near Valladolid is, once again, no more than a conjecture. The total sales of New Testaments in Castilla-Leon will therefore probably have been somewhat higher than the total of 1,130 arrived at here, but will not have risen beyond 1,150 copies.

IV.1.6 Castilla-La Mancha

THE NUMBERS for 'New Castile' (modern Castilla-La Mancha) suffer from another problem. The sales-figures as such are reasonably clear and certain, but since Borrow on various occasions was peddling his books on the very border between the Madrid community and the La Mancha province, it becomes near impossible to decide what part of the totals must be ascribed to one or the other area. The best I can do is the following:

Date	Section	Sold in or by	Madrid area	New Castile	Total on trip
Dec 37	II.2.2.xii	Toledo bookseller	0	13	13
Jul 38	III.2.1	Sagra of Toledo (trip 1)	100*	300*	400
Jul–Aug 38	III.2.2	Aranjuez-Ocaña (trip 2)	182	27	209
Feb 39	III.3.4	Guadalajara region (trip 5)	25*	21*	46
Total					361

*= assumptions

As we have seen above (III.2.1), Borrow specifically mentions 16 villages where he sold books during his 1st expedition to the Sagra. Four of these, on the road from Madrid to the Sagra, lie within the borders of the Madrid province. The average sale per village of 25 copies (400 : 16; see IV.2 for a justification of this assumption), urges the despairing investigator to ascribe 100 copies to the Madrid area, the remainder to sales in the Sagra.

Borrow specifies that of the 209 copies sold during his expedition to Aranjuez and Ocaña, 102 were sold on the road, and 80 in Aranjuez. All 182 belong to the Madrid area. Only the 27 sold in Ocaña before the local authorities pounced upon poor Juan Lopez and confiscated his stock were therefore sold in La Mancha.

How many of the 46 copies sold by Vitoriano Lopez on his doomed expedition to Guadalajara were disposed of between Alcalá de Henares and the border of La Mancha cannot be established with certainty, since the 'village of Arganza', where supposedly he sold his first 25, has not been identified. Assuming, however, that Knapp was right in supposing it was Daganzo, the 25 copies sold there belong to the Madrid area, and the remaining 21 copies will have been sold well into La Mancha, since Fuentelahiguera, where he was imprisoned, lies some 40 km into that province by the road which he travelled.

The margin of error which ought to be observed for total sales in Castilla-La Mancha will therefore roughly be 20 copies, so that the estimated total sales fluctuate between 340 and 380 copies.

IV.1.7 Sales in other Spanish regions and exports

In Asturias, 43 copies were certainly sold in the city of Oviedo (see II.2.2.ix), plus an unknown number of the 40 copies 'by private sale' which Borrow may conceivably have taken out of the province of Galicia in September 1837. Above (II.1.2.b), I assumed that half of those were sold within Galicia, which leaves another 20 for the road between the Galician-Asturian border and Oviedo, where Borrow was completely out of stock again. The total in Asturias may therefore have come to some 63 copies, but that number is very unsure.

In Valencia 24 copies were certainly sold through the local bookseller (II.2.2.xiv). There is no reason to believe that we 'missed' any other sales. Valencia was, essentially, the assigned fief of Borrow's colleague Lieutenant Graydon, and if Borrow – who never visited the city [L 23.7.1838] – trespassed there at all, it will have been because Borrego's *Compañia Tipográfica* already had an established working relationship with the bookshop of Jimeno.

There are no known sales at all in the other regions of mainland Spain. Extremadura was probably too poor to merit a sales-effort (compare Ford, *Handbook*, 770ff). Cantabria, the Basque Countries, Navarra and La Rioja were the scene of civil war. Aragon, Catalonia, and Murcia had been allotted to Lieutenant Graydon.

Finally 72 copies were certainly sold in Morocco, to which an unknown number, of perhaps 28, must still be added (see III.4.3).

A mere 20 copies may have been sent on to England by way of Gibraltar (see III.4.3). Note that there are no indications anywhere of other batches of the Scio New Testament having been sent over to England. The remaining unsold stock (some 800 copies) was, for all we can tell, integrally left behind in Madrid in April 1840 (see IV.7 below).

IV.2 Average village sales

Borrow's decision to sell his gospels in peasant villages was as daring as it was successful. By far the greatest part of the sales enumerated in IV.1.2 alone – 1,750 copies if one overlooks the cities of Toledo, Aranjuez and Ocaña – were sold in tiny peasant communities. And to that number should still be added the sales in the *pueblos* of Andalusia, Galicia and Asturias, which cannot be computed with exactitude, but which surely bring 'rural sales' close to half the edition, and certainly to half the total sales.

It was a success which nobody could have foreseen at the time; which shows the uncommon measure of the man; and which Borrow was sure to make the most of when he triumphed. Never one to miss an opportunity for self-promotion, he typically reminded the Committee of the Bible Society in his formal report of November 1838 'that until [I] myself solved the problem of the possibility [of distributing the Scripture amongst the peasantry], no idea had been entertained of introducing the Bible in the rural districts of countries exclusively Papist' [ROS]. He then went on to boast that 'every village in Spain will purchase from twenty to sixty [Testaments] according to its circumstances', and added that of 40 villages visited over the summer, only two – Mocejon, which had been celebrating a holiday, and Torrelodones, which Borrow considered an evil place by nature[77] – had purchased less than 30 copies [ROS]. This was, to say the least, a somewhat bold statement, seeing that of all the many *real* cities which he visited, each of them wealthy urban conglomerations with many thousands of inhabitants and an educated middle class, *only three* (Santiago, Lugo and Aranjuez) ever purchased 60 copies or more! Even if the city selling was mainly done in a passive way and for a considerably higher price, this hard fact still reflects wryly on Borrow's rural optimism.

The bold statement was, however, written down when Borrow was deliberately trying to impress his employers, who at the time were earnestly toying with the notion of laying him off. Hence it is only natural that the estimate got inflated just a little. In reality average sales in the villages were lower. Whenever we do see particular, concrete village sales take place, the total rather hovers around 20 or 25 per nucleus. Thus, Juan Lopez sells 'a large bundle of Testaments' of 20 copies in the village of Bargas in the Sagra [L 14.7.1838; *BiS* ch 43]; in mid February 1839, Vitoriano Lopez visits Carabanchel near Madrid, where he sells 12

---

77 He must have had some very nasty experience there, for the dismissive remarks he made in November 1838 [ROS] were repeated and even improved upon in chapter 46 of *The Romany Rye*, i.e. 15 years later!

copies in a hurried half an hour [L 15.2.1839; *BiS* ch 46]; a little later, the same man sells 25 copies in the village of 'Arganza' somewhere between Alcalá de Henares and Fuentelahiguera [L 4.3.1839]; somewhat over 20 Testaments get sold in total in several 'villages adjacent to Navalcarnero' [L 20.3.1839]; and Borrow himself, during a deliberate action to defy the *curas* of Abades, sells 'upwards of 30 Testaments' in its marketplace during a single evening session [L 1.9.1838].

These random, but in themselves indicative, figures may be shored up with the harder data we possess for his first expedition to the Sagra of Toledo. As seen above (III.2.1), the enumeration of villages given in a postscript to Borrow's letter of 3 August 1838, allows us to identify 16 villages where he distributed (5 on the road and 11 in the Sagra itself). In these 16 villages, Borrow sold a total of 400 copies. Hence the average sale per village was 25 copies.

One would like to make a similar calculation for the villages he visited on the way to Aranjuez during his second expedition (III.2.2), except that Borrow only identifies two of those – Pinto and Valdemoro – which is clearly too small a number. Borrow states specifically that he had been 'selling from 20 to 40 copies in every village that lay in the way or near it' [L 3.8.1838]; yet in his later expense account [Acc 10] he also reports, no less specifically, that total sales on the road to Aranjuez came to 102 copies. There must therefore have been other villages involved, but we cannot tell how many, and therefore cannot calculate a reasonable average. One more village would make it 34; two more villages would bring it down to 25 again; three more reduces the average to 20. I may leave the reader guessing the way I guess myself.

Yet however much a single village here and there may make an important difference to the numbers of a single expedition, the fact stands that farmer communities, on the average, purchased from 20 to 30 copies, rather than from 20 to 60; a result which, seeing the poverty of the times and the lifestyle of the 19th century Spanish peasantry, is already a small miracle.

IV.3 Bookseller sales

NEXT TO his own private sales, Borrow employed, either directly or indirectly, and with various levels of success, 16 booksellers in the provinces, plus an unknown, but insignificant, number of booksellers in Madrid. Their supplies and sales may be summarized in the following manner (note that several of the booksellers mentioned here have already been included in the regional calculations of IV.1):

Town	Section	Supply	Sold	Confiscated	Unknown
Burgos	II.2.2.xi	40	40		
Cadiz	II.2.2.xv	100			100
Coruña	II.2.2.vi	122*	58		64*
Ferrol	II.2.2.viii	20			20
Leon	II.2.2.iv	90	56		34
Lugo	II.2.2.v	130*	64		66
Malaga	II.2.2.xvi	100*		some	100
Madrid	II.2.2.i	52	52		
Oviedo	II.2.2.ix	140*	43	97	
Pontevedra	II.2.2.vii	25*	17*	8*	
Salamanca	II.2.2.ii	60*	3	some	57
Santander	II.2.2.x	200			200
Santiago	II.2.2.vii	125	98	27	
Seville	II.2.2.xiii	100	24	76	
Toledo	II.2.2.xii	13	13		
Valencia	II.2.2.xiv	100	24		76
Valladolid	II.2.2.iii	100	50	some	50
Totals		**1517**	**542**	**408+**	**567**

* conjectures, the results of a debatable calculation, or an educated guess

This inventory shows that Borrow was not wholly off the mark when he wrote at an early moment that the Spanish booksellers were rather 'short-sighted' and 'utterly unacquainted with the rudiments of business' [L 27.2.1837]. In spite of sales-conditions which any modern-day bookseller can only dream of in his most wistful moments (an abundant supply brought up to the doorstep; a valuable product at half the cost price; all postage and gate-dues picked up by the publisher; ample free advertisements; a commission of some 10 to 15 % on the retail price, and no obligation to reimburse the supplier until many months later!) sales through the bookshops are counted by the dozens rather than by the hundreds. Furthermore, in most known cases, from a third to half of the booksellers' sales were realized while Borrow himself was running around town, publishing advertisements, putting up posters, and shop-talking to the inhabitants; with the result that many of these bookshops sold about as many copies *a month* after Borrow had gone, as they used to sell *per day* while he was in town. One begins to understand why the good Bible-salesman, after only half a year's sales-experience, could grumble, very much with his booksellers in mind, that 'no work seems to prosper in Spain which is not closely attended to by the master' [L 1.11.1837].

Of course, the above inventory is not complete, nor wholly beyond discussion. Sales in Cadiz, Malaga and Ferrol are completely unknown, and may have been fair in the first two of these cities (although the small margins left in the total sales and the numbers for stock force me to assume only 5 copies for each in all further calculations). Sales in Salamanca were certainly higher than the '3' for which we have hard proof (a fair but still cautious guess would be 7 from the first supply, another 5 of the second, making 12 extra and a total of 15). And some of the sales-figures for Coruña, Valencia and Valladolid, and even for Oviedo and Pontevedra, may have been just a little higher still, seeing that we have no reliable data for the later periods in these cities. Purely by intuition, however, I estimate that the extra sales realized by these nine cities will not even have come to 75 copies in total, on the one hand because the margins for stock do not allow great sales through the booksellers (see IV.5), and on the other because Borrow surely had good reasons never to mention such results in his correspondence.

Such extra sales would bring the total sales through booksellers between May 1837 and May 1838 up to some 600 to 625 copies, or roughly two fifths of Borrow's outlay in supplies. This was obviously not the best available plan 'for promoting the *general* circulation of the Scriptures', as Borrow originally reckoned [L 27.2.1837]. Had he really relied exclusively on his bookshops, it would have taken until Kingdom Come for his edition to become exhausted.

For the sake of honesty, one somewhat moot point must here still be addressed. As noted above (section II.2.2.v), the 'little town of Lugo, in

Galicia' bought a remarkable 64 copies of the New Testament. Borrow credited this fine result to the salutary influence of its liberal bishop and various sympathetic priests and friars. So it may indeed have been, seeing that local priests often had a stimulating effect on sales-figures when they declared the Scio New Testament a worthy book (compare III.1). However, some 40 years later, the intelligent, knowledgeable and Catholic author Antonio Balbin de Unquera, in an otherwise sympathetic review of *The Bible in Spain*[78], wrote about this episode, that 'the good missionary obviously did not understand that many people probably bought these books in order to destroy them'! Was this pure conjecture? Or could it be that Balbin had picked up some local lore which he here revealed to the world in passing? It is difficult to tell. On the one hand, Balbin gives us no reason to think that this is anything more than a speculation; but on the other, it is a well-known fact that, much as bishop Sanchez Rangel himself and his second-in-command Padilla Aguila were both active and outspoken supporters of the new liberal regime, the rest of the Lugo clergy was not at all. Most of them were in fact 'massively Carlist', notoriously averse to the liberal tendency of their superiors and refused to obey Padilla in just about everything [Barreiro, *Carlismo*, 128, 144, 161f]. Hence it is indeed not unthinkable that they may have called upon their flock to perform an Act of Faith, and buy the heretical books so as to take them out of circulation.

One certainly begins to suspect so, seeing the truly remarkable *density* of sales in Lugo. With 64 copies sold among 6,000 to 7,000 inhabitants, Lugo acquired about one Scio New Testament to every 100 inhabitants, which is almost twice as high as in many more promising towns. In Madrid itself, for instance, Borrow's major sales-efforts over many laborious months, resulted in no higher a ratio than some 1:195 (1,150 copies among 225,000 inhabitants). Santiago de Compostela, with thrice Lugo's number of inhabitants and a high level of literacy due to its university, colleges and seminary, came only to a comparable 1:188 (98 copies to 18,500 inhabitants). And the other cities whose sales may be more or less computed, did no better: Oviedo – despite its elaborate

---

78 'Juicio de un Misionero Protestante sobre Galicia y Asturias', in *La Ilustracion Gallega y Asturiana*, (volume 1, nº 23, 20 August 1879, p. 274–279). A translation is available in Missler, *Judgement*, 30–42, and on the website *George Borrow Studies*.

educational system – seems to have reached only a ratio of 1:220 (43 copies to 9,000 inhabitants); Burgos 1:300 (40 copies on 12,000 people); Coruña 1:330 (58 copies to 19,500 inhabitants), and so on[79]. In fact, *the only other town* which shows an equally impressive result as Lugo is Leon, with its 56 copies to 6,000 inhabitants; Leon, that 'town remarkable for its ultra-Carlism' [APP], 'which perhaps may be considered as the least enlightened and most fanatic place in all Spain' [L 18.7.1839], and the only city where Borrow says he ever experienced any true opposition during his Northern Journey [APP][80]. In short: there are some indications that the cities where the sales were best, Lugo and Leon certainly, but perhaps also Santiago and Valladolid, were the most Carlist ones as well. And that suggests that *some* of the books may indeed have been bought, not out of interest in translated Protestant Scripture, but as food for inquisitorial flames!

IV.4 Confiscated copies

As THE list in IV.2 above shows, a total of 408 copies of the Scio New Testament were confiscated with certainty from five of Borrow's franchised bookshops (Oviedo, Pontevedra, Santander, Santiago and Seville) after the definite Prohibition of May 1838.

These 408 aside, 567 copies of those which were supplied to other booksellers are 'missing' from the sources. Some of these were probably still sold to clients; but seeing the snail's pace at which sales took place in the latter months of tolerance, by far the greater part of them must have remained unsold in May 1838, and – unless they were quickly and spontaneously returned to Borrow within days – will therefore have been caught by the authorities and placed in embargo. Without being able

---

79 The numbers of inhabitants for the different cities come mainly from Madoz's *Diccionario Geográfico* and Richard Ford's *Hand-Book for travellers in Spain*, both published in the mid 1840s on the basis of earlier research. Such numbers are notoriously uncertain, since proper demographic records were only just being kept in the 1830s. The numbers may, however, be taken as indicative.

80 This is not altogether correct. According to his own letter of 5 July 1837, in Valladolid 'evil-disposed, persons, probably of the Carlist or Papist party, had defaced or torn down a great number of [the advertisements] which had been put up.'

to calculate the *size* of the seizures, we do know for certain that stock was confiscated from the bookshops in Malaga (out of 100 supplied), Salamanca (an unknown stock), and Valladolid (out of the third supply of 50). The fate of the books in the remaining bookshops that had supplies lying about (Cadiz, Coruña, Ferrol, Leon, Lugo, and Valencia) is unknown. It is however more than likely that the left-overs in these places were also swept up by churchmen or *aguaziles*, since Borrow lamented at an early date that 'all [our] Bibles and Testaments [have] been seized throughout Spain, with the exception of my stock in Madrid' [L 26.6.1838].[81]

Apart from these bookshop confiscations, six lots are also known to have been seized from Borrow himself or from his aides during their countryside expeditions. They are the following:

At Ocaña in early August 1838 from Juan Lopez [III.2.2]	232
At Villallos in late August 1838 from Juan Lopez [III.2.4]	some
At Fuentelahiguera in February 1839 from Vitoriano Lopez [III.3.4]	15
Near Navalcarnero in early March 1839 [III.3.5]	20
At Navalcarnero (box) in early March 1839 [III.3.5]	50+
At Seville on 7 July 1839 in Borrow's Pila Seca house [III.4.1]	some

Which is to say that 267 copies were confiscated with certainty, plus three batches of unknown size, one large one of about 50, and two small ones, neither of which was probably bigger than 20.

Putting the numbers of seizures from the booksellers together with those from Borrow himself, we may say that 408 + 267 = 675 copies were confiscated with certainty. To this hard number, an estimated 40 copies

---

81 An enigmatic seizure of stock from a Murcia bookshop gets mentioned, together with the seizures at Malaga, Valladolid and Santiago, in a letter of 7 July 1838 from Prime Minister Ofalia to Ambassador Villiers (Jenkins, *Life*, ch. 17). In spite of the fact that Ofalia wrote that the booksellers 'uniformly stated that they belonged to Mr Borrow and that they were commissioned by him to sell and dispose of them', it is most unlikely that these Murcia copies were part of Borrow's franchise, since Murcia was very much the fief of Lieutenant Graydon, and there is no indication anywhere in the sources that Borrow ever supplied a bookshop there. They must have been Graydon's; the more because Graydon is known to have franchised a bookshop in Murcia (see Giménez, *Graydon*, 247).

may be added for the small lots caught at Villallos and Seville, and 50 for the box of Navalcarnero, making 765 copies; while the 567 bookseller's copies of completely unknown fate, brings the grand total of *possible confiscations* to some 1,332 copies, a very significant number, both in absolute terms (it represents over a fourth of the whole edition!) and for the conclusions which it allows us to draw about Borrow's later conduct (see IV.5 below).

IV.5 Development of the central stock

ONE OF the most intriguing questions which may be asked about the 1837 edition of the Scio New Testament is: what happened to the copies confiscated by the civil and ecclesiastical authorities of Spain in the summer of 1838 and early 1839? Were they ultimately exported from the land as the law prescribed? Were they simply left to rot in the damp cellars of state buildings, as one might suspect in the absence of all news about their fate? Or were they destroyed in savage, triumphant *Auto-da-Fé's*, as was occasionally proposed by the clergy, and is often suggested by 'Borrow-bashers' of the past and present such as Samuel Widdrington and Tom Burns Marañon?

No, none of that at all. In reality, these copies were quietly recovered by Borrow and ploughed back into his sales-effort, ultimately to be sold *almost one and all* to individual clients. This rather unexpected and even stunning fact (since Borrow was only allowed to take repossession of the books under the solemn promise that he would export them from the land!), can be easily demonstrated by drawing up the progress of his Central Stock in Madrid. If we add up all the batches which were removed from that reserve, either by sale, by supplies to booksellers or by confiscation during Borrow's countryside expeditions, we arrive at the results in the table opposite.

From this inventory we learn at a glance, that when push came to shove nearly 5,450 copies were removed from an original edition of 5,000 (and this without counting the roughly 800 copies which we know were left in stock when Borrow sailed from Spain, as IV.7. will show). Of course this is physically impossible, so an explanation is called for.

Barring the possibility that Borrow secretly printed 1,250 more Scio

Destination	Date	Section	Size	Stock Left	Stock Taken
Printed			5000	5000	0
Luxury Binding	Apr 37	I.2.a	2	4998	2
Madrid Booksellers	May–Oct 37	II.2.2.i	52	4946	54
Northern Journey first leg	May–July 37	II.1.2.a	200	4746	254
Coruña for Galicia	July 37	II.1.2.b	500	4246	754
Valladolid 2nd supply	July 37	II.2.2.iii & xi	50	4196	804
Seville	Mid 37	II.2.2.xiii	100	4096	904
Valencia	Mid 37	II.2.2.xiv	100	3996	1004
Cadiz	Mid 37	II.2.2.xv	100	3896	1104
Malaga	Mid 37	II.2.2.xvi	100*	3796	1204
Santander	Oct 37	II.2.2.x	200	3596	1404
Valladolid 3rd supply	Nov 37	II.2.2.iii	50	3546	1454
Leon 2nd supply	Nov 37	II.2.2.iv	50	3496	1504
Salamanca 2nd supply	Nov 37	II.2.2.ii	50*	3446	1554
Oviedo 2nd supply	Nov 37	II.2.2.ix	100*	3346	1654
Toledo	Dec 37	II.2.2.xii	13	3333	1667
Ambassador Villiers	May–Dec 37	II.3.1	50	3283	1717
Civil Governor	12 Jan 38	II.3.2	2	3281	1719
Madrid *Despacho*	Nov 37–Apr 38	II.3.2	331	2950	2050
Sagra (trip 1)	Jul 38	III.2.1	400	2550	2450
Aranjuez/Ocaña (trip 2)	Jul–Aug 38	III.2.2	209	2341	2659
Seizure Ocaña	Aug 38	III.2.2	232	2109	2891
Villages near Madrid	Jul–Aug 38	III.2.3	123	1986	3014
Segovia-Avila (trip 3)	Aug 38	III.2.4	884	1102	3898
Seizure Villallos	Aug 38	III.2.4	20*	1082	3918
Gift to BFBS	Nov 38	I.2.a	1*	1081	3919
Madrid city by Antonio	Jan–Feb 39	III.3.1	122	959	4041
Madrid 'purlieux' Vitoriano	Jan–Feb 39	III.3.2	27	932	4068
Cobeña region (trip 4)	Jan–Feb 39	III.3.3	167*	765	4235
Guadalajara region (trip 5)	Feb 39	III.3.4	46	719	4281
Seizure Fuente La Higuera	Feb 39	III.3.4	15	704	4296
Navalcarnero (trip 6)	Mar 39	III.3.5	20*	684	4316
Seizure near Navalcarnero	Mar 39	III.3.5	20	664	4336
Seizure at Navelcarnero	Mar 39	III.3.5	50*	614	4386
Madrid colporteurs & private	Mar 39	III.3.6	582	32	4968
Seville, Morocco, England	Apr 39	III.4.1–3	330	-298	5298
Seville	Oct 39	III.4.4	150*	-448	5448
Remaining stock in Madrid	Apr 40			**-448**	**5448**

* assumption or conjecture (see the pertinent sections for explanations)

New Testaments than the 5,000 always stated (which I consider unthinkable, seeing that we possess Borrego's bills and the exact quantity of paper used in the printing), there is only one place where Borrow might have found a sufficient number of books to perform his great sales in the Prohibited period, to wit: the copies which were confiscated from the Spanish booksellers and from himself in the summer of 1838. All other books were either in his own possession, or had been sold to clients and could not be retrieved.

That Borrow was not at all loath to add confiscated stock to his sales-reserves, we know for a fact from his Seville smuggling adventure (see III.4 above) and from the Santander franchise. As we have seen (II.2.2.x), not a single one of the 200 copies sent there in October 1837 was ever sold, and in July of 1839 Borrow stated explicitly in a letter to the Bible Society, after giving them a run-down of the available stock in Madrid, that 'the quantity of Testaments would not have been so large had I not recovered before leaving Madrid [for Seville in mid April 1839] upwards of 200, which had been placed in embargo at Santander and subsequently removed to the capital' [L 18.7.1839].

This somewhat apologetic statement (he was trying to make his employers understand why there was still so much unsold stock lingering about after two long, costly years of sales-efforts) is the only time we hear Borrow mention recovered stock from confiscations. In all other instances, he remains perfectly silent about such lots. We do not know why. Just possibly he may have been afraid that his mail was being read, and that he might get into trouble if his irregular doings got known[82]; and it is quite conceivable that he had already informed his employers of his intentions when consulting with them in London the previous November.

What we can trace, however, is *when* he added such batches to his central stock, because on four different occasions, Borrow specified the size of his reserves. These instances are the following:

---

82 This would have been no paranoid fantasy. One of the reasons Borrow gave for removing himself from his Seville hotel in early May 1839 was that 'I had a suspicion that I was watched' [L 12.6.1839]; and by the looks of it, he was! Lieut.-Col. E.E. Napier, who met him at this time, writes in his 1843 memoirs that 'in consequence of a suspicion being entertained that he was a Russian spy, the police kept a sharp look-out over him.' (Napier, E.E., *Letters from the shores of the Mediterranean*; a.k.a. *Excursions along the shores of the Mediterranean*, vol. ii , from 1842.)

- In his letter of 26 June 1838 he writes that all the Society's books have been seized throughout Spain 'with the exception of my stock in Madrid (upwards of 3000)';

- In his report to the Bible Society of 28 November 1838 he writes that 'there are at the present moment about 2,000 copies of the New Testament in Madrid' [APP]; something which is borne out by his expense account of the same month [Acc 10], where he claims 200 *reales* for the 'removal of 2,000 Testaments (…) to Society's store' in September;

- In late March 1839 – immediately following his great sales efforts in and around Madrid – he writes that 'the greatest part of those which still remain (about 1,000) I reserve for Seville, (…) and some of the other inland cities of Andalusia' [L 20.3.1839];

- Finally, from Seville on 18 July 1839, he passes on the inventory of the central stock made by his Madrid caretaker Maria Diaz, from which 'it appears that there remain unsold of Testaments 962' [L 18.7.1839]. This latter statement, the latest as well as the most precise, comes as a godsend for any investigator engaged in numbers.

If we feed this information into the above inventory and add the item of the 200 recovered books from Santander in the correct place, we are able to reconstruct approximately what steps Borrow took to ensure that he would have sufficient stock available for his various expeditions into the countryside. The first thing to observe is that all is in order until May 1838, at the time of the Prohibition and the confiscations, when Borrow states he has 3,000 copies in stock, and the above inventory (following on the sales from the Madrid *Despacho*) reaches 2,950. The list therefore does not need to be repeated up to that moment.

From there on, however, calculated and specified stock quickly part ways, and need correction.

Destination	Date	Section	Removed	Stock	Out of Stock	Reports
In stock June 1838				2950		3000+
Sagra (trip 1)	July 38	III.2.1	400	2550	2450	
Aranjuez/Ocaña (trip 2)	Jul–Aug 38	III.2.2	209	2341	2659	
Seizure Ocaña	Aug 38	III.2.2	232	2109	2891	
Villages near Madrid	Jul–Aug 38	III.2.3	123	1986	3014	
Segovia-Avila (trip 3)	Aug 38	III.2.4	884	1102	3898	
Seizure Villallos	Aug 38	III.2.4	20*	1082	3918	
Recovered 1	Unknown		-920	2002	2998	2000
Gift to BFBS	Nov 38	I.2.a	1*	2001	2999	
Madrid city by Antonio	Jan–Feb 39	III.3.1	122	1879	3121	
Madrid 'purlieux' Vitoriano	Jan–Feb 39	III.3.2	27	1852	3148	
Cobeña region (trip 4)	Jan–Feb 39	III.3.3	167*	1685	3315	
Guadalajara region (trip 5)	Feb 39	III.3.4	46	1639	3361	
Seizure Fuente La Higuera	Feb 39	III.3.4	15	1624	3376	
Navalcarnero (trip 6)	March 39	III.3.5	20*	1604	3396	
Seizure near Navalcarnero	March 39	III.3.5	20	1584	3416	
Seizure at Navelcarnero	March 39	III.3.5	50*	1534	3466	
Madrid colporteurs & private	March 39	III.3.6	582	952	4048	1000
Recovered 2 Santander	March 39	II.2.2.x	-200	1152	3848	
Recovered 3	Unknown		-140	1292	3708	
Seville, Morocco, England	April 39	III.4.1–3	330	962	4038	962
Seville	Oct 39	III.4.4	150*	812	4188	
Remaining stock in Madrid	April 40			812	4188	

* assumption or conjecture (see the pertinent sections for explanations)

From this inventory it is plain to see that Borrow somehow recovered stock at two different periods: first of all, between June and September 1838 he must have regained over 900 copies and added them to his central Madrid stock; if he had not, the reserve would have dwindled to less than 1,100 copies after his sales in the Segovia region, instead of the 2,000 he specified to the Bible Society in November 1838.

After the considerable sales in the first months of 1839, there were still some 1,000 copies in stock, exactly as Borrow states in his letter of 20 March 1839. To these were added the 200 copies retrieved from Santander, plus another 140 copies (approximately) at an unknown date from an unknown source, so that – after the removal of the 330 copies for Seville and Morocco – the 962 copies reported by Maria Diaz in July 1839 were still in the storehouse.

Cruising on these numbers, we may calculate that Borrow retrieved and re-used approximately 920 + 200 + 140 = 1,260 confiscated copies[83]; a number which comes remarkably close to the 1,332 calculated above (in IV.4) as the possible total of confiscated books. But to tell the truth, it is perhaps a little *too close* for comfort; for this implies that of all those 1,332 copies (which after all contained 567 books from bookseller's supplies whose fate is absolutely unknown), *barely any were ever sold*, beyond the mere 72 difference. That, in turn, implies that there were practically no (further) sales in Salamanca, Coruña, Ferrol, Valladolid, Cadiz, or Malaga. And that is perhaps more accuracy than we asked for.

I have no fault-proof, ready-made solution for this dilemma. But I suspect that we are dealing with a combination of two factors: first of all, that the further sales in the mentioned cities were indeed *very small*, less than 10 in most cases, which also goes a long way to explain why Borrow never once mentions them in his correspondence (far from being a source of pride, such dismal sales-figures were an embarrassment). And on the other hand, we cannot wholly exclude the possibility that Borrow had Borrego print *just a few more copies* of the Scio New Testament while he was at it, to be on the safe side. Not, of course, the 1,260 mentioned above, which would have freed him from the need to retrieve and re-use confiscated stock, but perhaps a dozen more. The otherwise unexplained 'three reams' of paper 'spoiled' which he entered in his expense account over the printing [Acc 4] could, with a little application, have produced some 22 copies more. And this would create some breathing space for

---

83 Or more correctly: books which had been confiscated or were returned to him by his booksellers *before* they could be confiscated. As we have seen in IV.3 and IV.4 above, some 765 were certainly placed in embargo by the authorities, while another 567 may have been seized, but were not necessarily. Some batches of this latter number may simply have been returned to Borrow as soon as the May 1838 Prohibition struck. We have no way of telling, for no such spontaneous shipments appear anywhere in the sources.

further sales in Salamanca and the other cities mentioned above[84]. With luck, new documents will pop up in the future, or old ones re-emerge, which allow us to solve this problem[85].

What is beyond all doubt, however, is that Borrow cheated the authorities, the government and the churchmen of Spain. Even though a fair part of the 567 'missing' copies from the booksellers may have been returned to him directly, without first having been confiscated, it is obvious that the remaining part – some 765 – were placed in embargo, and that he regained nearly 700 of these under the strict condition that he would export them from the land, which he didn't. It makes for a wry realisation, because in hindsight, and much against the romantic sympathy we often feel for the much-plagued Bible-peddler, we must conclude that his ecclesiastical enemies judged their man well. When Don Fermín of Santiago wrote that he feared the confiscated books would not really be exported from the land if they got handed back to their owner, the good canon was, quite simply, correct in his suspicions (see II.4). So was the fiendish Ecclesiastical Governor of Seville, who did not wish to yield the books to the heretic salesman (see II.2.2.xiii). And so were the authorities of Toledo who dreamed of destroying the consignment seized

---

84 In the case of the *Embéo*, the Gospel of Luke in the Gypsy language, Borrow did indeed pull off a trick of this kind. Having been authorised by the Bible Society to print 250 copies, he silently went ahead and printed 500! In hindsight it was a wise decision, since the Gypsy *Luke* sold – and still sells! – marvellously well.

85 Borrow's papers have been horridly cut up after his death, and spread thin over the globe. Consequently it is quite feasible that new information may in due time be discovered. There is, for instance, a manuscript page for *The Zincali*, kept by the archive of the Royal Geographical Society of Australia, which – according to the catalogue's description – contains on the verso 'a few memoranda of sales of the New Testament made while Borrow was agent of the Bible Society in Spain.' To my knowledge, no investigator has ever studied or published this page. Other sources which are not readily available to the modern investigator are those used by William Knapp, Borrow's first biographer, in the last few decades of the 19th century. Knapp spent half a life-time collecting Borrow's papers, then wrote his marvellous, if somewhat fault-prone, biography; and next left his Borrow papers (those, that is, which he did not burn to protect his idol from scandal!!) to the Hispanic Society in New York, where they are not easily seen. Somewhere in Knapp's collection there are receipts from Borrow's booksellers [Knapp, *Life*, I : 266], a file on the confiscations at Ocaña [I : 302], and a report by Usoz on the sales at Madrid during Borrow's 1837 Northern Journey [I : 359].

at Ocaña (see III.2.2). In the short run, this dubious behaviour carried the advantage that Borrow could sell off another 1,000 New Testament copies in the countryside of Spain. In the long run, however, it was to have rather more prejudicial effects, as we shall see in the conclusions to this study (V below).

IV.6 Total sales 1837–1839

AFTER ALL the above computations and calculations, we are now in a position to draw up the complete record of sales of George Borrow's 1837 edition of the Scio New Testament. The final results are not as complete, consistent or indisputable as one would wish; but given the often uncertain nature of the sources, it is the best we can do (see overleaf).

A word is needed on the column of assumed sales. In all instances of conjecture I have kept the assumed sales by booksellers and Borrow himself to the barest minimum (usually 5 copies), because – as already argued on many occasions above – the margin between certain sales and certain stock does not allow conjectured sales to be very substantial. As it is, the inventory below stays only just within tolerable limits if we include these minimum conjectured sales of 5 copies in each unknown instance; because the accumulated total of sales up to and including September 1839 – the number of 4,023 copies – must have been 4,038 in reality, this being the difference between the 5,000 copies printed and the hard number of 962 copies reported by Maria Diaz for stock on 18 July 1839[86]. This number of 962 ought to appear where – at the third line from the bottom – the number 977 stands at present. To put it differently: we have only a trifling surplus of 15 copies left; a very narrow margin indeed, which would have to accommodate all other unknown or undocumented sales.

As argued in the previous chapter (IV.5): that margin may have been just a little broader than is shown here, since Borrow may conceivably

---

[86] I admit the chronology of these statements is most confusing. It is perhaps helpful to point out that all the copies which Borrow sold in August and September 1839, had already been taken out of the Madrid stock months earlier, and were therefore subtracted by Maria Diaz in her inventory of mid July 1839.

Sold to or by	Date of sales	Section	Sold Certain	Sold Assumed	Total Sold	Stock Left
Printed						5000
Luxury Bindings	April 37	I.2.a	2	0	2	4998
Northern Journey private	May – Oct 37	II.1.2.a	118		120	4880
Madrid booksellers	May – Oct 37	II.2.2.i	52		172	4828
Salamanca bookseller	May 37 – May 38	II.2.2.ii	3	12	187	4813
Valladolid bookseller	June 37 – May 38	II.2.2.iii	50	5	242	4758
Satchel Sale Valladolid	June 37	II.1.3	15	0	257	4743
Leon bookseller	June 37 – May 38	II.2.2.iv	56		313	4687
Lugo bookseller	June 37 – May 38	II.2.2.v	64		377	4623
Coruña bookseller	July 37 – May 38	II.2.2.vi	58	5	440	4560
Santiago bookseller	Aug 37 – June 38	II.2.2.vii	98		538	4462
Satchel Santiago	Aug 37	II.1.3	15	0	553	4447
Pontevedra bookseller	Aug 37 – June 38	II.2.2.vii	17		570	4430
Ferrol bookseller	Sept 37 – May 38	II.2.2.viii	0	5	575	4425
Oviedo bookseller	Sept 37 – May 38	II.2.2.ix	43		618	4382
Santander Bookseller	Oct 37 – May 38	II.2.2.x	0		618	4382
Burgos bookseller	Oct 37 – May 38	II.2.2.xi	40		658	4342
Toledo bookseller	Dec 37	II.2.2.xii	13		671	4329
Seville bookseller	Mid 37 – May 38	II.2.2.xiii	24		695	4305
Valencia bookseller	Mid 37 – May 38	II.2.2.xiv	24		719	4281
Cadiz bookseller	Mid 37 – May 38	II.2.2.xv	0	5	724	4276
Malaga bookseller	Mid 37 – May 38	II.2.2.xvi	0	5	729	4271
Ambassador Villiers	May 37 – Dec 37	II.3.1	50		779	4221
Madrid Despacho	Nov 37 – Jan 38	II.3.2	331		1110	3890
Civil Governor of Madrid	12 Jan 38	II.3.2	2		1112	3888
Sagra (trip 1)	July 38	III.2.1	400		1512	3488
Aranjuez-Ocaña (trip 2)	July – Aug 38	III.2.2	209		1721	3279
Madrid 'villages'	July – Aug 38	III.2.3	123		1844	3156
Segovia & Avila (trip 3)	Aug 38	III.2.4	884		2728	2272
Bible Society	November 38	I.2.a	1		2729	2271
Madrid city by Antonio	Jan – Feb 39	III.3.1	122		2851	2149
Madrid purlieux	Jan – Feb 39	III.3.2	27		2878	2122
Cobeña region (trip 4)	Jan – Feb 39	III.3.3	167		3045	1955
Guadalajara region (trip 5)	Feb 39	III.3.4	46		3091	1909
Navalcarnero (trip 6)	March 39	III.3.5	20	0	3111	1889
Madrid colporteurs	March 39	III.3.6	582		3693	1307
Seville & surroundings (1)	May – July 39	III.4.1	200		3893	1107
San Lucar Customs	August 39	III.4.2	0	7	3900	1100
Consul Brackenbury	August 39	III.4.3	3		3903	1097
Morocco	Aug – Sept 39	III.4.3	72	28	4003	997
Exported to England	Aug 39	III.4.3	0	20	4023	977
Seville & surroundings (2)	Oct – Nov 39	III.4.4	0	150	4173	827
Totals			**3931**	**242**	**4173**	**827**

have printed a dozen copies or so more than the 5,000 always mentioned. In any case it may be pointed out that these 15 copies difference between the final calculation and the known documented reality represent only 0.3 % of the entire edition, which may be called an excellent margin of error for a statistical investigation which leans so heavily on casual and sometimes hazy information.

In conclusion: keeping well in mind that 242 of the sold copies are a conjecture, that roughly 20 copies were not sold but exported to England, and that at least 12 copies were gifts made by Borrow to various friends, acquaintances and officials[87], it is probably fair to say that Borrow sold 4,150 copies of the original 5,000 to individual, paying clients in the two and a half years of his book-peddling activity.

IV.7 Left-behind stock

BORROW LEFT a considerable stock of Scio New Testaments behind in Madrid when he definitely returned to England in April 1840 [L 24.12.1839]. The precise size of this stock cannot be calculated. The last reliable number we possess is the 962 copies which Maria Diaz reported to remain in the Madrid storehouse in the summer of 1839 [L 18.7.1839]. From there on, we only have vague indications.

As seen above, in the autumn months of 1839, after Borrow's return from Tangier and after Maria Diaz's store-house report, Borrow still performed the sales of 'a considerable number' of New Testaments in the neighbourhood of Seville (see III.4.4). These copies were taken from the Central Madrid Stock, but we have no idea how many they were. All we do know is that he originally planned to leave 400 copies in Madrid once he left for England, so that there might be a Bible Society reserve in case some unforeseen opportunity presented itself in the future [L 29.9.1839]. At the same time, he was still planning one more serious sales effort in La Mancha for late 1839, for which he surely had reserved the larger

---

87 Namely: 2 in 'luxury binding'; 1 to the Cura of Pitiegua; 1 to the Jewish merchant from Morocco in Vigo; 1 to Antonio Traba in Finisterre; 2 to the Madrid Civil Governor; 1 to the daughter of the *alcalde* of Villaseca; at least 1 to the Committee of the Bible Society; and 3 to consul Brackenbury in Cadiz.

part of the 962 − 400 = 562 copies. If he had in mind anything like the Sagra, Aranjuez or Segovia expeditions of the year before (III.2.1, III.2.2 and III.2.4 respectively), then it is probably not too much to say that he would have kept 400 of these 562 copies apart for this endeavour, and only sold some 150 more in Seville. And since the plan proved abortive, roughly 800 copies would then have remained in Madrid when he sailed away forever.

Naturally, this number of 800 also squares up well with the results we can derive from the list of Total Sales in IV.6 above, since the remaining stock of 827 copies there arrived at by computation (the number on the very right in the last line) must be lessened with the 15 'surplus' copies which were certainly still sold before 18 July 1839, making 812.

Depending on small variations (such as the true total of his later sales in Seville in the autumn of 1839), there may have been left behind 50 copies more or 50 less than these 812, but the number can, on the whole, be trusted as a reasonable estimate. These 'few hundred copies' – as he termed it himself – Borrow promised 'to leave in safe custody' [L 29.9.1839; L 24.12.1839], mainly because nobody seems to have had much of an idea where to go with them (see the letter from Browne to Borrow of 7 October 1839). He may have done so. We simply have no inkling what happened to this remaining sixth of the whole edition.

IV.8 Finances

ONE WOULD very much like to know how much money the 1837 Scio New Testament cost the Bible Society, and how much the edition ultimately brought in. Unfortunately, it is impossible to make much more than an approximate computation of finances over the whole of the enterprise[88]. As we have seen above (I.2.b) the total costs of paper, printing and binding of the 5,000 books came to nearly 90,000 *reales*. This was, however, only a fraction of the financial bleeding which the Bible Society took to bring the New Testament to Spaniards in their own language. A whole set of other costs ought to be added to it, such as Borrow's

---

[88] For a more extensive – if still inevitably incomplete – analysis see Collie, *Eccentric*, 159ff.

own salary over more than four years (200 Pounds Sterling or roughly 20,000 *reales* a year), his costs for travel to the Peninsula and back again on various occasions; the costs of his many expeditions (nearly 15,000 *reales* for the Northern Journey alone); the salaries for his collaborators Antonio Buchino, Juan and Vitoriano Lopez, Pepe Calzado the shop man, and Borrow's Basque servant Francisco; the rent of the Madrid *Despacho* and various store-rooms; the purchase, hire, gear and stabling of a small squadron of horses, and so on, and so forth.

The available data – i.e. those we find in Borrow's expense accounts, in the Bible Society ledgers (which do not specify costs very well) and in an occasional surviving personal notebook [Knapp, *Life*, I : 304f] – only allow us to compute part of these costs. Without going into lengthy but fruitless detail, the numbers are more or less as follows:

Preparatory year in Spain (1836)	50,000 *reales*
Printing of the Scio New Testament	90,000 *reales*
Costs between January 1837 and April 1840	145,000 *reales*
Total	**285,000** *reales*

Note that some of the costs cannot be determined and are therefore not included in this total[89]. Note also that neither the production-costs of the Gospel of Luke in Caló and in Basque (some 8,320 *reales* together), nor the costs of acquisition and binding of the 490 full Bibles which Borrow sold (4,265 *reales* approximately) are considered in the above total[90]. To compensate for this absence, income generated from the sale of these publications will likewise be ignored below.

The Bible Society, it may then be said with all due caution, will have disbursed some 285,000 *reales*, roughly 2,850 Pounds Sterling of the day, to carry out this little adventure.

---

89 E.g. the wages of Juan Lopez and the Basque Francisco, the gate-dues, portage and costs of advertisements during the Northern Journey; most of the packing, postage and gate-dues for the lots despatched to booksellers all over the country and back again; and the many taxes and dues needed to free the books from embargo.

90 For cost and income of the complete Bibles, see Appendix 2. For the income generated by the Caló Gospel, see Missler, *Underpriced*, 30f and Missler, *Gypsy*, 35ff. For its costs of production see Missler, 'Gypsy Luke Project, (2), further results' in *George Borrow Bulletin* 36 (2008), 34f.

When we next turn to income, a little more may be said, but the reliability of the numbers is really no greater. With the exception of a few gifts, the New Testaments were always sold for money, at prices which ranged from 2 to 12 *reales*, but in many cases we have no way of telling for how much. The following inventory is therefore only indicative. In order to help the reader judge the relevance and reliability of the numbers, a letter code is attached to each total, to wit:

A = a hard reliable number, taken from the expense accounts or book-seller correspondence

B = a fair guess which at least comes close to the true figure (e.g. 10 *reales* for a bookseller's copy)

C = a completely arbitrary guess, made when the price per copy is unknown, or when it is unclear how many copies in the same batch were sold for one price and how many for another

The margin of error in these numbers is of course huge, so it makes no sense to try to refine the results any further. All we may say is that there are good reasons to assume that the total income from the roughly 4,150 Scio New Testaments sold by George Borrow never reached 22,000 *reales*; something which is in fair keeping with the even lower estimate calculated by Bible Society officers at a later date, namely just 182 pounds, 2 shillings and 2 dimes, or some 18,210 *reales* altogether [Collie, *Eccentric*, 160]. The difference of some 3,800 *reales* between these two final numbers can mostly be explained by the fact that the Bible Society accountants astonishingly took no notice of – and never seem to have asked for – Borrow's sales in Seville and Morocco between May and November 1839![91]

---

91 As mentioned earlier, there is no account which records income from sales after 9 March 1839. From Borrow's financial record in Knapp, *Life*, I : 305 (III.3.6 and Appendix 3) we know that 443 full Bibles and 602 Testaments were still sold in Madrid between 9 March and late April. An account over these sales must have reached the Bible Society later, for the last ledger of Borrow's mission [Foreign Account Current, no 5, p. 79] records a sum of £48.12.0 for 'Sales of Scripture' dated 30 April 1839. This sum – roughly 4,860 *reales* at the exchange rate of 100 *reales* – squares up fine with the Knapp record: 4,430 for Bibles + 1,806 for Testaments = 6,236, minus costs of 886 for Bibles + 607 for Testaments = 1,493; makes 6,236 – 1,493 = 4,743. So the Bible Society's records were complete up to 30 April 1839; but after that date there is no sign anywhere in their books of income over Borrow's sales; which suggests that he was allowed to pocket the lot! Further study of the subject is clearly necessary (see also Collie, Eccentric, 159f).

Sold to or by	Date of sales	Section	Number	Price (reales)	Income	Code
Luxury Bindings	April 37	I.1.2a	2	0	0	
Northern Journey private	May – Oct 37	II.1.2.a	118	10–12	1224	A
Madrid booksellers	May – Oct 37	II.2.2.i	52	10	520	A
Salamanca bookseller	May 37 – May 38	II.2.2.ii	15	10	150	B
Valladolid bookseller	June 37 – May 38	II.2.2.iii	55	10	550	B
Satchel Sale Valladolid	June 37	II.1.3	15	4	60	B
Leon bookseller	June 37 – May 38	II.2.2.iv	56	10	560	B
Lugo bookseller	June 37 – May 38	II.2.2.v	64	10	640	B
Coruña bookseller	July 37 – May 38	II.2.2.vi	63	10	630	B
Santiago bookseller	Aug 37 – June 38	II.2.2.vii	98	10	950	A
Satchel Santiago	Aug 37	II.1.3	15	3	45	B
Pontevedra	Aug 37 – June 38	II.2.2.vii	17	10	0	
Ferrol bookseller	Sept 37 – May 38	II.2.2.viii	5	10	50	B
Oviedo bookseller	Sept 37 – May 38	II.2.2.ix	43	10	430	A
Santander Bookseller	Oct 37 – May 38	II.2.2.x	0	0	0	
Burgos bookseller	Oct 37 – May 38	II.2.2.xi	40	10	400	B
Seville bookseller	July 37 – May 38	II.2.2.xii	24	10	220	A
Toledo bookseller	Dec 37	II.2.2.xii	13	10	130	A
Valencia bookseller	July 37 – May 38	II.2.2.xiv	24	10	221	A
Cadiz bookseller	July 37 – May 38	II.2.2.xv	5	10	50	B
Malaga bookseller	July 37 – May 38	II.2.2.xvi	5	10	50	B
Ambassador Villiers	May 37 – Dec 37	II.3.1	50	10	500	B
Madrid Despacho	Nov 37 – Jan 38	II.3.2	331	10–11	3326	A
Civil Governor of Madrid	12 Jan 38	II.3.2	2	0	0	
Sagra (trip 1)	July 1838	III.2.1	400	3–4	1370	A
Aranjuez-Ocaña (trip 2)	July – Aug 1838	III.2.2	209	3–4	707	A
Madrid 'villages'	July – Aug 1838	III.2.3	123	3	369	A
Segovia & Avila (trip 3)	Aug 1838	III.2.4	884	2–4	2958	A
Bible Society	November 38	I.2	1	0	0	
Madrid city by Antonio	Jan – Feb 1839	III.2.5	122	4	488	A
Madrid purlieux	Jan – Feb 1839	III.2.6	27	3–4	104	A
Cobeña region (trip 4)	Jan – Feb 1839	III.2.7	167	3	501	A
Guadalajara region (trip 5)	Feb 1839	III.2.8	46	3	138	A
Navalcarnero (trip 6)	March 1839	III.2.9	20	3	60	A
Madrid by colporteurs	March 1839	III.2.10	582	3	1746	A
Seville & surroundings (1)	May – July 1839	III.3.1	200	3–10	1000	C
San Lucar Customs	August 1 1839	III.3.2	7	10	70	C
Consul Brackenbury	August 1839	III.3.3	3	0	0	
Morocco	Aug – Sept 1839	III.3.3	100	3–10	675	C
Exported to England	Aug 1839	III.3.3	20	0	0	
Seville & surroundings (2)	Oct – Nov 39	III.3.4	150	3–4	525	C
Totals			**4173**		**21417**	

(In the above list conjectured sales figures have been added up with the certain ones)

The numbers on all sides of the equation are also by far too shaky to reach any sort of reliable conclusions as to efficiency of Borrow's operations. Nevertheless so much can be said that the income from sales did not even rise to one quarter of the edition's costs of production. And if the total disbursement did indeed come to the 285,000 *reales* guessed at above, then sales returns did not even reach 10 % of total costs.

Nineteenth century Bible-peddling was a pretty expensive affair...

V

Conclusion:
Aims, means and morals

SPAIN WAS not converted to Protestantism by George Borrow's books, as his detractors rarely fail to repeat with glee. Perhaps this does not come as a complete surprise to anyone with a bit of common sense. A land which had been deeply Catholic for some 1,800 years, if we follow the hagiographies of Saint James the Elder and the famous Lead Books of Granada; or at least for 1,400 if we heed the more prosaic scholarly historians, is not, perhaps, to be tempted into another religion by 5,000 copies of vernacular Scripture.

Of course, it was never the object of Borrow's mission to convert all Spain; only to lay a kind of ground-work for religious improvement by the distribution of some Bible texts in the national language. Whether that aim was reached or not is simply impossible to say. How does one measure moral adjustments or the changes in people's world view? How can one say what modifications are due to what edifying input? Things of that sort can neither be quantified nor traced, so it is perfectly futile to assert – or deny – any influence of the Scio New Testament on the religious life of 19th century Spaniards.

This leaves only one, somewhat marginal, question to answer, namely: when all is said and done, was the thing at least done well? Was the net result of 4,150 distributed books really worth the effort, the hardship, the risks, the vast expense, the conflict, and the imprisonment – not to mention the life of Borrow's manservant Francisco, who died prematurely from a jail fever he would not have picked up had he not been serving George Borrow in the abominable Madrid prison?

137

Here, opinions will necessarily vary, depending on one's criteria. But giving credit where it is due, I may perhaps quote the words of hostile Samuel Widdrington who remarks rather sensibly that

'As to the object of the undertaking, it was not only a most complete and entire failure, but of such a nature as to defeat any future attempt of the same kind. No doubt can for a moment be entertained either of the good motives on which the mission was founded, or of the energy of the individual entrusted with it; but from what I heard, nothing was ever conducted in a manner more likely to ensure its certain and inevitable failure. The first great error was the printing without the Apocrypha[92]; to say nothing of the notes, which the Spanish law, both civil and ecclesiastical, as yet unchanged, requires indispensably to be annexed to those distributed amongst the people. (…) I have not the smallest doubt, that nearly every copy put in circulation, is either destroyed, or in the hands of the curas and others, who, from the mode adopted, were placed almost in a state of hostility to the [British and Foreign Bible] society. Had they commenced by reprinting either the Barcelona or Valencia Bible[93], at a reduced price, and asked the cooperation of the clergy in the distribution, no doubt whatever they would gladly have given it, and much good might have been done by such a course, provided that it be admitted, that a defective Bible is better than no Bible at all.'[94]

Two judicious things stand out in this unyielding discourse. First of all: one does indeed get the impression that if Borrow and his employers had only made some concessions, and followed the perhaps humiliating, but pragmatic, course of printing a New Testament which lived up to the laws of the land, open conflict might have been avoided and perhaps

---

92 As has already been noted in II.2.2.ix above, and will be further explained in Appendix 2 below: New Testaments – the only sort of Scripture Borrow printed – did not have, and therefore could not lack, *Apocrypha*. Widdrington is here scoring points by kicking balls into non-existent goals.

93 I.e. the giant 10-volume translation of the Old and New Testament by Father Scio, with all the notes, which appeared in Valencia in the latter years of the 18th century. What Widdrington means with the 'Barcelona Bible' remains to be determined; it may just have been the version of the New Testament which appeared in Barcelona in 1820 [Knapp, *Life*, I : 247].

94 Widdrington (a.k.a. Cook), S. E., *Spain and the Spaniards in 1843* (London 1844), quoted in the *George Borrow Bulletin* 31 (2005), 46ff.

even a guarded cooperation with the more liberal-minded part of the Spanish clergy and their political supporters might have been attained[95]. In the religious arena of the 1830s friction was surely inevitable; but with a little give and take, true carnage might perhaps have been avoided, and then many more common folk could have been provided with a Bible adorned, *ad nauseam*, with lengthy notes, something which would indeed be 'better than no Bible at all', since nobody needs to read notes if they do not want to[96].

Still more valid, however, is Widdrington's point that Borrow's undertaking was 'of such a nature as to defeat any future attempt of the same kind'. This was no hollow remark of an arrogant critic, but indeed the reality on the ground by the 1840s. Where Borrow and Graydon had passed through Spain, no missionary grass would ever grow again until the ultra-liberal 'Glorious Revolution' of 1868. The whole of the Catholic Church, and every Spanish conservative, had turned even more hostile to the Bible Society by the events of the 1830s than they had been to begin with. It needs to be stressed that this was not merely the opinion of hostile writers such as Widdrington, but that it was recognized by the professionals as well. James Thomson, another Bible Society agent, went to Spain in 1847 and found himself perfectly unable to accomplish anything, ten years down the road, because, as he wrote back to London, 'the ground was not in a neutral but in a hostile state. Had Mr Borrow and Mr Graydon hastened slowly, rather than rapidly, and perhaps rudely, it is probable that our real progress at this day would have been much

---

95 Borrow himself recognized so much. Long after the Prohibition he suggested that Scripture could quietly and peacefully be introduced in Spain 'with the consent, or at least with the connivance' of the clergy, a great part of whom were 'by no means disposed to offer any serious opposition to such a measure, they having sense and talent enough to perceive that the old system can no longer be upheld of which the essential part is (…) to keep the people in ignorance of the great sterling truths of Christianity' [APP].

96 Of course such a course of action is easier proposed *a posteriori* than performed at the time. Ms Kathleen Cann points out to me that the printing of Scripture without any additions was quite simply the fundamental law of the Bible Society, which it could not alter without losing its supporters. Only by 1968 (!) some denominational notes were allowed to be included in Bible Society publications. On top of that, printing Father Scio's very lengthy additions would at least have *doubled* the size of Borrow's New Testament!

greater, and we might still have had a sort of tolerance to go on slowly with our work'.[97]

Ever since 1899, when William Knapp penned the line that 'Lieut. Graydon's imprudence in the South (...) practically broke up the work in Spain for more than a quarter of a century' [Knapp, *Life*, I : 293], it has been common practice to put most of the blame for this increased hostility onto the shoulders of poor James Graydon. And there can be no doubt that the zealous Orangeman, with his provocative tracts that ridiculed the adoration of the Mother of God and painted the whole of the Catholic church as a simple money-making enterprise, deserves his fair share of reproach. But in Catholic eyes, George Borrow really was no better. For when we look at this cooler, less zealous, more reasonable man from their point of view, what do we actually see? We see a foreigner who came to Spain at its darkest hour to stir up religious trouble where there was so much already, and who then blatantly printed an incomplete version of Scripture, prohibited by Spanish Law; knowingly and willingly falsified the name of the printer on its title page; rode off into the countryside to sell his books when this had been expressly forbidden by a Royal Decree; and sold batches of confiscated books, sometimes smuggled back into cities like common contraband, which had been returned to him under the solemn pledge that they would be exported from the land. This – in Spanish eyes – was neither a gentleman nor a law-abiding guest, but rather one more faithless, law-breaking, not to say *dishonest* foreign *agent provocateur*. And looking at his list of sins, one cannot rightly blame them for seeing it that way.

Of course, Borrow 'rode on because of the word of righteousness' [*BiS* ch 44] as he himself defined it in paraphrase of a psalm[98]. He claimed to be serving a Higher Purpose, and to be heeding a Higher Law, than that of mere men; and this conviction may perhaps serve to some degree as an exoneration for his less admirable doings. And yet there is a problem with this claim; for exactly such an invocation of Higher Principles, in various different shapes and forms, also enables other self-righteous folk in this world to do pretty much as they please – and not always with

---

97 So Thomson's letter to the Bible Society of 14 February 1848, quoted in Cann, *Correspondent*, 10.

98 'Ride on, because of the word of truth, of meekness, and righteousness' (Ps. 45:5)

good intentions. One may think, for instance, of counterculture 'revolutionaries' who go steal in supermarkets, not to eat gratis but supposedly 'to battle monopoly-capitalism'; or of wealthy suburban householders who hire cheap, tax-free and conveniently *submissive* domestics under the guise of solidarity with the world's poor – to mention only the least offensive abuses of fake altruism. Consequently, one does not rightly know how to judge these lofty pretensions. It is always good to see a man throw himself unselfishly into battle for his most deeply held beliefs; yet to admit to the validity of such an argument for lawbreaking sets a dubious and dangerous precedent. In short: one would wish that Borrow had simply remained within the limits of the Spanish law, bothersome as that might have been for himself and for his mission.

In the long run, history still held one little irony in store for George Borrow. In the subsequent 19th and 20th century, Protestantism in Spain simply sailed in the wake of the Progressive cause. When the liberals gained power – as in the period from 1868 to 1874 after General Prim's *Glorious Revolution* – freedom of religion was granted in a fair or full measure, and the Protestant churches thrived. When the conservatives returned – most particularly in the 40 years of General Franco's dictatorship – everything was done to rot heresy out of the land. This never succeeded completely. Today a vast number of Protestant churches are established in the country, labouring calmly and quietly to gain adapts, forever hindered by the laws of the land and local customs, but under the protection of a respectable constitution. But what surely would have surprised Borrow most, is that these churches – instead of gaining a foothold among disillusioned Catholics – particularly make inroads among his beloved *Gitanos*, the Gypsies who after many centuries of racist mistreatment and several decades of seeing their young succumb to drug-abuse, find in Protestant religion the strength, dignity and strict self-discipline to face the plight of their nation. George Borrow, who on more than one occasion affirmed about his Gypsy friends that 'religion they have none' [*Zincali*, part 2, chapter 1], would surely have been as astonished as he would have been pleased by this most unexpected turn of events! Or, in paraphrase of his own words, one might say that *chachipé* is sometimes stranger than fiction!

Appendix 1: The monetary system of Borrow's Spain

Currency and coinage

Spanish currency of the 1830s was a nasty little affair. The impracticability of its subdivisions is only surpassed by the wild profusion of coins and denominations. To add to the confusion, English authors such as Borrow and Ford often substituted English terms (*'Ounce'*) for the original Spanish names (*'Onza'*), or alternated prices in Spanish money with those in the old English duodecimal system of Pounds, Shillings and Pence. Finally, the exchange rates between Spanish and international money was always reckoned in an imaginary coin, the *Peso*. The madness is therefore complete. It is more difficult to interpret a "note of bills" of a Madrid money-changer than it is to follow Max Planck on Quantum Physics.

There was no paper money in the 1830s, only coin; coin which was, in itself, in reasonable condition since the whole coinage was renewed under King Carlos III around 1770 (Ford, *Handbook*, p. 8). The following coins existed 'in the flesh':

The **Onza** (*Ounce* in English) which equalled 320 *reales*
The **Media Onza** which equalled 160 *reales*
The **Doblon** which equalled 80 *reales*.
The **Dos Duros** which equalled 40 *reales*
The **Duro** (a.k.a. *Peso fuerte*, or "strong weight", and *Dollar* in English) was 20 *reales*
The **Medio Duro** was 10 *reales*.

The **Peseta** (the "little weight") was 4 *reales*

The **Dos Reales** was – as the name implies – a coin of 2 *reales*

The **Real Vellum** was the standard currency unit and equalled a handy 34 *maravedís*

The **Dos Cuartos** was 8 *maravedís*

The **Cuarto** was 4 *maravedís*

The **Octavo** was 2 *maravedís*

The **Maravedí** was practically worthless (≈ 0.03 *reales*) and barely existed as a coin.

The *Onza, Media Onza, Doblon, Dos Duros* and *Duro* came in gold. The *Medio Duro, Peseta, Dos Reales* and *Real* in silver. The *dos cuartos, cuarto, octavo* and *maravedi* in copper; or in whatever piece of scrap metal – chopped from old canon and recycled bell towers – struck the fancy of the market. Richard Ford tells in his *Handbook*, p. 8 (and again in chapter 9 of his *Gatherings from Spain*) how in the late 1820s, by way of experiment, he changed a gold *Duro* on the Seville market-place, and received in return an astonishing collection of odd coins, which included all sorts of ancient Spanish denominations, and even some antique Arab and Roman ones, generally assumed to possess the value of a *maravedí*.[99]

So far things were reasonably orderly; but in practice, a number of legal and illegal variations ensured that chaos would reign. Ford mentions (*Handbook*, p. 12), that there was a special issue of gold *Media Onza, Doblon, Dos Duros* and *Duro*, with a narrow thread or "cord" stamped around the rim, and called "*de premio*" for possessing a small additional fractional value. On p. 10 he warns that many of the standard gold coins, particularly the giant *Onza*, were worth a fraction less for having been heavily clipped, and were therefore rarely accepted at their nominal value (he actually advised travellers to acquire a legal certificate for each *Onza* they carried, made out by a gauger, and specifying each coin's exact gold weight and value!) And on p. 9 he points out that there were still in

---

99 This old make-do habit took a long while to die, even if it lost a little in antiquarian appeal. In the early 1980s, it was still a common and accepted practice in Spanish shops, supermarkets and road-side stalls to give the client a few chewing-gums or sweets with his change if no 1 peseta pieces were at hand in the cash-register.

circulation some 18ᵗʰ century "quarter dollars" (5 *reales*) and "half quarter dollars" (2.5 *reales*)... Small surprise that the Spanish peasantry during the Peninsular War actually accepted as payment counterfeit 'gold dollars' which the British soldiers concocted by flattening their brass uniform buttons (Ian Robertson, *A Commanding Presence*, p. 293 note 24)! How could these poor folk possibly know that no such legal tender actually *existed*?

Next to these real *existing* coins, there were also three imaginary monetary units meant only for paper transactions:

The ***Peso***, for banking and exchange purposes, of 15 *reales*,

The ***Ducado***, merely used to talk about prices, of 11 *reales*, and

The phantom ***Doblon*** (not to be confused with its tangible namesake!) of 60 *reales*.[100]

Rates of exchange

THROUGHOUT THE 1830s, tourists, travellers and international bookkeepers (those of Borrow's Bible Society among them) equalled 100 *reales* with 1 Pound Sterling for all purposes of calculation and accounting. This was a fictitious rule of thumb, mainly inspired by the impossibility of keeping adequate everyday track of an exchange rate between the Spanish system, in which the non-existent '*Peso*' equalled 15 *reales* of 34 *maravedís* each, and the British coinage, in which 1 pound sterling equalled 20 shillings, each of which valued 12 pence[101]. For this ideal, fictitious situation, the following table may be drawn up to show the relative values between Spanish and British coins:

---

100 See Ford, *Handbook*, 12 and Jose Maria de Francisco Olmo: 'Conflictos bélicos y circulación de moneda extranjera en España 1808-1836', in: *Revista general de información y documentación*, vol 11, 1 – 2001, p. 130.

101 To make matters ever more incomprehensible, British bookkeepers and administrators in their bills and calculations sometimes call the imaginary '*Peso*' by the name of '*Dollar*' (symbol $), despite the fact that '*Dollar*' really ought to have been exclusively reserved for the '*Duro*' of 20 *reales*, otherwise known as the '*Peso Fuerte*'... The confusion is understandable, but the effect is truly awful.

	Maravedis	Reals	Peso-Dollar	Pounds	Shilling	Pence
Maravedi	1	0.03	0.002	0.0003	0.006	0.07
Real	34	1	0.067	0.01	0.2	2.40
Peso-Dollar	512	15	1	0.15	3	36
Pound	3400	100	6.67	1	20	240
Shilling	170	5	0.33	0.05	1	12
Pence	14.17	0.42	0.028	0.004	0.08	1

Of course, in real life, the exchange rates fluctuated considerably. Throughout the year 1837, for instance (a year for which I happen to possess data), 1 pound sterling stood at 97.6 *reales* in February, rose gradually to 101.4 *reales* over the spring, reached a top of 102.5 in late November, and dropped back to a neat 100 again in mid December. All of which reflects a hefty swing in exchange rate of 5 % within a year.

Purchasing power of Spanish money

It is always mighty hazardous to convert prices and wages of a distant yesterday into the currencies of the present. For one thing, such a conversion is only valid at the precise moment when the text is published, and quickly becomes obsolete. For another, such a conversion can never really take into account the different patterns of consumption and production of another macro-economic stage.

Consequently it makes better sense merely to give a broad indication of what people earned in the period in question, and what were the average costs of their livelihood. Such an outline has its short-comings, but does possess the great virtue of unchanging validity.

The average daily earnings of the common worker of the 1830s stood at 3 to 4 *reales* for a working day of 10 to 12 hours. These were the wages received by most city servants, by construction workers, and by normal, unskilled factory-hands in Spain's small-scale workshops. Skilled master workers in that same proto-industry earned a little more: between 5 and 10 *reales* daily depending on their responsibilities. Skilled masons received the same, while the highly specialised artisans in the fancy chocolate workshops received some 12 *reales* a day, just like a master architect, and a Greek manservant of awful temper but solid reliability. Military pay in the different ranks was roughly comparable. A private soldier earned 3 or 4 *reales per diem*, a corporal 5 and a sergeant 6; but all these received daily rations in addition to their wages. A lieutenant received a stipend of 10 *reales* daily, and a captain in command of a small garrison some 20 to 24, which may be called a substantial income. On the other, humblest step of the social ladder, stood, tellingly, the Spanish schoolmaster, who had to scrape by on slightly more than 2 *reales* a day, while charity institutions considered 24 *maravedís* – ⅔ of a *real* – sufficient for the daily keep of penniless prisoners. Finally, to top it all, there is the case of a Bible Salesman in the pay of a foreign missionary society, who received a yearly salary of 200 pounds, or 20,000 *reales*, which comes down to roughly 55 *reales* a day.

Naturally, commodity prices varied greatly depending on the season, the locality and the progress of the war-related crisis which hit Spain in the 1830s. The differences are sometimes quite pronounced and quite surprising. From Borrow's own writings, we learn that prices of first necessities in a distant inland metropolis like Madrid were lower than those in war-surrounded Santander on the north coast, even though this was a blossoming harbour town; while in the fertile, poverty-ridden Galician countryside food-prices were agreeably low, but this windfall was undone again by the fact that little more than coarse maize-bread and even courser *aguardiente* could be purchased. Consequently, it really is no more than indicative to mention that in Borrow's day a pound (i.e. 577 grams) of bread cost 8 *maravedís* when made from maize, 16 when made of rye and 26 when baked from wheat, and that for a single *real* one could buy a dozen eggs, four cabbages, a pound of meat, a litre and a half of milk or a single bottle of common country wine. To illustrate where this price-level left the average working man food-wise, I may quote an official inquest drawn up in the early 1840s by the town hall of Santiago de Compostela, which determined that local factory-hands spent some 2 *reales*, i.e. roughly half their income, on their own daily personal fare of *boroa* (maize-bread) and *caldo* (vegetable soup with beans, potatoes and a spoonful of pork-grease).[102] The remaining half

---

102 Archivo Historico de la Universidad de Santiago, legajo "*Estadistica. Fabricas e Industrias. Montes e Planteos 1836–1895.*" (no catalogue number assigned when I saw it). Excellent additional information for this place and time may be gleaned from the study by Leopoldo Martinez de Padin: *Historia politica, religiosa y descriptiva de Galicia*, vol. 1, Madrid, 1849 (particularly p. 192ff)

was left for rent, clothing and the keep of the family. This may seem little, but it ought to be added that houses were often owned, not rented, that clothes were mainly home-spun and -sewn, that most people went barefoot, and that the wives of these same factory-hands often earned money on the side by some form of piece-work, bringing in 6 to 10 *reales* a week. All these wages were notoriously erratic (if a factory received no orders, the workers got no pay); but, on the other hand yet again, many families owned a tiny kitchen garden where they grew some staples and kept some livestock. Therefore it probably comes close to the truth to say that the average lower class family had to subsist on 100 or 120 *reales* a month, complemented with a few commodities from their own household industry.

Appendix 2: Borrow's sales of complete Bibles

ACCORDING TO his own admission, George Borrow seriously misinterpreted Spanish attitudes towards Scripture in the early days of his assignment. In the spring of 1836, when he had only been in Spain a few months, he spoke out resolutely against the idea of distributing the entire Bible here, arguing that 'in these countries, until the inhabitants become Christian, it would be expedient to drop the Old Testament altogether, for if the Old accompany the New the latter will be little read, as the former is so infinitely more entertaining to the carnal man' [L 20.5.1836]. Beside this moral objection, there were also practical matters to consider. Borrow judged the only available Spanish copy text of the entire Bible – the so-called 'London Edition' from the 1820s – to be 'a Bible which does the editor no credit and the Society less' [L 20.11.1837]. It was deficient in matters like accentuation and punctuation, while 'words are frequently omitted or misspelt, and occasionally a short sentence is left out.' [L 25.12.1837; L 20.11.1837; L 28.11.1837]. On top of that, it would of course be more difficult to print the entire Bible than just the New Testament, which only represents about a fifth of the whole text. And finally, the troubles he could expect over the question of the 'Apocrypha'[103] if he decided to print the full Bible would be yet another

---

103 'Apocrypha' is the term which contemporary authors invariably use for the six books listed below. Yet it would really be better to speak of the 'deutero-canonical books' (even if that term is a veritable tongue twister). To put it in a nutshell: true Apocrypha are spurious and sometimes even silly pseudo-Bible books, often written centuries after the events by amateurs, which no church or serious ecclesiastic authority recognizes as being part of Holy Writ. The six books which are the bone of contention between Catholics and Protestants are, however, quite another case. The

hurdle rising between himself and success. The Spanish authorities, civil as well as ecclesiastical, would insist on the inclusion of the books of Tobias, Judith, the Wisdom of Solomon, Baruch, and Maccabees 1 and 2. Since the Bible Society could not possibly permit this, it would lead to a deadlock. 'An anticipation of that difficulty,' he explained later, 'was one of my motives for forbearing to request permission to print the entire Bible' [L 20.11.1837].

All these were surely valid arguments; except that Borrow failed to take into account one other quintessential aspect, namely the wants and wishes of his customers, and consequently the effect which his decision was to have on overall *demand*. Reading Spaniards with an interest in Scripture – mainly the educated city bourgeoisie and intelligentsia – clamoured for the full text of the Bible, and not only in a Spanish translation, but surprisingly even in the original languages and translations into other European tongues [L 28.11.1837; see also below].

Borrow discovered his mistake soon enough[104]. Shortly after he had printed the 5,000 Scio New Testaments and started distribution, he began to notice the discrepancy between what he offered and what he was asked for. 'I may here state,' he wrote soon after his return from his great Northern Journey of the summer of 1837, 'that if the books which I carried to the provinces had been Bibles, I could have sold ten times the amount of what I did' [L 28.11.1837]. And the point really got driven home to him when he inaugurated his '*Despacho*' in Madrid in the final days of November 1837. 'The shop opened yesterday, and several Testaments have been sold,' he told his employers after the first day of

---

5th century church-father Jerome, when making his famous Bible translation into Latin (known as the Vulgate), rejected these books because they were only known in a Greek version, and no Hebrew original could be located. While the Protestant churches followed Jerome in this, the Catholic church eventually accepted them as divinely inspired nevertheless. Thus, as a group, they form a 'second canon', coming on top of the 'first canon' of books which everybody accepts as divine.

104 In fact, he might have known all along. Already in his letter of 20 May 1836 quoted above, and *immediately following* on his remarks about the Old Testament being so much more 'entertaining to the carnal man', he informed his employers that 'Mr. Wilby in his [last] letter informs me that 30 Bibles have been sold in Lisbon within a short time, but that the demand for Testaments has not amounted to half that number.' Although this concerned the situation in another country, it at least ought to have made him give the matter some thought.

business, 'but three parts of the customers departed on finding that only the New Testament was to be obtained' and that no full Bibles were offered for sale [L 28.11.1837].

Borrow would not have been Borrow had he not taken immediate steps to remedy the situation. The very day he discovered the vast demand for complete Bibles from the customers of the *Despacho*, he begged his employers to furnish him with a large stock of books as soon as they could, and in whatever legal or illegal way possible. 'Send me therefore the London edition, bad as it is, say 500 copies,' he wrote in an almost dramatic tone. 'I believe you have a friend at Cadiz, the consul [John Brackenbury – PM], who would have sufficient influence to secure their admission into Spain. But the most advisable way would be to pack them in two chests, placing at the top Bibles in English and other languages, for there is a demand, viz.: 100 English, 100 French, 50 German, 50 Hebrew, 50 Greek, 10 Modern Greek, 10 Persian, 20 Arabic. *Pray do not fail*' [L 28.11.1837]. With this request he obviously did not only try to meet a rather surprising demand in a country and epoch little given to profound linguistic study, but also meant to add some lustre and variety to the stock of his *Despacho*.

Meanwhile, as he waited for the shipment to arrive, Borrow himself quickly combed the bookshops of Madrid and acquired a number of Spanish-language Bibles from a tradesman who did not dare to sell them himself. 'Since the opening of the establishment (…)' he wrote in late December, 'I have contrived to sell (…) between 70 and 80 New Testaments and 10 Bibles. You will doubtless wonder where I obtained the latter: in the shop of a bookseller who dared not sell them himself, but who had brought them secretly from Gibraltar. Of these Bibles there were two of the large edition, printed by William Clowes, 1828 (I would give my right hand for a thousand of them); these I sold (on the bookseller's account) for 70 *reals* or 17 shillings each, and the others, which were of the very common edition, for 7 shillings [some 30 to 35 *reales* – PM], which is, however, far too dear' [L 25.12.1837].

By late December there was still no news of a shipment of Bibles. Impatiently, Borrow repeated his dramatic plea, adding to his Christmas Day letter: 'Let me beg and pray that you will send Bibles, Bibles, Bibles of all sizes and prices, and in all languages to Madrid. You cannot conceive how helpless and forlorn I feel, 400 miles from the sea-coast, on being begged to supply what I possess not. I received an order the other day for 20 Hebrew Bibles. I replied with tears in my eyes, "I have nothing but the New Testament in Spanish".' [L 25.12.1837] The fact was that the Bible Society had set the machine in motion, but – perhaps put off by the uncommon invitation to engage in smuggling and underhand dealings – they moved prudently. As suggested, they contacted consul Brackenbury to see if he might assist them to import a shipment, but – much as the Cadiz consul was always most willing to help – he very sensibly pointed out that importing Bibles would be illegal, and that he therefore could not get involved. So instead, Borrow's letter of late November was referred to the General Purposes Sub-Committee, which decided to send him 500 unbound Spanish Bibles from the Society's depot at the Barcelona printshop of Antonio Bergnes[105]. Still eager, Borrow at first hoped to keep his *Despacho* running with this stock when the government forbade the sales of his Scio New Testament in early January [L 15.1.1838]. But unfortunately, the cargo – which must have been huge, very heavy and surely was transported in the most discreet way possible – took more than two months to arrive, only reaching Madrid by the middle of March [L 17.3.1838, postscript; Acc 8], when the conflict with the government was already in full swing. Borrow ordered a first small batch of 26 copies bound from the loose sheets at 5½ *reales* a piece sometime in the spring of 1838 [Acc 9; Collie, *Eccentric*, endnote 34 on page 262]; but – as far as we can tell – he never found the occasion to sell a single one of these at the time, and was left no other choice than to store the mammoth pile of sheets away with the rest of his secret stock, so as to avoid its confiscation.

It took a year for the stockpile to leave its hiding-place. For one thing, when Borrow resumed operations in the summer of 1838, he concentrated on peddling books in an underhand and ambulant manner among the peasantry of the countryside. Not only were complete Bibles 'far too bulky for rural journeys' [L 12.6.1839], but – much as he had seen the light as to selling full Bibles to the city bourgeoisie – he still maintained that

---

105 The information on the correspondence of the Bible Society with consul Brackenbury and with Antonio Bergnes (contained in a letter of the Rev. John Jackson to Bergnes of 8 December 1837) was kindly brought to my attention by Ms Kathleen Cann in personal communications of 21 and 23 May 2008.

the whole Scripture was not suitable to distribute among rural folk. 'The writer would by no means advise for the present an attempt to distribute the entire Bible amongst the peasantry,' he wrote in his formal report of November 1838, 'as he is of opinion that the New Testament is much better adapted to their understandings and circumstances' [ROS].

Not until early March 1839, when his gospel-peddling countryside expeditions around Madrid had come to an end, did Borrow's thoughts return to his stock of full Bibles for which he had been clamouring so anxiously 14 months earlier. He was already toying with the idea of moving his operations to Seville, where he could not of course carry the hefty stock of unbound Bibles. The stock itself was being gnawed away by rats, who were doing 'prodigous havoc to the stores' in its secret depot [L 9.3.1839]. And finally, Borrow had set his heart on making one more major effort at sales in the capital itself, where complete Bibles would presumably be a welcome merchandise. A first probe was made throughout January and February 1839 by Antonio and himself with the small batch of 26 Bibles bound in the spring of 1838. Happily, 17 of these were sold off without the least trouble, helped along by the extremely low price of 10 *reales* each which he asked for them [Acc 11; L 4.3.1839]. On 9 March he noted that 'I have disposed of all the Bibles bound already, and have been compelled on account of the demand to order the rest of the sheets to be got in readiness' [L 9.3.1839 to Hitchin]. To this purpose he found himself a trustworthy craftsman, 'in whose secrecy and honour I have perfect confidence' [L 20.3.1839], asked him to start binding the loose sheets into books, and handed them to his *colporteurs* and ambulant salesmen to be peddled house to house in the capital [see III.3.6 above].

It was a masterstroke. The costs of binding were considerable – 5 ¾ *reales* a piece for a book which would only fetch 10 *reales* – and so was the commission for his *colporteurs* – 2 *reales* on each copy sold – but the results easily justified the expenditure [Knapp, *Life*, I : 305]. Already on 20 March 1839, he could inform his employers that no fewer than 100 copies had been sold in the last 10 days. Demand was in fact so remarkable that 'the books are disposed of faster than they can be bound by the man whom I employ for that purpose', people even paying up front so as not to lose the opportunity to acquire one [L 20.3.1839]. Three weeks later again, he wrote to Jowett that yet another 200 copies had been disposed of, and that only some 150 remained to be dealt with [L 10.4.1839]. And by the 16th of the month, when drawing up his accounts for March and April just before travelling to Seville, he could record that a grand total of 443 Bibles of the original 500 had been bound and found their way to customers [Knapp, *Life*, I : 305]. This total he corrected upwards to 463 for the entire period from mid-January to April 1839 in his first letter from Seville, adding up the first 17 of February, the 443 of March and April, and an additional 3 which he may, conceivably, have carried to Seville and sold there [L 2.5.1839].

The secret of this success was without a doubt Borrow's excellent targeting of wealthy customers and his use of intermediaries who had access to their dwellings. 'The few copies of the entire Bible which I had at my disposal,' he wrote in conclusion at the end of the year, 'have been distributed amongst the upper classes, chiefly amongst the mercantile body, the members of which upon the whole are by far the most intellectual and best educated of the subjects of the Spanish monarchy' [L 24.12.1839]. Many of the books found their way 'into the best houses in Madrid', and as an illustration he offered the example of the household of his friend the Marquis of Santa Coloma, who 'has a large family, but every individual of it, old or young, is now in possession of a Bible and likewise of a Testament, which, strange to say, were recommended by the chaplain of the house' [L 20.3.1839]. The latter may or may not have been the same 'ecclesiastic' whom Borrow called 'one of my most zealous agents in the propagation of the Bible', and who, he explained, 'never walks out without carrying one beneath his gown, which he offers to the first person he meets whom he thinks likely to purchase' [L 20.3.1839]. Another excellent assistant was 'an elderly gentleman of Navarre, enormously rich, who is continually purchasing copies on his own account, which he, as I am told, sends into his native province, for distribution amongst his friends and the poor' [L.20.3.1839]. And elsewhere there is mention of a certain 'Don Santiago', who may just be Santiago Usoz y Rio, professor of Greek and brother of Luis, and of yet another 'Aragonese gentleman' who bought complete Bibles wholesale for further distribution [L 28.6.1839]. Seeing such a neat and well-designed marketing strategy and division of labour – gypsy *colporteurs* to peddle New Testaments to the poor and upper class intellectuals to distribute complete Bibles in wealthy neighbourhoods – one can only wonder what

George Borrow might have achieved in our more commercial, market-orientated modern era.

By now, Borrow thoroughly repented of his original mistake in speaking out against selling complete Bibles. The sheer, overwhelming volume of demand for the work left him no other choice. In Madrid, 'I was obliged to send away hundreds of people who wanted to purchase,' he wrote to his mother in April [letter to Ann Borrow from Seville on 27 April 1839, quoted in Shorter, *Life*, 122]. And he even pretended, on no less than three different occasions, that his 'inability to answer the pressing demands for Bibles which came pouring upon me every instant' was 'one of my principal reasons for leaving Madrid' [L 12.6.1839]; not to say that he was 'obliged to leave [Madrid] being unable to answer the demands for Bibles which assailed me'! [L 15.7.1839 to Hasfeld, in Fraser, *Hasfeld*, 36; see also L 18.7.1839] Surely not often was an innocent bookseller chased out of town by ferocious clients pursuing him for his merchandise, and forced to seek shelter in sunny Seville!

Even there, however, demand for the complete Scriptures kept haunting him. People in Seville proved likewise more interested in full Bibles than in the New Testaments. 'We are continually pressed for Bibles, which of course we cannot supply, Testaments are held in comparatively little esteem,' he wrote in June [L 12.6.1839]. And identical complaints reached him through his Madrid caretaker Maria Diaz, who wrote him of her plight in the summer of 1839, telling how 'the binder has brought me 8 Bibles, which he has contrived to make up out of *the sheets gnawn by the rats*, and which would have been necessary even had they amounted to 8,000, because the people are innumerable who come to seek more. Don Santiago has been here with some friends, who insisted upon having a part of them. The Aragonese gentleman has likewise been, he who came before your departure and bespoke 24. He now wants 25. I begged them to take Testaments, but they would not' [L 28.6.1839, quotation from a letter of Maria Diaz to Borrow translated by himself]. Since the whole remainder of the stock now available to her – not even taking into account the foraging parties of rodents – did not even amount to that number, the Aragonese gentleman will not have been satisfied in his demands.

In the end, the whole muddled business even forced Borrow into a rare moment of sincere self-criticism. 'Allow me to make here a remark which it is true I ought to have made three years ago,' he wrote in reference to his original rejection of the Old Testament for Spain [L 12.6.1839]. 'It is unwise to print Testaments, and Testaments alone for Catholic countries. The reason is plain. The Catholic, unused to Scripture reading, finds a thousand things which he cannot possibly understand in the New Testament, the foundation of which is the Old' [L 12.6.1839]. This, if anything, was the reason why his sales results were relatively modest! 'Pray inform me why the circulation has not been ten times greater?', he challenged his employers when they withheld the praise he thought was due to him. 'Surely you are aware that among the many peculiarities of my situation was this distressing one, namely, that I was scarcely ever able to supply the people with the books that they were in want of. They clamoured for Bibles, and I had nothing but Testaments to offer them. Had I been possessed of 20,000 Bibles in the spring of the present year [1839], I could have disposed of them all without leaving Madrid; and they would have found their way through all Spain' [L 29.9.1839]. Of Bibles he simply always had too few and of Testaments too many, 'the Spaniards, as is very natural, not esteeming the latter so much as the entire scripture' [Letter to Hasfeld, in Fraser, *Hasfeld*, 36]. 'Nevertheless when I take a large view of the subject,' he wrote elsewhere, 'I feel inclined to believe that we were right in commencing our labours in the interior of Spain by printing an edition of the New Testament at Madrid. I much doubt whether the astonishing demand for the Bible (…) would have arisen but for the appearance of the New Testament which awaked in people's minds the desire of possessing the entire Scripture. With great humility, however, I feel disposed to advise that provided at any future time the Society should think itself called upon to recommence its exertions here in the cause of a crucified Saviour, it employ, as its mighty instrument the Bible, the entire blessed Bible' [L18.7.1839]. It was, forsooth, an impressive change of mind. But then, as Borrow himself admitted: 'We live and learn' [L 12.6.1839].

Summary

To sum up, Borrow sold the following lots of complete Bibles between late December 1837 and the middle of July 1839, practically all of them in the city of Madrid:

From *Despacho* in December 1837	10	380 *reales*[106]	[L 25.12.1837]
By Antonio and GB Jan–Feb 1839	17	170 *reales*	[L 9.3.1839; Acc 11]
'Vanished' copies from first binding	9	-	[Acc 9; Acc 11]
By colporteurs Mar–Apr 1839	443	4430 *reales*	[Knapp I : 305]
Additional sales in late Apr 1839	3	30 *reales* (?)	[L 2.5.1839]
By Maria Diaz in June 1839	8	80 *reales* (?)	[L 28.6.1839]
Total	490	5090 *reales* (?)	

The total of complete Bibles which passed through Borrow's hands on their way to customers would therefore come to 490 copies. Of these, however, 10 copies came out of the stock of, and were sold in commission for, the skittish Madrid bookseller of December 1837. Furthermore, the fate of 9 copies of the original 26 bound in the spring of 1838 is not recorded anywhere in documents (these were clearly not absorbed in the 443 sold throughout March and April 1839, since all those were bound separately, as the below specification of costs will show). They may have been given away as presents, kept for personal use, or simply forgotten (but note that the three additional copies sold in late April may conceivably have come out of this small left-over lot). Taking all this into account, it may be said that Borrow disposed of 480 copies of his own complete Bibles, with a margin of error of 3 copies; while only between 23 and 20 copies remain unaccounted for.[107]

---

106 The income from the 10 copies sold for the Madrid bookseller in December 1837 came to approximately these 380 *reales* (2 copies at 70 plus 8 at approximately 30 as the letter of 25.12.1837 specifies). But Borrow states specifically that these were sold 'on the bookseller's account', which explains why neither income nor cost of acquisition ever figures in his Expense Accounts.

107 As stated at the end of chapter II.2.2.ix above, the possibility cannot be wholly excluded that Borrow organised a cargo of complete Bibles to be sent from England to a bookseller in Oviedo. Sales from such a batch ought to be added to the totals above, but no reliable information on this possible shipment has been located.

Borrow's verifiable income from these sales totalled 4,600 *reales*, but must have risen to 4,710 *reales* if the 3 copies of late April and the 8 copies of Maria Diaz also brought 10 *reales* each; and it may even have come to a total of 4,800 *reales* if all the 9 'vanished' copies brought the same price.

The costs of the operation were as follows:

Carriage of 500 Bibles from Barcelona to Madrid	625 *reales*	[Acc 8]
Binding of first 26 Bibles at 5 ½ *reales* each	143 *reales*	[Acc 9]
Binding of 443 Bibles at 5 ¾ *reales* each	2547 ¼ *reales*	[Knapp I : 305]
Expenses on sale 443 Bibles (2 *reales* commission)	886 *reales*	[Knapp I : 305]
Presumed costs of binding 3 additional copies	17 ¼ *reales*	[L 2.5.1839]
Presumed costs of binding 8 copies Maria Diaz	46 *reales*	[L 28.6.1839]
Total	**4264 ½ *reales***	

Since part of the rent of the *Despacho*, the salary for the shopman, the rent of various depots and the carriage of stock on several occasions from one storage to another should also be allotted to the costs of the sale of complete Bibles, it is no more than reasonable to say that no profit was made at all on the sale of George Borrow's Bibles. And if we add to this the unmentioned costs of paper and printing – which must have been in the region of 10,000 *reales* at the least[108] – we may conclude that Borrow's sale of complete scripture was no less of a financial bleeding than his sales of the Scio New Testament had been (see IV.8 above); something which comes as no surprise, seeing that he sold his complete Bibles for a rather ludicrous 10 *reales* only.

---

108 A tender of 17 October 1835 from Bergnes to Graydon for the printing and binding of complete Bibles in Spanish estimates the production price per copy between 27 and 63 *reales*, depending on the size (8° or 12°), the kind of leather for the binding (sheep or calf) and the number ordered (500, 1000 or 1500) [Bible Society Archive, Foreign Correspondence Inwards 1835, vol. 4, p. 51]. A later tender of December 1836 offers to print the entire Bible 'in Ream' for a price between 17 *reales* (5000 copies) and 26 *reales* (1500 copies) [Bible Society Archive, Foreign Correspondence Inwards 1837, vol. 1, p. 29]. Which one of these was actually printed and sent to Borrow in sheets, remains to be discovered. It will, however, be obvious that the cost price of Borrow's 500 unbound Bibles was already twice what he sold them for. (The above letters were once again unearthed by the inimitable Ms Kathleen Cann.)

Appendix 3: George Borrow's expense accounts

BELOW WILL be transcribed the twelve Expense Accounts which Borrow sent to the British and Foreign Bible Society in the course of his Spanish years, plus three bills from the printer Borrego and the banker O'Shea which accompanied these. They are presently found, together with Borrow's letters of the period, in the Archive of the British and Foreign Bible Society, kept by the Cambridge University Library, which most generously granted permission for the present reproduction. See 'Primary Sources' in the Bibliography for some additional information.

As might be expected, there are delicate sides to the transcription. The main problem is caused by the frequent notes, remarks, corrections and clarifications jotted down on Borrow's original pages by the Bible Society bookkeepers and accountants. Many of these annotations add considerably to our knowledge and help along our understanding of the expense accounts; consequently they ought to be kept. But the profusion of scribbles and the variety of hands confronts the transcriber with a dilemma how to reproduce them. So as not to make things more confusing than they are already, I have decided to reproduce – in the expense accounts – all writing in other hands than Borrow's own in an italic font. The same procedure will be followed in the three additional bills, with the understanding that the original author of the bill is not, of course, George Borrow.

Each document is headed by a short introduction which offers some philological and historical data. Original spelling is maintained throughout the text, except where no graphic sign was available to reflect it. Original lay-out is kept where possible, but could not always be followed. Additional notes are marked with *, †, etc, and their explanations will be found at the bottom of the page. These signs are not, of course, found on the original document. Neither are the recurrent remarks [signature], which simply mean that on that spot stands a signature or initial for approval by one of the Bible Society's officers.

The numbering of the expense accounts is fully my own. The order is chronological.

[Acc 1]   Expense Account of October 1836
[Acc 2]   Expense Account of 3 November 1836
[Acc 3]   Expense Account of 31 December 1836
[Acc 4]   Expense account of 5 April 1837
[Acc 5]   Expense account of 10 May 1837
[Acc 6]   Expense account of 20 November 1837
[BiBo 1] Bill of Borrego's *Compañia Tipográfica* of 28 November 1837
[Acc 7]   Expense account of 11 December 1837
[BiOSh]   Note of bills drawn by Borrow from the banker O'Shea
[Acc 8]   Expense account of 26 April 1838
[BiBo 2] Bill of Borrego's *Compañia Tipográfica* of 11 May 1838
[Acc 9]   Expense account of 9 July 1838
[Acc 10] Expense account of November 1838
[Acc 11] Expense account of 9 March 1839
[Acc 12] Expense account of (probably) April 1840

Account 1 of October 1836

THIS ACCOUNT, of three pages, covers the entire long period from the summer of 1835, when Borrow returned from St Petersburg, to 1 October 1836, a full year later, when he landed in London on return from his first stint in Spain, and was handed in personally by Borrow in London. The currency is in Pounds Sterling.

Account of Money disbursed
On various occasions in 1835–6

	£	s	d
Expenses in London on arrival from St Petersburg	1	18	0
For journey into Norfolk & return	2	10	0
In London before sailing for Lisbon	2	0	0
Fare to Lisbon	16	0	0
For passport	0	5	0
Expenses on board	2	12	0
For permission to land, and expenses on landing	0	15	0
For horse hire in excursion to Cintra & Mafra	2	18	0
Expenses whilst absent	2	7	0
For horsehire on various occasions	3	0	0
For lodging and living whilst in Portugal	26	0	0
For journey to Evora (self & servant	4	0	0
Expenses there	2	6	0
Journey back	3	5	0
For servant whilst in Portugal	3	0	0
Journey to Badajoz horses & g....*	5	0	0
Expenses by the way	2	8	0
Carried forward	80	4	0

* The word, which clearly starts with a 'g' is practically illegible; but it almost certainly reads 'guides' , as on several occasions below (see BiS chapter 6–8).

Brought forward	80	4	0
Stay at Badajoz of 3 weeks	5	1	0
Journey to Madrid by Diligence	3	17	0
Postillions &c. (guard on the way)	1	0	0
Expenses on the way	2	8	0
Various necessary articles purchased at Madrid	16	0	0
Expenses at Madrid for lodging & living during 8 months ½	110	0	0
For washing £ 127.10.0	9	10	0
For attendance *agreed by subcommittee*	8	0	0
For medical advice *as belonging to his Salary*	0	5	0
Fro medicines *see opposite page**	0	13	0
For excursions to neighbouring towns & villages	4	0	0
For purchase of donkey for Gypsy who rendered many services	0	9	0
For journey to Granada	5	0	0
Expenses	2	18	0
Stay at Granada	2	7	0
Journey to Malaga† horse & guide	3	12	0
Expenses	1	0	0
Stay at Malaga	2	8	0
Passport	0	5	0
Carried forward	259	11	0
Brought forward	259	11	0
For passage to England	20	0	0
Expenses on board, at Gibraltar Cadiz Lisbon	2	14	0
Landing in London	0	3	0
Custom house	0	3	0
	£ 282	11	0

*Deduct for items to be included
in Salary 127.10.0
one moiety only on a/c of peculiar circumstances*   63   15

£ 218   16   0

*Allowed by Finance Committee Ex^d [signature]‡
Oct 28th 1836 [signature]*

---

* This intrusive note by one of the Bible Society's bookkeepers is in another hand. The large bracket marks the three entries £ 110.0.0, £ 9.10.0 and £ 8.0.0 as the constituent sums. Borrow's contract stipulated that costs of living and personal expenses were to his own account. But see below at the end of this expense account.

† 'Malaga' is written above a crossed-out 'Granada'

‡ *Ex^d* means 'Examined' by one of the accountants, as on many occasions below.

Account 2 of 3 November 1836

AN ACCOUNT of a single page, drawn up in Pounds Sterling, which covers the period 1 October to 3 November 1836, a time Borrow spent in London for consultation with the Bible Society and in Norwich to see his mother. By the looks of it, the account was handed in personally just before sailing for Spain again on 4 November.

1836
Nov 3   Recd. of Mr Tarn 32*

Expenses at the Spread Eagle			
Gracechurch St from Octr 1 to Octr 4	2	0	0
D^o from Octr 17 to 25	4	15	0
D^o from Octr 25 to Novr 3 in Earl St	0	4	8
Coach to and from Norwich	3	10	0
Expenses at D^o	5	0	0
Sundry Expenses going to Spanish Emb^y to & from steamer etc	1	0	0
	16	9	8

Allowed by Subcommittee
Of Finance Novr 18th 1836   G Borrow
                    Ex^d [three signatures]

---

* Read: Received of Mister Tarn 32 (Pounds Sterling), as in the similar heading of Account 3 below.

Account 3 of 31 December 1836

A TWO-PAGE ACCOUNT drawn up in Pounds Sterling which covers the period 4 November to 28 December 1836, i.e. from the moment Borrow went aboard ship in London to his arrival in Madrid. The account was included in Borrow's letter to Tarn – one of the Bible Society's account-ants – from Madrid of 31 December 1836.

Account of Money disbursed in journey
From London to Madrid

Received in London from Mr Tarn
£ 50.0.0
*Ditto 32.0.0**

Expenses at Falmouth	0	8	0	
In steam-boat	0	15	0	
Subscription for sailors for good behaviour during tempest	0	10	0	
At Lisbon, stay of a week	2	18	0	
Landing at Cadiz, porterage &c.	0	6	0	
For passport	0	4	8	
Stay at Cadiz	2	2	6	
Passage to Seville	1	0	0	
Luggage	0	4	0	
Expenses by the way	0	6	0	
Custom-house expenses, porterage	0	3	6	
15 days stay at Inn at Seville	5	18	0	
Various expenses vizt , to Italian, mule-hire &c	0	15	0	
For passport	0	4	8	
For horses to Cordoba	3	17	0	
For guide	1	5	0	
3 days expenses by the way for self, horses and guide	2	13	0	
Carried forward	23	10	4	82.0.0

---

* 'Ditto 32.0.0' is written in another hand and refers to the advance Borrow re-corded at the head of Account 2 above.

Brought forward	23	10	4
For horse and guide whilst they rested at Cordoba	0	10	0
For their return to Seville	0	9	4
Stay at Cordoba of a week	2	14	0
To Contrabandista for the use of his horses from Cordoba to Madrid	8	3	8
For maintenance of Contrabandista and self during the journey, 8 days	4	16	0
Gratuity to Contrabandista at Madrid	0	9	4
Two days stay of Contrabandista and self at Inn at Madrid	1	3	4
	41	16	0

*Ex^d for Jos^h Tarn**

Allowed by Subcommittee   *Ex^d Ler 490 [signature]*
of Finance Feby 11.1837† [three signatures]   Retain in hand 8.0.0

---

* I.e. 'Examined for Joseph Tarn', the Bible Society's accountant who first handled Borrow's accounts. Tarn was gravely ill at this time and died early in 1837. Hence the examination was probably performed by his assistant and successor William Hitchin, whose signature is the first to follow.

† Where I transcribe 'Feb^y' stands an unreadable word, clumsily corrected on top of an earlier mistake. Seeing what happens elsewhere, this can barely be anything else than the date, i.e. February 11 1837.

Account 4 of 5 April 1837

A SINGLE PAGE account, the first drawn up in Spanish *reales*, and concerned exclusively with the costs of printing and binding the New Testament by Borrego's printshop between mid January and 5 April 1837.

Expenses
Connected with the publishing of the New Testament
At Madrid

	Rials
For the composition and printing of 1000 copies of the New Testament at 180 rials per sheet, say 67 sheets	12060
For the printing of 4000 copies of the said 67 sheets at 85 rs per 1000	22780
To Doctor Luis De Usoz for literary assistance afforded	732
For 670 reams of paper consumed in the impressions, at 45 rials per ream	30150
For three reams spoiled	135
For the binding in calf of 5000 copies at 4 ½ rs per copy	22500
	88357

Allowed by the Sub
Committee of Finance May 10.1837
Ex^d [three signature]

Paid on account

21 January	*Bill 200-0-5-Exc.97.**	19400	
21 Februy	*Ditto Ditto*	19400	38800
	Balance to settle†		49,557

George Borrow

We have examined this account which is conforma (...)‡ to the agreement entered into in our presence with the printing company......H.O'Shea

---

* This line refers to the 'Bill' of the Bible Society's Madrid banker O'Shea's (BiOSh below) which records these £ 200, 0 shillings and 5 pennies, against an exchange rate ('Exc.') of 97 *reales* to the pound. The following sum of 19,400 *reales* likewise figures in that bill. Since O'Shea's bill was not made out until 28 November following, these scribbles must have been added later.

† I.e. the balance to settle with Borrego. O'Shea took care of this over the next months. BiOSh below charges the Bible Society for two more sums: 27,057 *reales* on 5 April and 22,500 *reales* on 21 April, which – together with the 38,800 *reales* here recorded – add up to a total payment of the 88,357 (compare L 16.3.1837).

‡ Before the edge of the page was damaged, the word probably read 'conformable' or 'conformably'.

Account 5 of 10 May 1837

A TWO PAGE expense account over the period January 1837 – when the first of the horses was bought – to early May 1837, when Borrow's foot was already in the stirrup to leave on his Northern Journey. Mainly concerned with preparations for travel and some other private expenses, it was sent to the Bible Society accompanied by the letter to Brandram of 10 May.

	Rials
For the purchase of a black stallion	2100
For the purchase of bay horse from Contrabandista	900
For two saddles	700
For two mangers	40
Two horse cloths	50
Two bridles	200
Crib, sieve, and various stable articles	120
For four months stable hire	160
Keep of one horse for four months	648
Of another for ten weeks	432
For man to carry proofs and attend horses at 8 rs per diem	
Janry	248
Febry	224
March	248
April	240
	6310
For one quarter's salary due on the 11th Febry	5022
	11332*

---

* Borrow's own total – 11432 *reales* – here gets crossed out and replaced by the correction 11332. The totals below are likewise adapted to this better number.

	Rials
Cash drawn for up to the present moment	11000
	Accounted for 11332

	11000
	<u>11332</u>
	Balance in my favour <u>332</u> rs
	George Borrow
	10 May 1837

Total Expenses	*11332*	*Reals*	
*3 mo Salary to 11 Feb*ʳʸ	*5022*	,, ,,	*say 50.0.0*
*Travg Exp*ˢ *abroad*	<u>*6310*</u>	*@ 97 to £*	*65.1.0*

*Ex*ᵈ *& Cor*ᵈ *
Allowed by Finance
Sub Committee Jan 10/38 [three signatures]

---

* A sequence of abbreviations of rather difficult interpretation and transcription. Following other comparable scribbles (particularly in Acc 11 below) it ought to be read: 'Examined and Corrected'.

Account 6 of 20 November 1837

THE FIRST expense account which mentions both money disbursed and money received by the sale of Scio New Testaments. Both columns are jotted down on a single page, on the reverse side of Borrow's letter to Brandram of 20 November 1837. The period is mid-May to 20 November 1837, i.e. the Northern Journey plus the three weeks immediately following on Borrow's return to Madrid.

**Account of money received and disbursed
during the last six months.**

Received	Reals	
From Mess.ⁱˢ O Shea & Comp.ʸ	15000	
By sale of horse at Coruña	3000	*deduct from Travg Exp.*
By private sale of 118 Testaments	1224	*1924 Rials*
By sale of 30 at Valladolid	300	*@ 100 to £*
„ „ „ 40 at Oviedo	400	*say £ 19.4.9*
Total	19924	

Disbursed	
Expenses of self, servant and two horses during journey of 195 days at 70 *reals* (17 shillings) per diem	14650
For horse hire from Coruña to Ribadeo	200
„ „ „ „ Ribadeo to Gyon	180
„ „ „ „ Oviedo to Santander	320
For horse purchased at Santander	700
Servant's wages for 6 months (the half of which was paid by Mess.ⁱˢ O Shea to wife and family at Madrid)	2160†
For fixtures of shop now hired at Madrid	950
Two months rent advanced	400
	19560

Allowed by Finance Ex.ᵈ [three signatures]
Comee Jan.ʸ.10.1838

Balance in hand 362 *reals*.
George Borrow 20 Novr 1837

---

* The three numbers joined by the } add up to the 1,924 reales mentioned here.

† I.e. the wages of Antonio Buchino at 12 *reales* a day (see *BiS* chapter 19).

Bill of Borrego of 28 November 1837 (BiBo 1)

THE BILL of Borrego's *Compañia Tipográfica* over all the services lend in Borrow's absence during the Northern Journey. It is written in a beautiful hand but seems to contain a number of mistakes. It is unclear when Borrow sent this in to the Bible Society. It may have gone with his next expense account of 11 December 1837 – Account 7 below – or may have been added to the other bill of Borrego's which recaptures this sum – BiBo 2 – when that was dispatched on an equally unknown date

El Señor Don Jorge Borrow a La Com.ª Tipografica

	Debe
Por el esceso de precio de cuadernacion con dorada de ochocientos ejemplares del Nuevo Testamento a 1 real uno	800*
Por la encuadernacion de lujo de dos ejemplares	160
Por la impresión y el papel de cuatrocientos carteles de anuncios remitidos a Cadiz, Sevilla, Malaga y Valladolid†	90
Por el cajon y embalaje para los cuatrocientos ejemplares de la Biblia embiados a la Coruña	50
Por el cajon que fue a Valladolid para Leon	25
Por los cuatro cajones y el embalaje de los ejemplares enviados a Cadiz, Sevilla, Malaga y Valencia a 30 rs.	120
Por el cajon y embalaje de los ejemplares enviados a Santander	40
Por los portes y gastos que ha cargado D. José M. Perez de la Coruña	403
Por los portes y gastos que ha cargado D. Juan B. Jimenez de Valencia	84
Por los portes y gastos que ha cargado Caro y Cartaya de Sevilla	110
Pos las portes que carga Riesgo de Santander	157
Por la impresión y papel de color de 300 carteles para Madrid	120
Madrid 28 de Noviembre de 1837	2159

Nota – Los corresponsales de Valladolid, Malaga y Cadiz han avisado el recibo de los libros sin fijar el valor de gastos y portes y quedan pendientes para otra cuenta

José de Revolled & Gª (?)

---

* The number 800 has been heavily deleted, but was not subtracted from the final total. Borrow did subtract it later from the 3,884 *reales* due in the statement of his current account [BiBo 2], which includes this bill for 2,159 *reales* [L 9.7.1838]. The result, 3,084 reales, was transported to his expense account of 9 July 1838 [Acc 9].

† Seeing the sequence below, Valladolid may be a writing mistake for Valencia.

Account 7 of 11 December 1837

An account of a single sheet covering the period 21 November to 11 December 1837. The original is drawn up in two columns, with 'Money Received' on the left, and 'Money Disbursed' on the right. It was sent to William Hitchin – one of the Bible Society's accountants – apparently without any further comment, on 11 December 1837, just as Borrow returned from his rapid excursion to Toledo.

Money Received

	Rials
By money in hand at period of last account	364
By M^r O'Shea's Bill	2000
By sale (private) of 13 Testaments at Toledo	130
By 26 Testaments (two gilded) sold at Society's Establishment just opened at Madrid	262
Rials	2756

Money Disbursed

	Rials
Gate dues at Toledo for the introduction of 102 New Testaments at 8 per cent upon supposed value	56
Nine days expense at Toledo of self horses and servant	590
Rials	646

Ex^d [three signatures]

Allowed by Finance
Com^{ee} Jany 10.1838

In Hand
Rials 2110

George Borrow

Bill of O'Shea 18 December 1837 (BiOSh)

THIS SUMMARY of the Bible Society's Madrid banker, the only one to survive, lists the sums disbursed by O'Shea in 1837. It proves that 19th century Spain made blatant madness pass for a numismatic system, whose niceties could at times even baffle professional bookkeepers. I limit my comments to the minimum. When this bill was sent to the Bible Society is unknown.

Note of Bills drawn by Mr Borrow to the order of H^y O'Shea & c

1837		£							R.^{y}	
February	3	200	0	5	at the exchge of	36 ⅞	less charges 1.0 %*	of comm^n Postage &c		
								x 19400		
,,	3	70	8	8	,,	36 ⅞	,,	6835	4	
,,	24	200	0	5	,,	36 ⅞	,,	*x* 19400		
April	5	275	0	7	,,	36 ⅜	,,	*x* 27057		
,,	5	40	13	5	,,	36 ⅜	,,	4000		
,,	21	224	15	10	,,	35 ¾	,,	*x* 22500†		
May	16	150	0	0	,,	35 ½	,,	15118		
,,	16	55	0	0	,,	35 ½	,,	5544		
		£ 1215	19	4	Sterlg producing net			R.^{y} 119854	4	

M^r. Borrow has since drawn for

Novemb	28	20	0	0	exchge	35 ⅛	net	2037	
Decemb	16	20	0	0		35 ⅞		1994	
		£ 1255	19	4	Ster producing net			R.^{y} 123885	4

Madrid 18th December 1837

H. O'Shea

1 real de vellon 34 maravedis
512 maravedis 1 Dollar
1 Dollar so many pence‡

---

* The impressive mathematical skills of Paul Durrant have proven beyond doubt that this tiny illegible scribble must be read as 1 %.

† The four *x*'s mark the sums which make up the 88,357 reales paid to the *Compañía Tipográfica* to settle the debt of Account 4.

‡ An annotation by the poor Bible Society bookkeeper who had to disentangle this. Since 512 : 34 ≈ 15 reales, the 'Dollar' meant here is not the Duro of 20 reales, but the imaginary Peso of 15. The '1 Dollar so many pence' means that there were roughly 35 or 36 Pence to every 'Peso' (see also Appendix 1)

Account 8 of 26 April 1838

A MEGA-ACCOUNT DRAWN up at the end of Borrow's letter to Hitchin of 26 April 1838, right in the middle of the unfolding diplomatic crisis over his sale of New Testaments and other vernacular Scripture. It covers all costs and income, new and so far overlooked, between Mid 1837 to late April 1838, and has all the appearance of a hurried final account, just in case…

Money Received on the Bible Societys Accompt

	Rˢ	
By 52 copies of New Testament, at 10 ʳˢ, sold at Madrid during my absence in the North of Spain*	520	
By 291 copies of New Testament, sold at Madrid, since last accompt, partly in Society's establishment nᵒ 25 Calle del Principe, partly by private sale	2910	
By 14 copies (gilded) at 11ʳˢ	154	
By 23 copies of St Luke in Rommany to the Gipsies of Madrid at 4ʳˢ each	92	
By 12 copies ditto at the Societys Establishment at 16 rials each	192	
By books	3,868	Rs
By Bills of Messʳˢ O Shea since 28 Decʳ 1837	12000	
	15868	

Bills for 50 £
       30 £
       40 £
120 exch of 100 Rials to £ Sterling

---

* I.e. by Luis Usoz y Rio

Money Disbursed on the Societys Accompt

	Rs
Various expenses defrayed by Don Luis Usoz, during my absence in 1837. Namely porterage at various times of Madrid edition of the New Testament, advertizements in Newspapers, percentage to Booksellers, and 4 months hire of room for general depot.	372
Rent for depot from the 1 Octr 1837 to 1 May 1838*	120
For the printing of 500 copies of Saint Luke in Rommany, 11 sheets at 160^{rs} per sheet	1760
For reprint of 1 ½ sheet spoiled	200
For 13 reams of paper for same	780
To Doctor Oteiza for translation of St Luke into Basque	800
For 12 reams of paper for same	720
For 4 Months rent of Societys Establishment in Madrid at 12 dollars per month	960
For two months (Jany Feb^y) salary to shopman at 4^{rs} per diem	236
Carriage of 500 Bibles from Barcelona, expenses of porterage &c in Madrid	625
For binding of 300 copies of Rommany Gospel 3^{rs} per cop^y	900
Extraordinary binding ,, ,, ,,	40
,, ,, 100 copies of Basque Gospel	300
26 advertisements of New Testament in Diary of Madrid 10 r^s each	<u>260</u>

           Allowed by Sub Com^{ee}   8073
           of Finance May 16 1838
           Ex^d [three signatures]   <u>15868</u>

         In hand   Rs 4495   GB

---

* I.e. seven months, which may well be a writing mistake for 1 November to 1 May, 6 months at 20 per month

Bill of Borrego of 11 May 1838 (BiBo 2)

A STATEMENT OF Borrow's current account with the *Compañia Tipográfica*. It lists the earlier debt over printing (BiBo 1), adds a number of costs over advertisement and shipments, and credits the proceeds from two booksellers' sales. After correcting the resulting debt to 3,084 *reales* (see note to BiBo 1 above) Borrow included the saldo in his expense account of 9 July 1838 (Acc 9), writing to Hitchin that 'the original bill I shall forward as soon as it has been signed and vouched for by Messrs. O'Shea, who paid the money'. This was done on an unknown date.

El Editor del Nuevo Testamento D. Jorge Borrow s/c corriente con La Compañía Tipografica

Debe

			Rˢ.vⁿ.	mª
1837				
Novᵉ	28	Por el importe dela cuenta de esta fecha*	2,159	
1838				
Febrero	6	Por los gastos de portes y demas que carga el Sʳ Medina de Malaga	146	
	3	Por derechos de Aduana que ha satisfecho D. José Mª Perez de la Coruña por las Biblias que se le remitieron según s/c 30 Dicᵉ.	120	
Mayo	11	Por la composicion de 11 pliegas del Evanjelio de Sⁿ Lucas en Vascuence y el tirado de 500 ejemplares 160 rˢ uno	1,760	
			4,185	

Haber

			Rˢ.vⁿ.	mª
1838				
Marzo	11	Por liquido producto de venta de 24 ejemplares, hecha por Jimeno de Valencia	220	24
„	„	Por liquido de venta de 10 ejemplares hecho por Caro y Cartaya de Sevilla	80	
Mayo	11	Saldo que resulta a favor de la Compañía	3,884	10

S.E. u O. Madrid 11 de mayo de 1838 José de Revolled & Gª (?) 4,185
Rmo. José de Revolled & Gª (?)

---

* I.e. BiBo 1 above.

Account 9 of 9 July 1838

A SOMEWHAT COMPLICATED double-page account covering the period
20 March to early July 1838. Sent to Hitchin on 9 July with a lengthy
explicatory note.

Account of Money received and Disbursed on the account of the Bible Society since 26th April last.

	R^s
	7,795*
20th April in hand	
Subsequently drawn at	
various periods	10,084
	17,879

Money Disbursed

	Rs
For shophire from 20th March to 20th April	240
D° to 20th May	240
D° ,, ,, June	240
Salary to shopman, March, April, May, June at 4^{rs} per diem	492
To Doctor Oteiza for further assistance in the case of the Basque Gospel (principally variations in the translation)	160
Carried forward	1,372

---

* This may correspond to the sum of 4,495 *reales* 'in hand' at the end of account
8. Borrow's own copy of that account was lost when his papers were seized in late
April (see his letter to Hitchin of 9 July 1838), so he worked from memory. It would
be a rare instance of Borrow erring to his disadvantage when it came to money
matters!

	Rs
Brought forward	1,372
For binding of 200 copies (last) of Gypsy Gospel	600
For second hundred of Basque Gospel	300
For 26 copies of Bible at 5½ *reals*[*]	143
By Mr Borregos bill[†]	3,084
To Unfortunate (on Mr Brandrams account) £ 1.16.[‡]	180
For porterage[§]	60

Allowed by Sub Com^{ee}   5739
of Finance Sept 5.1838 [two signatures]

Personal Account	5739
11th Decr 1837 By salary due	7,060
11th Feby 1838 ,, ,, ,,	5,000
11 June ,, ,, ,, ,,	5,000
By prison expenses	940

Ex^d [signature]   23739

For Balance &c   Balance due Rs 5,860
See Statement   George Borrow, Madrid
Made by WHit   July 9, 1838

---

* Other than one might think, this sum does not represent the *purchase* of Bibles, but the costs of binding some of the 500 Bibles in loose sheets received from Bergnes in Barcelona in March 1838 (see Appendix 2).

† I.e. the saldo of Borrego's bill of 11 May 1838, minus the 800 *reales* for gilded copies Borrow refused to pay (see BiBo 2 above, and L 9.7.1838).

‡ I.e. the renegade Catholic priest Pascual Marin (see Jenkins, *Life*, 225–227).

§ I.e. the costs of moving stock to a secret store-house (see the letter to Hitchin of 9 July 1838)

Account 10 of November 1838

A LENGTHY ACCOUNT, spread thin over four pages, covering the Gospel-peddling expeditions to the countryside of July and August 1838, plus the travelling expenses to return to England in September-October 1838. Borrow handed it in personally to the Bible Society when in London for consultations. Hence there is no accompanying letter.

Proceeds from the Sale of 1616 New Testaments in the Provinces of Old and New Castille

	rs
By sale of 230 Testaments in Sagra of Toledo at 3 *reals* each	690
Do ,, ,, 170 at 4rs	680
Do ,, ,, 102 on the road to Aranjuez at 3rs	306
Do ,, ,, 80 at Aranjuez at 4rs	320
Do ,, ,, 27 at Ocaña at 3rs	81
Do ,, ,, 123 in villages in the vecinity of Madrid at 3rs	369
	2446

Carried forward

	rs
Brought forward	2446
By 546 copies in the districts of Segovia and Avila in Old Castile at 3rs	1638
Do 16 at 2rs	32
Do 322 at 4	1288
	Rs 5404
By 5 copies of St Luke in Rommani at 16rs	80
Do 2 ,, ,, in Basque at 12rs	24
	Rs 5508

[three signatures]

Extraordinary expenses during six weeks journey
in old and new Castile, Vizt. 3 persons, 2
horses and 1 burrico.   1800
For carriage of books on various occasions   120
Removal of 2000 Testaments and shop-furniture to Society's store.   200
Advance of two months rent for store at 4^{rs} per diem   240
Horse keep 9 months at 220^{rs} per month   1980
Stabling at 40   do ,,   ,,   360
Final advance to Marin*   500
Fare from Madrid to Saragossa   380
Baggage   100
Passport   <u>40</u>
                                                              5720

                                       B^{t} for^{d} 5720
Expenses on the road, Postil^{ns}, Conductor, and diet   227
Expenses at Saragossa   118
Fare to Oleron in France   240
Expenses on the road (4 days)   227
From Oleron to Bordeaux   180
Expenses at Bordeaux   462
Fare from Bordeaux to Paris by mail   510
Expenses   90
D° at Paris   340
From Paris to Boulougne   200
Expenses   125
D° at Boulougne   80
From Boulougne to London   68
Expenses on board, landing, Custom house   <u>50</u>
                                                            R^{s} 8637

             [two signatures]
Decr 12.1838   Ex^{d} [signature]

---

* See the note to account 9 above.

Account 11 of 9 March 1839

Wɪᴛʜ ɪᴛs many remarks of the Bible Society's bookkeepers scribbled all over the page, this is probably the most complicated account to transcribe and interpret correctly. It consists of two large pages which cover the period 21 December 1838, when Borrow left London to sail to Spain the last time, to 9 March 1839, when he had just returned from his last expedition in the neighbourhood of Madrid. It was sent to Hitchin on 9 March 1839 with an explicatory note, which Darlow reproduces. This is the last of the documents in the Bible Society Archive which record income from sold books. William Knapp, however, possessed a personal record of Borrow's which brings the numbers of sales etc. up to 16 April, i.e. three or four days before Borrow took the mail-coach to Seville. For sake of completeness, the additional parts from that record will be added separately following the transcribed account.

Money disbursed on the account of the Bible Society

	Reals	
For Baggage by Diligence to Falmouth	115	
To Drivers and guards	62	
Personal expenses	48	
Expenses at Falmouth	145	
Dº on board and in landing at Cadiz	190	
Dº at Cadiz	112	
From Cadiz to Seville by steamer	60	
Personal expenses, custom house, porterage etc	37	
Expenses at Seville 11 days	440	
Passport	20	
From Seville to Madrid by Courier	740	
Postillions	60	
Gratuity to couriers	60	
Expenses by the way, 4 days	98	
Keep of two horses, 6 weeks, at 3 dollars per week	360	£
Purchase of pony for Vitoriano	240	*sold for 5.6.0*[*]
Saddle for self	190	

---

[*] Not only the modern investigator gets confused by this jungle of numbers; so did the very accountants of the Bible Society. Once the expeditions from Madrid were over, Vitoriano's pony was sold for 230 *reales* [Knapp, *Life*, I : 305], which makes £2.6.0, not £ 5.6.0!

Horse cloth and halter   27

For Vitoriano, since the period of his entering the
service of the Bible Society, namely from the 22
Jany to the 1st of March, for wages, expenses in journies
board, lodgings etc   448

Journey of Antonio to Guadalajara, 3 days   90

D^o of myself, Antonio & Vitoriano to
Naval Carnero, 5 days   <u>235</u>
                                                                        3777
1839   @ *100 to the £*   *37.15.4*
March 11. By One Quarter's Salary due this day   <u>*50. 0 .0*</u>
Mr George Borrow   *£ 87.15.4*

Cr By Cash for the Balance down   *3.1.7*

Money received on the account of the Bible Society

By Cash received in London Decr 21 1838   *20.0.0*

                                                          Reals

By Bill on M^r O'Shea   5000   =   *50.0.0*

By the sale, in country, of 213 Test^nts at 3^rs   639

D^o ,, in town, of 122 at 4^rs   488

In the purlieus* of Madrid, vizt at the
Puente de Segovia, Embarcadero &c. of 27
at various prices   104   }   *= 14.13.9*

By 17 Bibles at 10^rs   170

By 3 copies of St Luke in Gipsy, at 16^rs   48

By 2 D^o ,, ,, in Basque at 10^rs   <u>20</u>

                                                          6469
To Balance due to Mr Borrow   *3. 1. 7*

Balance in hand 2692 Rs.

                    June 14.1839
Ex^d & corrected [signature]   *[two signatures]*   *£ 87.15.4*

---

* Borrow spells 'purlieus' for the modern French plural 'purlieux'.

Knapp, *Life*, I : 305 adds the following items to the above

Money disbursed

Total of Acc 11:	3,777
Hire of magazine (storage) 5 months	630
Binding of 443 Bibles at 5 ¾ rs. each	2547 ¼
Victoriano from March 1st to April 1st, keep and wages	248
Horse keep 7 weeks at $ 3 per week	420
Stable hire 3½ months at $ 2 per month	140
Shoeing etc.	36
Removal of Bible Society's property from Magazine	50
Porterage on three chests of books for Andalusia	19
Expenses on selling Bibles	886
Expenses on selling Testaments (9 persons employed at Madrid for 16 days)	607 ½
	9,360 ¾

Money received

Total of Acc 11:	6,469
Bill £ 40	4,000
Sale of 443 Bibles at 10 rs. each	4,430
Sale of 602 New Testaments in country at 3 rs.	1,806
Sale of Victoriano's pony ($ 11.50)	230
	16,935
Due to the Bible Society, Madrid, April 16th, 1839	7,574 ¼

Account 12 of April 1840

BORROW'S LAST expense account, probably handed over personally to his employers during their last interview on 20 April 1840 in London. It covers the entire period from late April 1839 when he moved to Seville, to his landing in England on 16 April 1840, a full year later. Since Borrow expected to be paid in English money it is drawn up in Pounds Sterling; and seeing that the bill is huge one suspects that a 'creative' exchange rate was occasionally applied. Sadly, there is no sign of money received over the sales of books in Seville and Tangiers during the spring, summer and autumn of 1839, nor do we find the sometimes considerable sums which Borrow's Spanish booksellers must have send him (or O'Shea) after the final reckoning of their accounts. Another expense account – reflecting those receipts and the ones over the Madrid sales of March and April 1839 as seen in Knapp's record reproduced above - may have existed and may have been sent in; but if it was, it has not survived.

Account of Money Disbursed

	£	s	d
Journey from Madrid to Seville in the spring of the year 1839 of myself, servant and two horses distance 300 miles	16	14	0
Stay at posada of the Queen at Seville (15 days) of myself, servant and horses	11	11	0
Hire of felouk to San Lucar for conveyance of scriptures after they had been liberated on the pledge of guarantee that they should be removed from Seville	2	10	6
Gratuity to Guarantee	0	14	0
To the Englishman John Plant who went in charge of the Scriptures from Seville to San Lucar, absent 5 days	1	0	0
To Muleteer for assistance rendered at various times in introducing books into Seville from San Juan d'Alfarache, a village down the river	1	2	0
To various individuals employed in circulating scriptures in Seville during the year 1839	3	6	0
	36	17	6

	£	s	d
	36	17	6
For 27 journeys of myself, at intervals, during the year 1839 in the kingdom of Andalusia absent 4 days and for assistance rendered by various individuals	16	0	0
For return of servant to Madrid from Seville	5	0	0
For 9 months keep of horses	11	0	0
For 6 months rent of apartment in Madrid where Societys books were deposited	15	4	0
Journey from Seville to Tangier and expenses there; passports, custom house, expenses at San Lucar, conveyance of scriptures from latter place to Gibraltar &c	29	12	0
Prison expenses at Seville	4	16	0
Journey to Madrid from Seville and return	18	0	0
Sundry expenses at Madrid during a stay of 3 weeks	5	0	0
	141	9	6*

	£	s	d
	141	9	6
Journey from Seville to Cadiz by land	2	6	0
Expenses at Cadiz whilst awaiting packet	3	0	0
Passport and embarkation	0	10	0
Passage to England	20	0	0
Expenses, landing, custom house	1	15	0
Money left in hand of Mr Brackenbury for the passage of valuable horse purchased on my own account for the use of Bible Socy	15	10	0
Expenses in London	4	4	0
£	188	14	6

Exd & Corrected [signature]
[two signatures]

---

* Borrow's own £142.15.6 was corrected to £141.9.6. Consequently the total below, which Borrow had calculated at £190.0.6 had to be amended to £188.14.9

Bibliography and sources

D ue to the nature of this study and the quality of the sources, I need to use an unconventional, and somewhat ambiguous, system of reference.

Practically every other sentence throughout the text will need a reference to what we may call the 'primary sources', namely: George Borrow's letters to the British and Foreign Bible Society; his expense accounts to that same body; his two 'general reports' to the same, and finally the chapters of his 1843 travelogue *The Bible in Spain*. In order not to burden the book with hundreds of footnotes, these references will be made in the text itself, between square brackets, in the shortest possible manner. Of course, this is not beneficial to the 'readability' of the text; but I trust that readers will soon learn to overlook sign-groups such as '[L 18.7.1839]', '[Acc 8]' and '[*BiS* ch 11]'. The meaning of these abbreviations will be explained in the section 'Primary Sources' below.

As for the other sources used: those which are referred to regularly will receive a similar treatment, i.e. references will be made between square brackets in the text itself by the name of the author, a catch-word, and a page number. For the full list of these consulted works, plus the abbreviations used, see below under 'Secondary Sources'.

Lastly, sources which get mentioned only once or twice will be relegated to footnotes and written out there in full in the customary manner.

Primary sources

THE LETTERS which George Borrow, throughout the period of his Spanish mission, wrote to his employers of the British and Foreign Bible Society, have been published by T.H. Darlow, ed., *Letters of George Borrow to the British and Foreign Bible Society* (London, 1911). Recently, this book – as well as many others on the subject of Borrow – has been made partly available on the internet by the excellent Gutenberg Project (http://www.gutenberg.org/), in a manner which makes it easy to download. The letters will be referred to by a simple 'L' between square brackets, followed by the date of writing. Thus [L 14.1.1837] means the letter which George Borrow wrote to his employers on 14 January 1837. Unless otherwise stated, the letter was addressed to Borrow's main Bible Society contact, the Rev. Andrew Brandram.

The expense accounts which Borrow sent, with some regularity, to the accountants of the Bible Society to justify his disbursements and keep track of the salary they owed him, are an integral part of his letters, but were not reproduced by Darlow in the publication mentioned above. They are at present kept by the Cambridge University Library, in the Archive of the British and Foreign Bible Society, section 'Borrow papers BSA/D2/5'. A transcription is published here, in Appendix 3, for the first time ever and with kind permission of the CUL. The twelve known expense accounts – our best and most reliable source for sales-figures – will be referred to with an 'Acc' between square brackets, followed by a number. Two bills from Borrow's printer Borrego and one from his banker O'Shea, sent along with his accounts by way of justification, receive a different code. The full list of the 15 documents plus their coding will be found in the introduction to Appendix 3.

In late November 1838, Borrow wrote two 'general reports' for the Committee of the Bible Society, in order to explain what he had been doing and what he still planned to do in Spain. Both of these are included in Darlow's publication of Borrow's letters.

The first of the two is usually titled 'Account of Proceedings in the Peninsula'. This report was, however, withdrawn soon afterwards for being too outspoken. It will be referred to with a simple [APP].

The second report replaced this withdrawn version within days, and is titled 'Mr. G. Borrow's Report on Past and Future Operations in Spain'.

Covering the same ground, but worded in milder terms, it was formally endorsed by the Bible Society Committee on 28 November 1838. It will be referred to as [ROS].

Three years after his return to England, Borrow published his Spanish memoirs in the travelogue *The Bible in Spain* (first published 1843). The text of this book follows that of his letters very closely, sometimes even verbatim. There are, however, important differences both in formulation and in detail, and a number of episodes in each are absent in the other. *The Bible in Spain* is available in a great number of printed editions, and equally in the Gutenberg Project, where it may be downloaded for free. In order to enable all readers to locate the passages referred to, independent of the edition at hand, I refer to the chapters of the book, rather than to the page numbers of one arbitrary edition. Thus [*BiS* ch 43] means chapter 43 of *The Bible in Spain*.

Secondary sources

THE FOLLOWING are the books and articles used in the writing of this study, ordered according to author's name and the abbreviated catch word which I use throughout the text. In each case of reference, the catch word will be followed by the page number to the passage in question. Hence [Ford, *Handbook*, 398] refers to page 398 of Richard Ford's *A Handbook for Travellers in Spain*. Those articles and books which are at present (autumn 2008) or will soon be available on the internet are marked at the end of the entry with a '[Website: ....]' in which the title of the website comes in place of the dotted line. Since most websites are short-lived and very ephemeral, I will not go through the laborious trouble of typing out internet addresses (http://www.iamanuglyblemishonthispage.org etc). A digitally published book or article is always best found by feeding author and title into a search machine, and pray for the best.

[Barreiro, *Carlismo*] Barreiro Fernández, J.R., *El Carlismo Gallego* (Santiago 1976).

[Barret, *Mission*] Barrett, K.: 'George Borrow's mission from the Bible Society to distribute a Bible without notes in the Spain of 1836-1840', in: *George Borrow Bulletin* 33 (2006), 9-22.

[Campos, *Náufragos*] Campos Calvo-Sotelo, J., *Náufragos de Antaño* (Barcelona 2002)

[Cann, *Correspondent*] Cann, K., *An Astonishing Correspondent, George Borrow and the Bible Society*, lecture delivered at Bible House, London, on 22 July 1981. [Website: George Borrow Studies]

[Collie, *Eccentric*] Collie, M., *George Borrow: Eccentric* (Cambridge 1982).

[Collie & Fraser, *Bibliography*] Collie, M., and Fraser, A.: *George Borrow, a Bibliographical Study* (Winchester 1984).

[Fernandez, *Crónicas*] Fernández de Castro, D., *Crónicas Ibéricas: Tras los pasos de George Borrow, vendedor de biblias en el siglo XIX* (Barcelona 2008)

[Ford, *Handbook*] Ford, R., *A Hand-Book for Travellers in Spain* (text of the 1845 edition), edited by Ian Robertson (Centaur Press: London 1966).

[Fraser, *Hasfeld*] Fraser, A. (ed.), *George Borrow, Letters to John Hasfeld 1835–1839* (Tragara Press: Edinburgh 1982).

[Fraser, *Mol*] Fraser, A., 'Benedict Mol, treasure digger of Saint James', in: *George Borrow Bulletin* 12 (1996), 69–82.

[Fraser, *Sleeping*] Fraser, A., 'Sleeping under the Angel's Wings: George Borrow's Imprisonment in Madrid', in: *Proceedings of the 1991 George Borrow Conference* (Toronto 1992), 25–47.

[Fraser, *Taylor*] Fraser, A., 'Baron Taylor and Judah Lib: two displaced persons', in: *George Borrow Bulletin* 28 (2004), 3–17.

[Fraser, *Unsung*] Fraser, A., 'Borrow's Unsung Collaborators in Spain', in: *Proceedings of the 1993 George Borrow Conference* (Toronto 1994), 29–44. A Spanish version of the same is also available: see Fraser, A., 'Los olvidados colaboradores de George Borrow en España', in: *Cuadernos Hispanoamericanos*, n°. 524, February 1994, 39–55.

[Giménez, *Graydon*] Giménez Cruz, A., 'James N. Graydon, Comisionado de la Sociedad Biblica de Londres: controversias sobre su actuación de España (1835–1840)', in: *Hispania*, XLVII (1987), 225–250.

[Giménez, *Prensa*] Giménez Cruz, A., *La Prensa española de la época y George Borrow*, separata de Anales del Instituto de Estudios Madrileños, Tomo XXX (Madrid 1991), 361–379. This is a translation of Giménez's 'Borrow and the Spanish Press', in: *Proceedings of the 1989 George Borrow Conference* (Toronto 1990). I decided, however, only to use the Spanish version, since this includes the original Spanish texts from the contemporary newspapers.

[Jenkins, *Life*] Jenkins, H., *The Life of George Borrow* (London 1912). [Website: Gutenberg Project.]

[Knapp, *Life*, I and II] Knapp, W. I., *Life, Writings and Correspondence of George Borrow*, 2 volumes (London 1899). [Website: Gutenberg Project, forthcoming.]

[Madoz, *DG*] Madoz, P., *Diccionario geográfico-estadístico-histórico de España y sus posesiones de ultramar*, 16 volumes (Madrid 1846–1850). [Website: various complete or partial versions of this colossal work are available on the internet; all, however, are scanned and arduous to handle.]

[Missler, *Considerable*] Missler, P., 'The most considerable of them all: Rey Romero, Borrow's bookseller in Santiago', in: *George Borrow Bulletin* 16 (1998), 32–45. [Website: George Borrow Studies.]

[Missler, *Gypsy*] Missler, P., 'Gypsy Luke Project: preliminary results', in: *George Borrow Bulletin* 32 (2006), 32–48. A further instalment was published under the title 'Gypsy Luke Project, (2), further results' in *George Borrow Bulletin* 36 (2008), 29–35. [Website: an integrated version of both instalments will soon appear on the website George Borrow Studies.]

[Missler, *Judgement*] Missler, P., 'A Partial Judgement', in: *George Borrow Bulletin* 30 (2005), 30–42. [Website: George Borrow Studies.]

[Missler, *RRT*] Missler, P., 'Rey Romero's Testaments', in: *George Borrow Bulletin* 28 (2004), 22–37. [Website: George Borrow Studies.]

[Missler, *Underpriced*] Missler, P., 'The Case of the Underpriced Testaments', in: *George Borrow Bulletin* 29 (2004), 17–31. [Website: George Borrow Studies.]

[Ridler, *GBaaL*] Ridler, A., *George Borrow as a Linguist* (Warborough 1983, 1996).

[Ridler, *Seville*] Ridler, A., 'George Borrow in Seville, Granada and Córdoba', in: *George Borrow Bulletin* 24 (2002), 54–69.

[Ridler, *Sidelights*] Ridler, A., 'Sidelights on George Borrow's Gypsy Luke', in: *The Bible Translator*, volume 32, n° 3 (July 1981), 329–337.

[Robertson, *Tour*] Robertson, I., 'George Borrow's Tour in North-west Spain from mid-May to late October 1837', in: *Proceedings of the 1993 George Borrow Conference* (Toronto 1994), 63–84.

[Shorter, *Circle*] Shorter, C.K., *George Borrow and his Circle* (London 1913) [Website: Gutenberg Project]

Issues of the George Borrow Bulletin, which is by now the greatest modern treasure-house of Borrovian studies, may be ordered through the *George Borrow Society* website. This website also offers additional information on the life and works of Borrow, and a comprehensive index of materials published over the last fifteen years in the near 3,000 pages of the *Bulletin*.

Index

T**HE FOLLOWING** index is brief and far from exhaustive. It concentrates exclusively on items of interest but rare occurrence which are scattered throughout the text and do not possess a chapter of their own. Hence there is no entry for 'Borrow' or 'New Testament', both of which appear on every page. Nor will there be an item 'Madrid', since this subject is easily located by looking at the list of contents. References are to page number. Items found in footnotes will be marked as '64n'. Items found both in the body text and in a footnote on that same page will be marked '64+n'.

Lightning Source UK Ltd.
Milton Keynes UK
22 November 2010

163251UK00002B/179/P